The Multi-Agency Approach
to Domestic Violence:
New opportunities, old challenges?

The Multi-Agency Approach to Domestic Violence:

New opportunities, old challenges?

edited by
Nicola Harwin, Gill Hague & Ellen Malos

Whiting & Birch
mcmxcix

002836

]62·8292

Published by Whiting & Birch Ltd,
PO Box 872, London SE23 3HL, England.
USA: Paul & Co, Publishers' Consortium Inc,
PO Box 442, Concord, MA 01742.
British Library Cataloguing in Publication Data.
A CIP catalogue record is available from
the British Library
ISBN 1 86177 002 2 (cased)
ISBN 1 86177 003 0 (limp)

Printed in England by Watkiss Studios

Contents

Acknowledgements

This book has been a challenge to produce and we are very grateful to the many people who have offered us support and assistance to make it possible. All three of us have been active in the Women's Aid movement for many years, and we would like to express our deep thanks to both women within the movement and women survivors of domestic violence with whom we have worked over these years and from whom we have learnt so much. Many local domestic violence activists and Women's Aid workers have also shared their experiences and understandings to make this book possible.

In this new endeavour, we have been supported by our colleagues within both the Women's Aid Federation of England and the Domestic Violence Research Group of the School for Policy Studies, University of Bristol. We must also thank the Joseph Rowntree Foundation for financially supporting the national research studies of housing authority responses to domestic violence and of multi-agency domestic violence initiatives, in which all the editors were involved in different capacities, and which acted as a springboard for this book. Particularly special thanks to Barbara Ballard of the Joseph Rowntree Foundation and to the Research Advisory Groups of the two studies.

We are particularly grateful to our contributors for their work on this project, and for their time and patience. Our thanks also go to Valerie Douglas for secretarial assistance with some of the chapters, and Mark Cox for computing assistance. The contribution to this book of David Whiting of Whiting & Birch has gone far beyond the normally accepted duties of a publisher.

Our thanks also go to all those friends who have nurtured and supported us over the years, including:

For Ellen Malos: To my parents who taught me to recognise injustice and oppression and let me take my own path even though they did not always understand or approve, to John, Rob and Anna and to all my friends for their support in difficult times.

For Nicola Harwin: To Bill Gaines, for all the years of love and friendship, to Jeremy, Jason and Sammy, for the challenge of raising sons, and for cuddles and laughter, to Joan and Dennis for letting me go free.

For Gill Hague: My thanks as always to Dorothy, Dave, Cassie, Keiran, Jac and Alison. I couldn't manage without you.

Contributors

Thangam Debbonaire
Thangam Debbonaire was National Children's Officer for the Women's Aid Federation of England from 1991 to 1997. In this role she ran a national training programme for refuge children's workers, provided briefings, information, resources and telephone advice for work with children to local refuge services and other agencies throughout England, as well acting as advisor to several research initiatives. Thangam has written and spoken widely on the needs and experiences of children and domestic violence including contributing to the first UK publication on children's experiences of domestic violence (Mullender and Morley, 1994). Thangam now works as a freelance trainer and consultant.

Jennifer Gardiner
Jennifer Gardiner is a Lecturer in the School of Social Work at Curtin University of Technology, Perth, Western Australia. She is interested in a wide range of theoretical and practice issues including interpersonal violence, individuals in society, feminist/qualitative research, Aboriginal and multicultural issues, community work and social policy. She is active in the local women's movement and is finalising her PhD, which documents and analyses her experience as a key player in attempting to establish inter-agency coordination on domestic violence in Western Australia.

Jane Geraghty
Jane Geraghty has previously worked with Probation Services in Middlesex, Nottingham, Lincolnshire and Inner London, and is currently Divisional Chief Officer with the South Yorkshire Probation Service. From 1989-1991 she was seconded to the Home Office Crime Prevention Unit.

She has been a member of a number of committees for the Association of Chief Officers of Probation including Crime Prevention, Family Court Welfare, Partnership and Gender Action, and is currently a member of the Sex Offender Committee. She is also involved in the South Yorkshire Domestic Violence Forum and Sheffield's Domestic Violence Forum.

Sharon Grace
Sharon Grace is a Senior Research Officer in the Home Office Research and Statistics Directorate, where she has worked for the last eight years in the field of domestic and sexual violence, child abuse, pornography and obscenity. She is the author of the following Home Office research reports: *Policing Domestic Violence in the 1990s, Rape: From Recording to Conviction, and Testing Obscenity:* and *An International Comparison of Laws and Controls Relating to Obscene Material.*

Sue Hanley
Sue Hanley worked in teaching and in residential social work before joining West Midlands Probation Service as a Probation Officer in 1973. Since 1987, she has worked as an Assistant Chief Probation Officer, in a variety of generic and specialist contexts, including Family Court Welfare. Throughout her career in the Probation Service, she has taken a particular interest in gender issues and in work with the victims and perpetrators of domestic violence. She carries lead policy development responsibility in both of these areas for West Midlands Probation Service and is a member of ACOP's Domestic Violence Action Group. She was recently a panel adviser to the ESRC Violence Programme.

Charlene Henry
Charlene Henry has been involved in the domestic violence field for eleven years. She is a founder member of Hadhari Nari Women's Project in Derby and of the Derby Domestic Violence Action Group. She is very committed to equal opportunities and takes an active stance against racism in society. Currently, Charlene works as a project manager within Hallmarks Community Housing Association and is a Council of Management member of National Council of the Women's Aid Federation of England.

Robyn Holder
Robyn Holder currently works in Australia as the Victims of Crime Coordinator for the Australian Capital Territory where she is implementing a Duluth-style programme. She is also Chair of the ACT Domestic Violence Prevention Council and Chair of Victim Support Australasia. From 1987 -1994, Robyn worked at the London Borough of Hammersmith (UK) in the Community Safety Unit. She was responsible for developing the Borough's Corporate Programme on Domestic Violence as well

as setting up the Domestic Violence Forum. Robyn enjoys crossing boundaries in her work and, with her young son, has a vested interest in challenging dominant (and dominating) masculinities.

Davina James-Hanman

Davina James-Hanman works as the Coordinator for the Greater London Domestic Violence Project, which aims to develop a London-wide inter-agency domestic violence strategy. Previously, she was employed by the London Borough of Islington as the first local government Domestic Violence Coordinator, a post which she took up after doing domestic violence voluntary work abroad, and working in a refuge. Davina has also acted as a consultant for a number of statutory and voluntary organisations. She has written a variety of domestic violence manuals and handbooks for both abused women and practitioners.

Barry Johnson

Barry Johnson is currently Assistant Chief Probation Officer at Hereford and Worcester Probation Service with a range of responsibilities that cover partnership arrangements, including Community Safety and Domestic Violence. He coordinates the probation service contribution to addressing domestic violence, which has included an initiative to change attitudes amongst people at school, the publication of a Directory of Services for women, multi-agency training, and an inter-agency group for perpetrators.

Liz Kelly

Liz Kelly has been a feminist researcher and activist in the field of violence against women and children for over 20 years. She has been active in establishing local services including refuges and rape crisis centres, and in local and national campaign groups. She is the author of *Surviving Sexual Violence*, and of many articles on domestic violence, sexual abuse of children, rape and sexual assault, pornography and feminist methodology. Since 1987, she has worked with other feminists (currently Sheila Burton and Linda Regan) at the Child and Woman Abuse Studies Unit, University of North London. Liz also chaired the Council of Europe Group of Specialists on Violence against Women.

Martha McMahon

Martha McMahon is an Associate Professor of Sociology at the University of Victoria, BC, Canada. She teaches in the areas of feminist theory, qualitative methods, and women and the environment. She is the author of *Engendering Motherhood* (Guilford, 1995) which won the 1996 American Sociological Association's Sex and Gender Section Book Award.

Annie Moelwyn-Hughes

Annie Moelwyn-Hughes works as an independent Domestic Violence Policy Consultant, and as a Senior Health Promotion Officer with Lothian Health in Edinburgh. She is interested in working with agencies to encourage effective provision and policy change that reflects women's needs and experience. She is a member of the Scottish Needs Assessment programme which undertakes work on Domestic Violence as a public health issue and co-author of *Domestic Violence* (Scottish Forum of Public Health Medicine).

Audrey Mullender

Audrey Mullender is Professor of Social Work at the University of Warwick. She has nearly twenty years experience of teaching social work in higher education, prior to which her background was in statutory social services. She has been Editor of the *British Journal of Social Work* and has herself produced over seventy publications in the social work field. Her books include: *Children Living with Domestic Violence: Putting men's abuse of women on the child care agenda* (1994, edited jointly with Rebecca Morley) and *Rethinking Domestic Violence: The social work and probation perspective* (1996).

Pragna Patel

Pragna Patel has been a member of Southall Black Sisters (SBS) since 1982. Until 1993, she was also a full time case worker for the organisation. She has contributed articles to a number of books and journals arising from SBS case work and campaigning experiences, on the subjects of Asian women and domestic violence, policing, the criminal justice system, the politics of multi-culturalism and religious fundamentalism.

Ellen Pence

Ellen Pence is one of the founders of the Duluth Domestic Abuse Intervention Project, which has become the internationally recognized model for a coordinated, inter-agency community response to woman battering. She has worked with this project since its inception in 1980. She earned her PhD from OISE,

Toronto, Canada, and is the author of many articles on domestic violence. She is the designer of training and educational curricula, and has conducted training seminars in many countries around the world.

Andy Stelman

Andy Stelman is currently Assistant Chief Probation Officer in Merseyside, with responsibility for work in the Criminal Courts, and for Community Safety issues. Andy worked as a regional training officer in Leeds before coming to Merseyside. He helped set up the first domestic violence perpetrators programme in Merseyside in 1992, and has written and spoken extensively at national conferences about the subject. He is a member of the Liverpool Domestic Violence Forum.

Andrea Tara-Chand

Andrea Tara-Chand was until recently manager of the Leeds Inter-Agency Project (Women and Violence) - LIAP - and was a key player in developing LIAP's work from 1990 when funding for the project was secured. Andrea is a management committee member of Sahara black women's refuge, and of PATH Yorkshire, a positive action training organisation for black ethnic minority people in Leeds. She has a long history of work in the women's and black voluntary sectors and is totally committed to working for the rights of black people and women.

Ann Webster

Ann Webster is an Equalities Advisor at Derby City Council where she has worked in the Equalities Unit since 1989 on a range of equality work, specialising in women's and disabled people's issues. As a disabled woman, Ann recognises the oppression and discrimination faced by many people in society, and, for many years, has campaigned to blow away the many myths and stereotypes faced daily by equality groups. In 1993/4, Ann was Derby's mayoress which enabled her to raise women's and disabled people's issues even higher in Derby and beyond. A survivor of domestic violence from a previous marriage, Ann was active in the Derby Domestic Violence Action Group from 1992.

Gill Hague

Gill Hague is a long-term activist against domestic violence and member of the women's movement. She has worked for many years in women's groups and projects, and has been employed as a community organizer, social worker, lecturer and researcher. She has many publications on domestic violence and on other issues, mainly concerning women, and has been an active participant in the politics of the refuge movement. With Ellen Malos, she is a founder member of the Domestic Violence Research Group at the University of Bristol. Gill's publications include the popular overview book, *Domestic Violence: Action for Change* with Ellen Malos and many chapters, articles and reports , particularly on the multi-agency approach.

Nicola Harwin

Nicola Harwin is National Co-ordinator of the Women's Aid Federation of England, the leading national charity working to end domestic violence with a national network of over 250 local services. With over 20 years experience of providing local and national services, Nicola has played a key role in monitoring and responding to legislation and policy affecting abused women and children, including giving evidence to the 1992 Home Affairs Select Committee Inquiry into Domestic Violence, responding to numerous government consultations, working as an expert advisor with a wide range of statutory and voluntary bodies, and acting as a consultant to several research projects into domestic violence. She also provides training on domestic violence and is the author of numerous publications: advice leaflets for survivors, training resources and handbooks for service providers, briefing papers for government and the public, and contributions to recent and forthcoming books.

Ellen Malos

Ellen Malos has been involved in the women's movement since the 1960s and has been a teacher and writer on women's issues for many years. Her 1980 publication *The Politics of Housework* has been recently republished in a new edition by New Clarion Press (1995). She is a Research Fellow and a founder member of the Domestic Violence Research Group at the University of Bristol (in the School for Policy Studies). With Gill Hague and Wendy Dear she conducted a national study of multi-agency domestic violence initiatives in the UK, and subsequently published a guide for good practice. She is also joint author, with Gill Hague of *Domestic Violence: Action for Change*, which is widely used by practitioners, students and many others.

1
Introduction

Ellen Malos, Nicola Harwin and Gill Hague

Context and beginnings

Domestic violence by men against women is now a public issue. During the late nineteenth century, it became the subject of campaigning activity and of new legislation in Britain, the United States and elsewhere, but this concern waned in the first part of the twentieth century (see e.g. Hague and Wilson, 1996). Then, in the early 1970s, women experiencing violence in the home and their children began to seek support from women's centres which were springing up under the impact of the women's liberation movement of the time (Pizzey, 1974; Dobash and Dobash, 1980; Rose, 1985). By the mid-Seventies, refuges had been set up by activists and survivors in towns and cities throughout the UK, and similar developments were occurring in other Western countries. In Britain, these refuges were mainly coordinated through the Women's Aid federations which have led the struggle against domestic violence for more than twenty-five years since that time.

It rapidly became clear to women activists within the refuge movement that domestic violence was an issue which cut right across the responsibilities of almost all local and national statutory agencies, and one to which none of them responded at all adequately. As research studies started to be conducted on violence in the home, unsympathetic, non-existent or inconsistent agency responses were recorded time and time again (see eg Binney, Harkell and Nixon, 1981; Borkowski et al, 1985; Pahl, 1985). Social services, for example, very much saw their brief at the time as directed towards working with so-called 'problem families' to keep them together, including those in which domestic violence was occurring, unless there was clear and direct abuse or neglect of the children (Maynard, 1985). Women and children who were forced to leave their homes due to domestic violence were not considered to be homeless by local authority housing departments prior to the homelessness legislation of 1977 (Rose, 1985, Binney, Harkell and Nixon, 1981, 1985, Malos and Hague, 1993), and the police would very often treat even severe and repeated violence as a minor incident (Dunhill, 1989, Edwards,1989). At worst, the woman herself might be treated as if she was wasting police time or was herself the offender, as Amina Mama (1996) documents in relation to black women, a reaction which has by no means disappeared today, especially where issues involving immigration or asylum might be at stake.

In this adverse situation, Women's Aid groups and refuges attempted to raise the issue of domestic violence in an empowering way and to work with statutory and voluntary agencies, often against the odds, to expand and improve the services offered to women experiencing domestic violence and their children. Inter-agency work between Women's Aid groups, the Women's Aid federations, and other agencies with the potential to provide services thus began as far back as the mid 1970s, as the new Women's Aid movement became aware of the massive problems which women seeking assistance encountered (Hague, Malos and Dear, 1996) .

At this time, there was no clearly developed concept of inter-agency or multi-agency cooperation in the United Kingdom. Indeed even now, as may be seen from some of the chapters of this book, there is no clear distinction drawn between inter-agency work (which can involve no more than two agencies in principle, and may be very informal), more formal work between two or more agencies, and complex, elaborate multi-agency work involving a number of agencies and aiming to include all those whose work is relevant. In practice (and within this book), the terms 'multi'- and 'inter'-agency are often used interchangeably.

A useful working definition, however, might be one which distinguishes between 'inter-agency' work involving a selection of two or three agencies working in cooperation and 'multi-agency' work which includes all relevant agencies and attempts to develop coordinated policy and practice in relation to a given area of social policy response.

In fact, the growth of the Women's Aid movement in the

second half of the 1970s coincided to some extent with the development of new concerns about the physical abuse of children in the family and the development of formal multi-agency child abuse procedures and panels (although these have sometimes excluded some voluntary sector agencies). Another strand in the development of the recognition of work across traditional boundaries was the development of joint health and social services initiatives from the mid-1980s onwards, which were initially inter-agency initiatives but with a wider multi-agency impact. The mid-eighties also saw the development of greater cooperation in some local authorities between statutory and voluntary agencies at a community level, as well as the development of police initiatives on community policing which are discussed elsewhere in this book.

The beginnings of multi-agency approaches to violence against women and domestic violence

By the mid 1980s, the scene was set for a number of parallel developments in different parts of the country and with different emphases. A variety of women's services and campaigning groups were in existence which were concerned with domestic violence, with rape, and with violence against women more widely, and which were working together for change (within the criminal justice system in particular). At the same time, there was also a growing volume of criticism of policing, some of which was expressed through systematic research (Bourlet, 1990; Edwards, 1989; Hanmer and Saunders, 1984) and which coincided with, or was a reaction to specific events, such as the serial murders of women in Yorkshire by Peter Sutcliffe or a television documentary on the Thames Valley Police in the early 1980s which showed the unsympathetic treatment of a rape victim. Simultaneously in some areas, there were more or less cooperative or acrimonious examinations of police practice in local authority and joint local authority/police committees (Hague and Malos, 1998).

By 1986-7, the need for changes in police practice had been accepted in Parliament by the Under-Secretary of State at the Home Office, and was given shape by a Home Office Circular in 1986 (Home Office, 1986) and an influential working party of the Metropolitan Police which reported in 1987 (although the widely leaked report was never published in full). By 1988, police domestic violence units and a police multi-agency approach to responses to domestic violence had begun to develop in some areas of London and in a few other areas of the country such as West Yorkshire (as a result of women's movement campaigns and police links with critical feminist researchers and/or local government initiatives). Developments in domestic violence work were documented in an important Home Office publication in 1989 (Smith, 1989).

Not all such developments were linked specifically to policing. In Portsmouth, Nottinghamshire, and Cleveland, for example, Women's Aid groups and local councillors or local authority officers began regular meetings during this period which were well-placed to develop into more formal multi-agency initiatives covering a variety of subject areas subsequently. A few pioneering multi-agency projects began to develop and to lead the way forward, for example, in Leeds, the London Borough of Hammersmith and Fulham, Nottinghamshire and Wolverhampton.

More official encouragement then developed after the issuing of the influential Home Office Circular 60/90 (which attempted to improve the police response and recommended police participation in multi-agency initiatives). This was followed by the National Inter-Agency Working Party Report (1992), produced by a coalition of agencies including Women's Aid, which included some guidelines on multi-agency work, and the House of Commons Home Affairs Committee Report in 1993. A number of initiatives from government departments and official bodies also contributed, most notably the Safer Cities projects and preventive projects on repeat victimisation, giving rise to a substantial number of inter-agency forums. In 1995, the Home Office published the Inter-agency Circular, *Inter-agency Co-ordination to Tackle Domestic Violence* (Home Office, 1995), which encouraged all relevant agencies to engage in multi-agency work. This important circular (currently being extensively revised) gave an impetus to the further development of initiatives which were already numerous and which had developed in a variety of ways from a variety of beginnings.

We also have to remember that these developments are not confined to the United Kingdom, but have been dynamically related to those which have taken place in a number of other regions, most notably in North America and Australasia, but in an increasingly wide selection of countries. It is that variety which this book wishes to illustrate, though it would by no means claim to be representative or exhaustive, and for various reasons contributions are not present which we had wished to include. In some cases, this is because the projects concerned have lost their funding or have succumbed to cutbacks in women's services and in welfare provision, both in other countries and in this one. Thus, it is important to remember that, while this book celebrates much that has been achieved and the general transformation, since the 1970s, in the level of provision and of inter-agency initiatives, these advances have also been accompanied by inadequate resourcing, budgetary cuts, and loss of services. Many refuges, domestic violence projects and multi-agency domestic violence forums currently face a perilous future.

Also, like many books, this one has been some time in the making and there have been important developments since some of the chapters were written. New legislative provisions and government guidance have been developed: for example, Part IV of the Family Law Act 1996, and the Protection from Harassment Act 1997, to improve legal protection for women experiencing domestic violence and their children; the Crime and Disorder Act 1998, which may raise the profile of domestic violence within community safety strategies. While we do not yet have a comprehensive national strategy on domestic violence, important new measures are also outlined within *Living Without Fear*, the new government document setting out integrated approaches to tackling violence against women, including continued public awareness initiatives and a revised multi-agency circular to all statutory bodies.

It is anticipated that both national and international encouragement of the inter-agency approach to tackling domestic violence will continue in the future. The approach has much to recommend it, but is also rife with potential problems. This book attempts to address these issues and to offer some ideas and potential avenues for the future development of multi-agency domestic violence work into the twentieth first century.

Contents

The contributions to this book have arisen from the authors' descriptions and analyses of developing practice in multi-agency initiatives in several different countries. The chapters are not all written from the same perspective. Some are more guarded or more critical of the approach than others. We hope that the book will offer to its readers information that will enable them to make their own assessments.

The first section of the book (Chapters 2- 7) discusses general matters relating to inter-agency work, in particular, issues for the women's movement against domestic violence and issues concerning racism and other types of discrimination, power and equality. The second section (Chapters 8-12) describes a variety of different approaches to multi-agency domestic violence work. The third section (Chapters 13-17) discusses multi-agency work in various service sectors (eg the police, housing and social services).

In chapter 2, Gill Hague provides a description of the national research study into multi-agency responses to domestic violence (see Hague Malos and Dear, 1996) which has been one strand informing the development of this book. This chapter highlights both key features of multi-agency forums and key issues for the development of inter-agency work.

In chapter 3, Nicola Harwin examines the role of Women's Aid in the development of multi-agency responses to domestic violence, drawing on local and national experiences and concerns, and critically discusses their potential effectiveness in improving responses to women and children in the context of current law, policy and practice.

In chapter 4, Thangam Debbonaire discusses the links between domestic violence against women and children and child protection work, and identifies some policy implications for the development of new multi-agency responses.

In chapter 5, Pragna Patel gives a provocative account of the development of multi-agency community policing, its connections with the development of multi-agency responses to domestic violence, and the implications for social justice and equality.

In chapter 6, Liz Kelly takes a critical look at the concepts of 'inter-agency work' and 'partnership' from a feminist perspective, and suggests ways forward for the development of more democratic and accountable ways of working.

In chapter 7, Charlene Henry and Ann Webster (in an interview with Gill Hague) describe the importance of, and the difficulties involved in, developing equalities work as an integral part of the multi-agency response. They detail the concrete steps taken up until 1998 by the Derby Domestic Violence Action Group to develop an equalities perspective within all aspects of its work.

Chapters 8 and 9 by Robyn Holder and Andrea Tara-Chand, respectively, discuss the work of the Hammersmith Domestic Violence Forum and the Leeds Inter-agency Project, two of the most creative and pioneering multi-agency initiatives in the UK.

In Chapter 10, Annie Moelwyn-Hughes discusses ways of reaching joint agreements on domestic violence policy in the light of the development of the Multi-agency Strategy on Domestic Violence in Central Scotland.

Chapter 11 by Martha MacMahon and Ellen Pence, describes the contributions made by the pioneering and highly influential Duluth Domestic Abuse Intervention Project in Duluth, Minnesota, currently recognised as one of the most innovative, world-wide.

Chapter 12 by Jennifer Gardiner details the historical and social background to domestic violence work in Australia, looks at developments in government action on domestic violence and multi-agency approaches, and describes some specific Australian multi-agency projects.

Chapter 13 by Ellen Malos and Chapter 15 by Andy Stelman, Barry Johnson, Sue Hanley and Jane Geraghty discuss the roles, respectively, of housing and probation services in multi-agency initiatives on domestic violence. Both chapters place the issue in a wider context of specific policies and practices both nationally and locally within the agencies concerned.

Chapter 14 by Sharon Grace details developments in the police response and in police contributions to multi-agency work using a Home Office research project which she conducted to assess the effectiveness of these responses.

Chapter 16 by Audrey Mullender discusses social services and multi-agency responses and engages in a wide-ranging discussion of the role of social services and social workers in relation to domestic violence and to child protection.

Finally, in Chapter 17 by Davina James-Hanman, inter-agency initiatives are discussed in relation to education services and to the development of education packs on domestic violence for use in schools.

References

Binney, V., Harkell, G. and Nixon, J. (1981) *Leaving Violent Men.* Bristol: Women's Aid Federation of England.

Borkowski, M., Murch, M., and Walker, V. (1983) *Marital Violence:*

The community response. London: Tavistock

Bourlet, A. (1990) *Police Intervention in Marital Violence.* Milton Keynes: Open University Press

Department of Health (1997) *Local Authority Circular: Family Law Act 1996, Part IV Family Homes and Domestic Violence.* London: Department of Health

Dobash, R. and Dobash, R. (1980), *Violence against Wives.* London: Open Books

Edwards, S. (1989) *Policing Domestic Violence.* London: Sage

Dunhill, C. (1989) *The Boys in Blue: Women's challenges to the police.* London: Virago

Hague, G. and Malos, E. (1996) *Tackling Domestic Violence: A guide to developing multi-agency initiatives.* Bristol: The Policy Press

Hague, G. and Malos, E. (1998) *Domestic Violence: Action for change.* (2nd Ed) Cheltenham: New Clarion Press

Hague, G., Malos, E. and Dear, W. (1996) *Multi-agency Work and Domestic Violence: A national study of inter-agency initiatives. Bristol:* The Policy Press

Hague, G. and Wilson, C. (1996) *The Silenced Pain: Domestic violence 1945 - 1970.* Bristol: The Policy Press

Hanmer, J. and Saunders, S. (1984) *Well Founded Fear: A community study of violence to women.* London: Hutchinson

Home Office (1995) *Inter Agency Circular: Inter-agency co-ordination to tackle domestic violence.* London: Home Office and Welsh Office

Home Office (1990) *Circular 60 / 90: Domestic Violence.* London: Home Office

Home Office (1986) *Circular 69 / 86: Violence against Women.* London: Home Office

House of Commons Home Affairs Committee (1993), *Report of Inquiry into Domestic Violence.* London: HMSO

Law Commission (1992) *Family Law, Domestic Violence and the Occupation of the Family Home.* Report No. 207, London: HMSO

Malos, E. and Hague (1993) *Domestic Violence and Housing: Local authority responses to women and children escaping violence in the home.* Bristol: WAFE and University of Bristol

Mama, A. (1996) *The Hidden Struggle: Statutory and voluntary responses to violence against black women in the home.* London: Whiting and Birch

Maynard, M. (1985) 'The response of social workers to domestic violence', in Pahl, J. (ed) *Private Violence and Public Policy.* London: Routledge and Kegan Paul, pp 125-41

National Inter-Agency Working Party (1992) *Domestic Violence.* London: Victim Support

Pahl, J. (1985) *Private Violence and Public Policy: The needs of battered women and the response of public services.* London: Routledge and Kegan Paul

Pizzey, E. (1974) *Scream Quietly or the Neighbours will Hear.* Harmondsworth: Penguin

Rose, H. (1985) 'Women's refuges: Creating new forms of welfare?', inUngerson, C. (ed) *Women and Social Policy.* London: Macmillan, pp 243-59

Smith, L. (1989) *Domestic Violence: An overview of the literature.* Home Office Research Studies 107. London: HMSO

Ungerson, C. (ed) (1985) *Women and Social Policy.* London: Macmillan

The Women's Unit (1999) *Living Without Fear. An integrated approach to tackling violence against women.* London: Cabinet Office.

2
The multi-agency approach to domestic violence: A dynamic way forward or a face-saver and talking shop?

Gill Hague

Introduction

This chapter presents a brief overview of some of the issues involved in developing multi-agency responses to domestic violence. It is designed as a 'context-setter'. Many of the issues raised, the advantages and disadvantages, the innovations and the difficulties, are considered in more detail - and from a variety of different perspectives - in later chapters and are not developed in any depth here.

The chapter is based on the findings of a major research study by the University of Bristol Domestic Violence Research Group. This national study, completed in 1996 and generously supported by the Joseph Rowntree Foundation, examined multi-agency responses to domestic violence (see Hague, Malos and Dear, 1995; Hague, Malos and Dear, 1996; Hague and Malos, 1996; Hague, 1997).

The Development of the multi-agency approach

Multi-agency work as a response to domestic violence is currently being encouraged in many parts of the world. In various countries in Africa, Asia and Latin America, for example, agencies have begun to come together to start to coordinate existing projects, to set up previously non-existent services, including shelters / refuges and women's support groups in some areas, or to engage in awareness-raising and campaigning work about violence against women. In the United States and Canada, multi-faceted inter-agency domestic violence intervention projects have been established in several areas including London, Ontario; Duluth, Minnesota; King County, Seattle; and Quincy, Massachusetts. Similarly in Australia and New Zealand, a variety of coordinating multi-agency projects are developing. Some of these initiatives are discussed in this book. However, it is significant in this context that a few domestic violence intervention projects in both Western and developing countries initially committed themselves to writing for the book but had to pull out due to funding crises or closure, precipitated, in some cases, by the advent of right wing governments. Despite these difficulties, however, inter-agency work on domestic violence is encouraged by international bodies including, for example, the United Nations and the Beijing Conference Platform for Action (UN Department of Information, 1995; UNICEF, 1997), and was promoted by a variety of speakers at the large international conference on violence against women held in Brighton in the UK in November 1996.

In the UK, the British government is in the process of attempting to develop domestic violence policy, although not without contradictions (see for example, Hague and Malos 1994). The impact of the new Labour Government cannot yet be gauged at the time of writing. However, Inter-departmental Ministerial and Officials Groups now exist, with the Home Office as the lead ministry. These groups were responsible for initiating an Inter-agency Circular entitled *Inter-agency Coordination to tackle Domestic Violence*. This Circular, produced in 1995 by the Home Office and the Welsh Office and currently being reworked by the present government, encourages all relevant agencies to work together on an inter-agency basis to build a coordinated response to domestic violence (Home Office, 1995). The establishment of multi-agency forums has also been recommended by the Women's Aid federations, by the House of Commons Home Affairs Committee *Inquiry into Domestic Violence* (House of Commons

Home Affairs Committee, 1993) and, earlier, by the National Inter-agency Working Party Report, *Domestic Violence* (1992; see also, in this early context, Smith, 1989).

The terms, 'multi-agency' and 'inter-agency' tend to be used interchangeably in this field, and normally refer to initiatives which should properly, perhaps, be called 'multi-agency' since they consist of a wide-ranging group of agencies working together. In many areas, there have been one-off multi-agency initiatives on domestic violence (for example, the holding of specific training courses), and informal liaison may have been developing over many years and be just as effective as a more structured approach. Nevertheless, more formal, on-going multi-agency domestic violence forums have now been established all over the UK. In our research study, there were at least 200 such forums in existence in 1996, bringing together relevant local agencies in both the statutory and voluntary sectors on a regular basis to attempt to coordinate domestic violence responses.

The name of the game

Women's Aid and the refuge movement have been at the forefront of the struggle against domestic violence in the UK for twenty five years, and have been attempting to get other agencies involved for much of that time. It must be said that, until recently, few others were interested. Now, however, inter-agency work has become the name of the game, not only in domestic violence work but in many other fields as well.

Local multi-agency work has been encouraged by both central and local government in a whole variety of social and welfare services, often without any input of resources. These areas of work include child protection, crime prevention, community safety, community care, action on drugs, and so on. A considerable amount of both government and independent research has been done on multi-agency responses to social problems, much of which, while noting potential opportunities for improved practice, has also taken a rather sober approach in elaborating the many complex difficulties involved. These difficulties include power differences between agencies, the tendency of participating organisations to 'defend their own turf', differences in working ethos and practice, lack of resources, controversies over whether there should be a lead agency, and differences regarding gender, race and other equalities issues (see eg Sampson et al, 1991;

Smith et al, 1993; Liddle and Gelsthorpe, 1994; Lloyd, 1994; Arblaster et al, 1996). This kind of joint working is clearly a hard thing to do. Nevertheless, 'inter-agency' is now something of a 'buzz-word'. We are all meant to be doing it. But does it work in relation to domestic violence?

Some pros and cons

The fact that statutory and voluntary sector agencies are finally taking on domestic violence is encouraging, and the findings of our research were clearly that inter-agency coordination can lead to very creative and innovative new developments (Hague, Malos and Dear, 1996). In contrast to some types of joint work between agencies, multi-agency work on domestic violence rarely concentrates on individuals. Fears by some women's organisations that inter-agency coordination would result in increased 'surveillance' of abused women and children, and in inappropriate conferring between agencies about individual cases, appear to be largely unfounded so far. There are few statutory responsibilities in relation to domestic violence (partly because the use of state powers to protect women from violence is taken massively less seriously than their equivalent use regarding children). A positive side to this otherwise disturbing situation is that the creative, informal dynamism and innovation which characterise many inter-agency forums may be facilitated by the lack of formal statutory control (as compared with the situation for child protection where much more formal inter-agency approaches are in place).

Nevertheless, while much dedicated inter-agency work is occurring in different areas of the country, the approach is only worth pursuing if services for women and children experiencing domestic violence are improved and if their safety is enhanced - in other words, if things get better. Unfortunately, there are plenty of examples of the 'talking shop' approach to inter-agency coordination in which nothing actually happens.

Our research showed that, as well as being a creative development in many localities, a commitment to inter-agency work could act as:

• a face saver for local and central government - a way of appearing as if you are doing something about domestic violence without having to put in any real resources; and

- a smokescreen to disguise ineffectual action or the lack of any action at all, a way of looking (and possibly feeling) good while nothing much really changes and abused women and children continue to have few services available to them, and those which do exist face cutback.

There are very real drawbacks to an uncritical embracing of the 'multi-agency solution', and it is vital, in this context, that we ask ourselves why inter-agency work is being encouraged at a time of resource shrinkage. Is it merely a con and a cheap option?

It is also vital that we consider what it means to be attempting to coordinate services and structures if those services and structures are inadequate, piecemeal and imbued with conflicting attitudes to domestic violence. An addressing of these issues can assist us in building multi-agency responses which are effective and useful, cognizant of both their own potential and their own pitfalls, and able to carry both individuals and agencies forward in tackling domestic violence. If, on the other hand, an analysis of this type leads to the conclusion that the multi-agency project under consideration is nothing but a face saver for local or central government or a sop to those campaigning for effective domestic violence policy, then such a project is probably not worth pursuing.

Who is involved in forums?

At the moment in the UK, more and more multi-agency initiatives are being established, often without the critical analysis suggested above. Many inter-agency forums have been initiated by the police as a result of Home Office Circular 60/1990 (Home Office, 1990) which laid out the parameters of an improved police response to domestic violence, including participation in inter-agency initiatives. Women's Aid refuge groups and local authorities have also been active in domestic violence forums, in the latter case often through the auspices of community safety, equalities or policy units. In our research, refuges and the police were most often involved. Social services, probation and housing authorities and agencies participated significantly less often, although these agencies were taking an active, or even a major, role in many forums (see also Hague, Malos and Dear, 1995; Hague and Malos, forthcoming, 1998). In some forums, solicitors and other practitioners in the criminal justice system were very active.

Where are health and education services?

During the research study, it became clear that health services were absent from many local domestic violence forums. Health visitors sometimes take an active role, but in general doctors and other health service personnel participate very rarely. This lack is reflected in the fact that there is no separate health chapter within this book, despite approaches by the editors to several health practitioners. However, health services are of key importance in building sensitive and effective responses to abused women and their children, and one of the findings of the study was that these services need to take a more active role in inter-agency work. On the positive side, some health workers are developing good policy and practice guidelines and protocols for domestic violence work. Recent guidance from the Department of Health on both inter-agency work and on the development of practice guidance will be of some assistance (Department of Health, 1997), but more guidelines specifically on health issues are needed.

Education departments are similarly absent. While such departments play a less key part in responding to domestic violence on an emergency basis, they have a vital role in education and future prevention. In addition, the effect on children of witnessing, and being involved in, domestic violence against their mothers is an issue which has 'found its time' (Mullender and Morley, 1994; Hague, Kelly, Malos and Mullender, 1996). Some domestic violence forums have children's needs subgroups and may engage in work on youth and education issues (see the chapter by James-Hanman in this volume).

What do inter-agency forums do and how are they structured?

The types of work done by inter-agency forums include:

* facilitating the provision of refuges and other emergency women's services;
* the coordination of services overall (eg setting up coordinating procedures, conducting monitoring and research, producing directories of services and practice guides);
* the identification of gaps in services (by eg conducting service audits) and, in some cases, the provision of new services (eg telephone helplines and women's support groups)
* the development of improved services, of good policy and

practice guidelines within individual agencies and of domestic violence training initiatives for practitioners and policy-makers across agencies;
- the conducting of public education and awareness-raising work (for example, Zero Tolerance campaigns); and
- other educative and preventative work (for example, establishing perpetrators programmes, working in the education services and producing education packs for schools etc).

In order to conduct this work, some forums have developed formal structures, management committees and subgroups, and have produced written guiding principles, aims and objectives, procedural guidelines and other terms of reference including equal opportunity policies. Some then organise their work around detailed action plans, regularly reviewed, or, in a few cases, longer term strategic plans. In several areas of the country, two-tier systems have been set up with a county-level forum evolving wider domestic violence strategy, and smaller grass-roots or practitioner forums feeding information into it. Such arrangements had achieved limited degrees of success at the time of our study, but the approach appears to be worth pursuing.

The support and commitment of managers
The research found that some degree (at least) of involvement at policy-making level was usually important in order to make changes. It should be noted, here, that a few forums are campaigning or grass-roots groups or women's networks and are seeking to develop through a different route and with a different agenda to the 'policy / management' one (see also the chapters by Harwin, Kelly and Patel). The issue of management involvement in inter-agency initiatives is clearly a complex one.

Such involvement can detract from the creative dynamism and grass-roots appeal of an initiative, but was clearly identified as important by many forums in our study. On a general level, practitioners in both statutory and voluntary sector agencies often participated in inter-agency forums during our research, but gaining the support and involvement of managers and policy-makers was substantially more difficult (with the possible exception of the police).

However, it was clear from the study that in order to enable effective inter-agency coordination and the adoption of specific improvements in agency policy and practice, the active commitment (if not the participation) of senior managers to multi-agency domestic violence work was essential. With clear management support, inter-agency domestic violence work could then become part of the agreed policy of the organisation, with officers delegated to attend forums, rather than participating in an ad hoc way.

Gaining the support of agencies at management and policy-making level in this way, raising the profile of the local forum, and being in a position to facilitate policy and practice changes in a local area and within individual agencies were identified by many in the study as essential for the meaningful development of the approach. There was evidence that, where these developments had occurred, multi-agency forums could participate actively in evolving domestic violence policy and strategy across a whole locality and could also act as an effective 'watchdog' on the quality of local service delivery.

Resources and policy development

One of the largest issues facing inter-agency initiatives is lack of resources. As a result of this and other complex factors, many forums get stuck at the networking stage (although networking can be helpful in itself). Both statutory and voluntary sector agencies will normally donate and share whatever resources that they can, but the development of meaningful policy and practice work, and the coordination and development of services and of awareness raising and preventative initiatives, are almost impossible without further resource input. A difficult issue can then be competition for resources with refuge, advocacy and support services for abused women and their children. While best practice is clearly to support improved direct service provision rather than to act as a competitor, and many inter-agency forums avoid such competition as a matter of agreed policy, it can still occur as funding pressures increase.

In general, a principled commitment to inter-agency domestic violence work can often happen only where agencies see tackling domestic violence as one of their core responsibilities. Our research found that, if inter-agency domestic violence initiatives are to become effective on a widespread level, further guidance from, and policy development by, other government departments and agencies apart from the Home Office (and the police), to amplify the Inter-agency Circular, would be useful. It is vital to understand that inter-agency approaches can only work if they are embedded within a wider supportive policy framework. Further guidance and advice would also be of help from the Women's Aid federations, to expand that already available, and from national voluntary sector agencies, local authorities and health bodies.

Power differences

During our study, power differences between agencies participating in multi-agency forums were clearly difficult to deal with. While some forums were able to overcome these difficulties and evolve meaningful guiding principles, joint understandings of domestic violence and collaborative ways of working, in many, power differences and their possibly corrosive effects were overlooked or sidestepped.

It is also undoubtedly true that inter-agency work can dilute feminist or women-centred ideas about domestic violence, perhaps ending up with a 'lowest common denominator effect', even though many forums have struggled to evolve common visions, to develop women-centred analyses of domestic violence based on ideas about gender and power in relationships, and to evolve practices which are empowering of abused women and children.

Statutory agencies in multi-agency forums have a tendency to attempt to 'own' or to lead the work done, even though many are aware of this difficulty and do their best to avoid it. It happens, however, almost by default as a result of different working practices, procedures, patterns of hierarchy, and expectations of control. Voluntary sector agencies, for their part, may not prioritise the work, or see that they, too, must adapt and change alongside the statutory sector. The struggle, then, is to maintain the dynamism of inter-agency work while engaging all agencies equally, gaining the commitment of higher management, but avoiding statutory agencies 'taking over'.

In particular, it has been suggested that difficulties can be experienced in trying to evolve a working multi-agency response with the police. Many of the study interviewees described how the police have engaged in a great deal of sensitive inter-agency work, especially where specialist police domestic violence units or domestic violence liaison officers posts are in existence. Where the police take a continuously dominating role, however, leading the initiative at all times, for example, or holding all meetings on police premises, the outcomes according to our research were less happy. Various women's organisations and others have raised general issues about the potentially racist or discriminatory nature of some policing work, as well as the masculine ethos of police services, which can make inter-agency coordination with them difficult or even inappropriate (see Patel in this volume; also Hague and Malos, 1997).

The women's movement against domestic violence

The site of women's resistance to domestic violence in this country and worldwide has been, and continues to be, the international movement of women against violence. Women have always resisted male violence, and this resistance of course takes different forms in different countries, cultures and time periods. Currently, developments in women's resistance to domestic abuse are taking place in different ways all over the world with the formation of grass-roots campaigns, and new services and responses. In the UK, the Women's Aid federations and other women's refuge groups, organisations and campaigning bodies, such as Southall Black Sisters and Justice for Women, form part of this movement. A key issue then becomes: how can a social movement of women be part of a mainstream multi-agency response? How can this social movement of resistance articulate with statutory and voluntary sector joint working? (See also the chapters by Harwin and by Kelly in this volume.)

In our research, we found that Women's Aid and the refuge movement were often isolated or marginalised within inter-agency forums, sometimes finding themselves in the position of giving credibility to such a forum while being powerless to prevent their ideas being diluted or coopted beyond recognition. However, creative possibilities to ensure that Women's Aid remain in a central position were being tried out in some areas of the country. The Women's Aid federations, and the Women's Aid Federation of England in particular, offer consultancy and advice on multi-agency work, and, in some areas, Women's Aid inform and nourish all the inter-agency work which takes place. These issues are discussed more fully in the next chapter.

Equalities issues and the involvement of abused women and children

Our research suggested that, when it was conducted, power and equalities issues were only being taken on by a small number of forums in a meaningful way with the result that organisations of black women, disabled women, or lesbians, together with children's groups, community groups, and various others, often felt left out and pushed to one side. Multi-agency work on domestic violence could then become something which was somewhat cut off from grass-roots organisations and which felt unwelcoming to some individuals and groups with an interest in the issue.

The involvement of abused women and their children, and informal accountability to them, were issues of concern in our research. Disappointingly, only five out of 70 women interviewed had heard of their inter-agency forum even in passing, and only two were involved in any way. Even where refuges were very active in their local forum, women from the refuges rarely knew anything about it. In this context, questions then have to be asked about what it means when inter-agency coordination of services is occurring without the involvement of women and children who have experienced violence, or any consultation with them. Where, in such a situation, is the power? It is clearly not with those who have experienced abuse. Women's Aid and the refuge movement have always had policies of attempting to raise the voices of abused women and children and to promote their views and needs, but the translation of such ideas into the work of inter-agency forums is slow in coming.

The positives

On the bright side, some forums are developing innovative new practice to involve abused women and to seek their views through, for example, survivors advisory groups which monitor the work of the forum. Alternatively, in some areas, local refuges are involved, as an agreed principle of forum policy, as conduits of information from groups of abused women to the local forum and vice versa. Some forums are also developing general equalities work as an integral part of all the training, awareness raising, educative work and service provision that they do. Equalities then becomes, not only part of the work done, but also an integral part of the structure and organisation of the inter-agency project. The multi-agency initiatives which are engaged in this work point out that domestic violence affects all communities and that building a multi-faceted, community response means just that. Everyone - and all communities - need to be involved. Therefore equalities work is viewed as an essential part of the multi-agency approach (see also chapter 7 by Henry, Webster and Hague).

Many forums are chaired by Women's Aid and local refuge groups or, alternatively, these groups may take a central role in the management of the initiative. Local policy and practice has been transformed in some areas, especially, where long-established forums have pioneered the work, as in Leeds, Hammersmith and Fulham and Islington, and in particular where the forum has been able to employ coordinators and development workers. In some local areas, particularly active and committed support from the top management of statutory and voluntary sector agencies has assisted in giving inter-agency work a high profile leading to effective and dynamic policy and practice development.

At its best, therefore, and especially where the women's movement against domestic violence stays centre stage, inter-agency work on domestic violence can be a way of finally getting the state to take on the issue. It can be a creative 'next step' in combating domestic violence, and in moving forward from the provision of refuges and support services for women and children to spreading the work more widely, improving policy and practice and conducting preventative, educational and consciousness-raising work.

The provision of services, and the development of coordinating, campaigning and educative initiatives can then go hand in hand as two sides of the same coin as we move slowly forward towards a society where domestic violence is no longer tolerated. How far this is happening in practice, and the stumbling blocks and positive staging posts along the way, are discussed in detail in the rest of this book.

References

Arblaster, L., Conway, J., Foreman, A. and Hawtin, M. (1996) *Asking the Impossible? Inter-agency working to address the housing, health and social care needs of people in ordinary housing*. Bristol: The Policy Press

Department of Health (1997) *Local Authority Circular: Family Law Act 1996, Part IV Family Homes and Domestic Violence*. London: Department of Health

Hague, G. (1997) 'Smoke-screen or leap forward', *Critical Social Policy*, 17(4)

Hague, G., Kelly, L., Malos, E. and Mullender, A. (1996) *Children, Domestic Violence and Refuges.* Bristol: WAFE

Hague, G., Malos, E. and Dear, W. (1996) *Multi-agency Work and Domestic Violence: A national study of inter-agency initiatives.* Bristol: The Policy Press

Hague, G., Malos, E. and Dear, W. (1995) *Against Domestic Violence: Inter-agency initiatives.* Bristol: SAUS Publications

Hague and Malos, E. (forthcoming, 1998) 'Inter-agency approaches to domestic violence and social services', *British Journal of Social Work*, 28, pp369-386

Hague, G. and Malos, E. (1997) 'The police: Inter-agency initiatives as a response to domestic violence' *Police Journal*, LXX, 1

Hague, G. and Malos, E. (1996) *Tackling Domestic Violence: A guide to developing multi-agency initiatives.* Bristol: The Policy Press

Hague, G. and Malos, E. (1994) 'Domestic violence, social policy and housing', *Critical Social Policy*. 42

Home Office (1995) *Inter Agency Circular: Inter-agency Co-ordination to Tackle Domestic Violence.* London: Home Office and Welsh Office

Home Office (1990) *Circular 60/90: Domestic Violence.* London: Home Office

House of Commons Home Affairs Committee (1993) *Report of Inquiry into Domestic Violence.* London: HMSO

Liddle, M. and Gelsthorpe, L. (1994) *Crime Prevention and Inter-agency Cooperation,* Police Research Group Paper 53. London: Home Office

Lloyd, C. (1994) *The Welfare Net.* Oxford: Oxford Brookes University

Mullender, A. and Morley, R. (1994) *Children living with Domestic Violence.: Putting men's abuse of women on the child care agenda.* London: Whiting and Birch

National Inter-Agency Working Party (1992) *Domestic Violence.* London: Victim Support

Sampson, A., Smith, D., Pearson, G., Blagg, H and Stubbs, P. (1991) 'Gender issues in inter-agency relations: Police, probation and social services', in Abbott, P. and Wallace, C. (eds) *Gender, Power and Sexuality.* London: Macmillan

Smith, L. (1989) *Domestic Violence: An overview of the literature.* Home Office Research Studies 107, London: HMSO

Smith, R., Gaster, L., Harrison, L., Martin, L., Means, R. and Thistlewaite, P. (1993) *Working Together for Better Community Care.* Bristol: SAUS Publications

UN Department of Information (1995) *The Beijing Declaration and The Platform for Action. New York:* United Nations

UNICEF (1997) *The Progress of Nations.* London: UNICEF

3
New opportunities, old challenges? A perspective from Women's Aid

Nicola Harwin

In this chapter I will look at the role of Women's Aid in the development of multi-agency responses to domestic violence, the impact of multi-agency work on, and advantages and disadvantages for, Women's Aid's role and services, and the opportunities and challenges we face in developing effective responses to abused women and children. This chapter draws on my own experience of working locally and nationally for the last 25 years, as well as on feedback from local Women's Aid refuges and individual activists through conferences, workshops, and informal surveys.

Introduction

For more than 25 years, Women's Aid groups scattered throughout the country have provided practical and emotional support as part of a range of services to women and children experiencing violence and other abuse from those with whom they are living. Women's Aid grew out of the women's liberation movement of the late 1960s and early 1970s: the 'great mobilisation of women' described by Rebecca and Russell Dobash (1992). As women came together, the issue of violence in the home, as well as other forms of sexual and interpersonal violence to women, became highlighted. In those early years, there were very few options available to women seeking alternatives to living with violent men. Protection under civil or family law was almost impossible to get (except in the context of divorce);

domestic violence was not accepted as a reason for homelessness; the police dismissed 'domestics' as a trivial and time-wasting use of their resources; and the response of most agencies was 'go back home and make it up'.

The first Women's Aid groups were set up in response to women's desperate need for a place to stay with their children, where their violent partners could not find them. Those early refuges were run entirely on the voluntary labour of committed women, activists and survivors. Premises were often in poor condition and usually overcrowded, but they provided safety and support and enabled many of the women who used them to break away and start a new life free from abuse. By 1974, thirty five groups in different parts of England had managed to set up refuges, and gave advice to women who contacted them. From then on, Women's Aid was and remains the key support agency for women and children experiencing domestic violence. (Fuller accounts of the development of the Women's Aid movement are given in Hague and Malos, 1998, and Dobash and Dobash, 1992, but a brief discussion of this is necessary to set in context some of the contemporary issues for Women's Aid in relation to multi-agency initiatives.)

Early forms of response within the refuge movement were linked to the emerging understanding of many activists themselves about the nature of sexual and interpersonal violence and patriarchal relations ('the personal is political'), and to the values and methods of work - promoting empowerment, and self determination - being developed in the late 1960s and early 1970s by civil rights and liberation movements across the world. One guiding principle for the refuge movement from the beginning was to recognise that there is no 'them' and 'us', that any woman can be at risk from domestic violence, regardless of race, ethnic or religious group, class, sexuality, disability or lifestyle, and that women working together could change things together.

By sharing our experiences, survivors and activists quickly learnt that 'domestic violence' included a range of physical, emotional and sexual abuse - not all of which was immediately recognisable as violence - but which was intended to dominate and control an abused woman's behaviour and choices. As our understanding of the dynamics of domestic violence grew, we acknowledged its origins within the traditional and patriarchal family structures of domination and subordination, and within a global framework of discrimination against women, and denial of women's human rights. In the late 1960s and early 1970s, relationships between men and women were already under scrutiny against a new feminist vision of equality, of the creation of non-violent and non-abusive relationships. Responding effectively meant therefore recognising the gender and power dynamics of women abuse, and creating autonomous women-only services which were both protective and empowering, as well as challenging gender inequalities that provided infra-structural support for male violence. Our approach, which challenged explanations of domestic violence as located in the individual or psychological characteristics of abusers or survivors, was for many years in conflict with the mainstream social welfare ideology and understanding of representatives and practitioners of statutory agencies (see for example, Pahl 1985, Dobash and Dobash 1992, Hague and Malos 1998), and has only been relatively recently ratified and supported by national and international directives on gender and human rights (see for example, the Convention on the Elimination of Discrimination Against Women - Violence Against Women Directive, 1993; the Global Platform for Action from the United Nations Fourth World Conference on Women in Beijing, 1995).

Over the last 25 years, a diverse range of women working together - activists, survivors, and women from a wide variety of backgrounds, from statutory and voluntary agencies - have developed and expanded the network of support services to women and children experiencing domestic violence. Despite a variety of services and management structures and styles across the UK, some core beliefs for working with abused women and children remain. Women's Aid's advocacy role and services are based on a common approach: to believe women and children and make their safety a priority; to support and empower women to take control of their own lives; to recognise and care for the needs of children affected by domestic violence; and to promote equal opportunities and anti-discriminatory practice. The majority of local women's services share this approach, although there are a few projects with approaches that conflict with these values: for example, those that prioritise family reconciliation rather than women's advocacy services, which are run on paternalistic lines, or which focus mainly on housing services (see the discussion below and in chapter 13 on recent worrying developments in refuge provision).

There are now over 300 locally-based Women's Aid and independent projects across the UK, providing specialist support and advocacy for abused women and children, as well as a range of services: emergency and temporary accommodation, specialist services for children, specialist services for Black and minority ethnic women, telephone helplines and a variety of outreach support to women and children in the community. In England alone, more than 52,000 women and children stay in refuges each year, and over 100,000 contact us for help and support (WAFE, 1995). Across the UK, support and resources for local services are provided by the four Women's Aid federations: Welsh Women's Aid, Scottish Women's Aid, Northern Ireland Women's Aid and the Women's Aid Federation of England.

It is largely in response to this feminist direct action and associated campaigning over the last 25 years that the legislation and other agencies' practices have gradually changed. Lobbying for changes in the legal framework for protection led first to the Domestic Violence and Matrimonial Proceedings Act in 1976, which allowed a married or cohabiting woman to obtain a court order aimed at preventing further violence and to exclude her violent partner from the shared home. Then, a year later, domestic violence was specifically included in the homelessness legislation: women and children who were experiencing abuse were classed as 'in priority need' and the local authority had a duty to provide alternative accommodation. Police policies and practices have been slower to change, with the need for a major change in approach being clearly signalled by the Home Office Circular in 1990, which emphasised the importance of ensuring the safety of those experiencing abuse, and recommended arrest in appropriate circumstances. Women's Aid has continued to monitor policy and legislation and has in recent years influenced the introduction of the Family Law Act 1996, the Housing Act 1996, and other civil and criminal legislation.

25 years ago there was a resounding silence on the issue of domestic violence across most criminal justice and social welfare agencies. Today, the issue of domestic violence has become increasingly prominent. It is no longer of concern only to women's groups and voluntary organisations, but, largely as a result of our activism, it is also discussed by politicians and legislators, and in the media. The questions taken up by, for example, the Law Commission, the Home Office, the Home Affairs Select Committee, and the Inter-agency Working Party are very similar: how to increase the effectiveness of civil protection; how should the police best respond to domestic assaults, how to overcome some of the difficulties in the prosecution process? How can

violence against women and children be prevented in the long term? (Law Commission, 1989, 1992; Smith, 1989; Home Affairs Committee 1993; Victim Support, 1992). There is also now the beginnings of shared agreement as to the answers. Public interest in the issue has grown significantly, as indicated by the presence of domestic violence as a key storyline in all the major British soaps in the last four years, as well as now regular coverage in local and national media.

After more than two decades of campaigning, it is important to acknowledge our achievements. Any satisfaction is, however, tempered by an awareness that - despite heartening signs of welcome change - the surrounding context is in some respects even more inhospitable than it was a decade ago. In particular, the dominant ideology of the last two decades has structured the debate (and legislative and practice responses) in ways that are not always favourable to women (Harwin and Barron, in Itzin and Hanmer (eds), 1999, forthcoming). Within this context, the multi-agency initiatives on domestic violence which have developed over the last decade must be both welcomed and critically evaluated.

Women's Aid and the development of multi-agency responses

In one sense inter-agency work on domestic violence is not new - since the late 1960s there has been a history of feminist and community networking across a range of organisations to create new service responses to violence against women and to lobby for social change. From the early 1970s local Women's Aid groups had contact with a wide range of agencies through the development of referral systems, advocacy and public education work. In the early 1980s some Women's Aid groups also began to set up semi-formal inter-agency liaison involving police, social services, and housing agencies; others began to develop more formalised public education and institutional advocacy work through running conferences or training involving different agencies. These initiatives, developed and expanded through the establishment of local authority women's units, equalities units and community safety units in the 1980s prefigured the rapid development of more formalised multi-agency work in the 1990s.

Some of the earliest formal multi-agency initiatives (for example in Nottinghamshire, Leeds, London and

Wolverhampton) were the result of new alliances being formed by committed feminists working across voluntary sector and local authority boundaries, in the context of the radical reappraisal then taking place of the role of the police and the criminal justice system in relation to domestic violence. The changes in the police response to domestic violence, partly fuelled by activist criticism, led to a new focus on domestic violence as a crime and coincided with other developments - a number of research studies carried out by feminist academics, into both police responses and women's safety in the community, and the strong and growing feminist activism on violence against women. Across the country, a variety of domestic violence fora began to be set up, some spearheaded by police, others by local authorities or Women's Aid, often very different in focus or structure (see Hague, Chapter 2). However, the experiences of working with and for abused women and their children in the 1970s and 1980s left many Women's Aid activists deeply ambivalent about these developments.

Throughout the 1970s and 1980s, domestic violence was (and in many ways still remains) a difficult and unpopular issue that most agencies simply did not want to address. Through day to day support and advocacy work with women and children, many Women's Aid activists frequently found themselves in conflict with social workers, housing officers, police and other agency practitioners, often frustrated and critical of the lack of understanding shown by agency staff of women's needs and experiences, and of responses which frequently undermined women's safety and protection (see for example: Binney et al, 1981; Pahl, 1985). Many practitioners still find it hard to understand the emotional pressures and practical difficulties abused women face, especially why many find it hard to leave, or go back to live with violent men and often, like abusers themselves, minimise or deny women's fears and the dangers they and their children face.

In many areas the process of establishing a need for refuge services, and determining how they should be run, had already brought local groups into conflict with local authorities who not only had the power to give or withhold buildings, funding and other resources but sometimes attempted to dictate who should or should not be using the services (for example, attempting to exclude women from outside the local authority area). Ideological differences in relation to our own analysis of violence against women as well as our non-hierarchical working methods meant

Women's Aid groups often found themselves marginalised and ignored by statutory agencies.

There were of course some positive responses from within statutory services from the very beginning, but these were ad-hoc and largely dependent on the interest, concern, or commitment of isolated individuals working within these agencies (some of whom themselves became part of the emerging Women's Aid movement). Formal policy development on domestic violence by statutory agencies did not begin in most areas until the early 1980s, and this was mainly confined to some Labour local authority housing departments.

Contact with police, for example, was usually related to referral to, or defence of, the refuge building itself, or attempts to get belongings, and the limitations of police responses pre-1990 are well-documented (Dunhill, 1989). The grass roots nature of the movement, and its links to civil rights and women's liberation movements meant that many activists also had an ambivalent attitude to the state and, in particular, to the role of the police. There were and are, of course, radical differences in terms of agency values, culture, and personnel which inevitably lead to tensions and antagonism: the police are predominantly a white, male, rigidly hierarchical organisation; the Women's Aid movement, female, feminist, and overtly embracing alternative values, sexual identities and culture. In some areas, there was a wholesale rejection of working with police - especially in London and other inner city areas where black and ethnic minority communities were experiencing the impact of a high level of police presence and intervention - which was seen by some local Women's Aid groups as collusion with state repression (see also Patel Chapter 5).

Making the transition from a critical and defensive position, which less powerful individuals and organisations within any community are often forced to adopt, to one of developing new forms of joint working while still maintaining a challenging and feminist perspective on the issues has therefore been a difficult process for many activists, but for many it has been an empowering and worthwhile enterprise undertaken as part of a core aim of ending violence against women and children and of improving their options and choices.

Women's Aid: the national role in multi-agency work

Women's Aid's national role, like that of local groups, has been to keep a focus on the needs and experiences of women and children experiencing domestic violence and to improve policy and practice responses. At national level new opportunities for institutional advocacy and inter-agency liaison on domestic violence were both influenced by, and also drove forward, local initiatives within Women's Aid. From the late 1980s the Women's Aid national office in England had a key role in supporting a number of local Women's Aid groups in the development of multi-agency work through a number of mechanisms: for example, presentations at local and national multi-agency conferences provided a national overview of policy and practice issues and a national perspective on action needed to tackle domestic violence.

This work helped to raise the profile of Women's Aid with other agencies, to promote the need for funding of vital refuge support services, and to support local Women's Aid groups in raising difficult and controversial topics within the local multi-agency context. At the same time feedback from the national refuge network enabled national Women's Aid to represent local concerns to government and other national bodies.

At annual national Women's Aid conferences across the UK, the four federations began to address the new opportunities for multi-agency work and the issues and concerns these raised. Our perspective was also influenced by international developments and connections. In 1988 Welsh Women's Aid organised an international conference on domestic violence, with representation from women trying to develop services in 33 countries. The emphasis of the conference was also on participation by women from non-Western and developing countries, many of whom were sponsored by Women's Aid groups across the UK (with admirable lack of self-interest, as only a few delegates from the four federations were permitted so that the conference was not over-represented by UK women). Sharing information and experiences with women from countries as diverse as, for example, Uganda, Papua New Guinea, Brazil and India enriched our perspectives on the need to promote a diversity of community responses, which would not be dependent solely on increases in service provision and legal prerequisites for change.

At the same time our visions for change were influenced by work taking place within the United States, Canada and elsewhere attempting to create more holistic approaches within the criminal justice system. In 1989 a week long training by Ellen Pence from the Duluth Domestic Abuse Intervention Project, Minnesota, at Stirling University organised by the CHANGE project, marked the beginning for Women's Aid in England of a reassessment of criminal justice opportunities and the role of men's programmes as a part of developing community responses to domestic violence. Although the Scottish initiatives in both Stirling and Lothian (based on community intervention and perpetrators' programmes in Duluth) were not viewed uncritically by Scottish Women's Aid for a number of reasons, nevertheless the publicising of the Duluth experience over the next few years (and the feminist analysis that underpinned the project) did provide support and a number of useful counter-arguments to some of the non criminal justice-based and often worrying voluntary men's programmes and groups operating in the UK, which had already begun to attract interest from probation officers.

More recently, feminist activists, citing the multi-agency work of Ellen Pence and others in Duluth, have been promoting the concept of undertaking *institutional audits* within multi-agency work, to examine the way individual attitudes, organisational ethos, and existing procedures and protocols can interact to prevent an effective focus on women's safety or offender accountability. While the need for such 'audits' has been recognised by Women's Aid activists and trainers for many years, it is only now that the recent changes in statutory agencies' awareness of domestic violence, and the growth of multi-agency work, have led to this approach, whereby *institutional audits* as well as *tracking* (setting targets and monitoring the progress of each agency within the system to identify good and bad practice) may begin to be implemented (see Pence and McMahon, chapter 11 for fuller discussion). It has been suggested however by some activists that the focus on service audits and tracking is more useful than on 'changing attitudes' or 'raising awareness' of domestic violence. It may well be true in many instances but there are still areas of women's lives (going to court for injunctions or child contact orders, for example) where outcomes will only be changed if court personnel (solicitors, barristers, judges and magistrates) are required to have domestic violence awareness training.

From 1987 onwards the Women's Aid Federation of England lobbied for an interdepartmental approach to domestic violence, for the development of a national strategy, and for more effective coordinated service provision, at local and national level. We also made representations to the first Ministerial Group on Women in 1988 on the need for a coordinated strategy for local refuge services and funding, and for the need to support our National Helpline and other vital national work. As a result of a government response to our request for Helpline funding which indicated that Victim Support was funded to meet the needs of all victims, and by implication women and children experiencing domestic violence, we approached Victim Support for clarification of their service provision and referral policies, and a new era of work began.

This led, following discussions with Victim Support on the mutual lack of information and inter-agency cooperation to date, to a change in Victim Support referral policies which recognised the role of Women's Aid, locally and nationally. From 1990, some local Victim Support schemes were beginning to get an increase in referrals from police as a result of Circular 60/90 and changing police responses. This raised other practice issues for Victim Support, in particular, whether it was either safe or ethical in terms of confidentiality for a voluntary agency to receive or follow up referrals of women experiencing domestic violence, without their consent.

With the support of Women's Aid, Victim Support then convened an Inter-Agency Working Party on Domestic Violence, with a wide and representative membership: the Law Society, the British Association of Social Workers, the Association of Chief Police Officers, the Royal College of General Practitioners, the Association of Chief Officers of Probation, Relate, the Women's Aid Federation of England, and Welsh Women's Aid were among the members, and the Home Office, Department of Health and the Crown Prosecution Service sent representatives to observe the proceedings. These meetings gave Women's Aid representatives the opportunity to share their understandings and experience of domestic violence with senior representatives of other organisations and this led to a greater recognition among the statutory sector of key practice issues and the vital role of Women's Aid and the work of refuge support services. One beneficial outcome has been the Position Statement from the Association of Chief Officers of Probation, developed in consultation with the Women's Aid Federation of England, which was drawn up partly in response to concerns raised on the Working Party about the role of the probation service (and in particular court welfare officers) in cases of domestic violence.

This national multi-agency work, which reviewed service provision and responses across England and Wales, not only drew on local experiences and knowledge but also had a positive impact on local developments. The development of the formal position statement by ACOP, led in Leeds, for example, to the involvement of the local probation service who until then had been dragging their heels on domestic violence and multi-agency work. After the publication of the Report, and the Home Affairs Select Committee Inquiry that the Report helped instigate, Women's Aid was inundated with requests for information and support from multi-agency initiatives setting up across the country, as well as from individual agencies.

With government attention, 20 years after the last Select Committee, once more focused on domestic violence, evidence of the vital role of refuge support services, and representations on the need for proper funding and resources for them, were made to the 1992 Select Committee, not only by the Women's Aid federations, but also by representatives of police, probation and other statutory and voluntary agencies. In the event, the recommendations of the National Inter-agency Working Party, and consequent public attention, did lead to some government financial support, for the first time, for the Women's Aid National Helpline.

Though subsequent government action has, so far, been limited to short-lived public awareness campaign, the 1995 Inter-agency Circular and various further initiatives in 1998/99, nevertheless support for more comprehensive action has continued to grow, alongside the explosion of multi-agency initiatives, and an increased interest in the issue both nationally, and internationally. Successful national campaigns on domestic violence and the inequities of homicide law by Southall Black Sisters, Justice for Women, Women's Aid groups and others increased public awareness and led to new interest in domestic violence by more traditional women's organisations such as the National Federation of Women's Institutes. Work within a number of women's organisations, including the Women's National Commission, of which Women's Aid is a member, alongside international feminist networking, has helped develop international links and a global focus on violence against woman as a human rights issue - highlighted by the United Nations Global Platform for Action on Women drawn up by world governments at Beijing in 1995.

Local Women's Aid experiences of the impact of public attention to domestic violence and multi-agency work

Research in 1996 identified a number of issues for Women's Aid groups in the development of multi-agency initiatives (Hague, Malos and Dear, 1996): for example, power differences between statutory and voluntary agencies and the impact on multi-agency agendas and focus; and the marginalisation of Women's Aid groups in some areas for a number of reasons including insufficient staff time and resources to fulfil a wider advocacy and education role as well as to run an already under-funded crisis service. The research confirmed concerns we expressed during the Home Office consultation on the Inter-agency Circular in 1994, which did then subsequently contain references to the need to enable the participation of Women's Aid in multi-agency forums. However, recent feedback from a number of local Women's Aid groups through informal surveys, workshops and conferences suggests that while these problematic issues are still current, other aspects of multi-agency working have been beneficial and helpful.

Many activists report that there is improved recognition of the nature and extent of domestic violence, and of all the problems women face in getting free. The development of agreed terms of reference, of both single agency and joint policies on domestic violence (even though this has sometimes been a slow and difficult process), has led to better efforts to coordinate services, and to improvements in practice responses. In particular multi-agency work has improved inter-agency contact: practitioners in all agencies have been able to gain insight into the work of other agencies and realise the pressures and limitations on them; agency stereotypes have been challenged by information exchange and improved liaison; new designated roles and regular contact between people have led to better informal networking and liaison, and quicker access to the right person in each agency to deal with specific issues.

Although there has been a noticeable improvement in many areas in responses to domestic violence, some groups recently surveyed did express concern that despite a 'hardcore' of regular agency representatives on the forum, there was still a lack of commitment from the organisations from which they came. In particular, lack of ongoing training and education for service providers within different agencies was identified as a problem.

Lack of funding, coordination and commitment by the local authority was also a concern in some areas. Confirming findings of Hague and Malos in their research, in some areas Women's Aid groups, with the least resources of all the agencies, were the motivating force behind the forum, one group reporting that they were carrying all the administrative costs, and that staff were providing the human resources on a voluntary basis. In this area, and others, worries were expressed that pressure on and under-funding of refuge work might leave Women's Aid unable to sustain their input and that the multi-agency initiatives would dissipate.

While input to multi-agency work can vary enormously from refuge to refuge, in some areas new joint work was being developed which was perceived as leading to big improvements in, for example, the police response, though this has also had costs in terms of expanding workload and human resources for the local group. The opposite view was also expressed: that the forum was still mainly a 'talking shop' where agencies exchanged statistics and information about current work but that the real difficulties and dangers facing abused women were not being addressed and monitoring of adequacy of responses to abused women and children was simply not on the agenda.

In some areas, integration of equalities issues into the work of the forum was felt to be reasonably effective (see also Henry, Webster and Hague, chapter 7); in others local Women's Aid groups saw this as an uphill struggle to keep issues of race, sexual identity, disability and gender on the agenda. Representation of survivors was, by and large, through individuals who were often staff, ex-residents or volunteers with the local Women's Aid group, although some attempts were being made to establish survivors' groups. It may be that new forms of outreach work now being developed by local Women's Aid groups, in particular survivor support groups, may be a useful source of feedback to help monitor improvements needed in agency policy and practice. ESRC-funded research in the Domestic Violence Research Group at Bristol University into user and survivor involvement, and perceptions of multi-agency initiatives, taking place over the next three years, should offer useful insights for the development of better mechanisms for ensuring this.

New opportunities for Women's Aid in multi-agency work?

Many activists feel that involvement in multi-agency work has helped to raise Women's Aid profile and to improve the professional image and value of the organisation: by being able to make personal contact with policy makers; by liaison with, and training of, front-line staff; and through Women's Aid expertise being promoted by other agencies who have benefited from it. Improving the local group's reputation has in some areas helped expand the range of services and fund-raising capacity, particularly where Women's Aid's role as speaking for women and children survivors is explicitly recognised and valued. But others report that there is still a problem of not being seen as 'professionals' despite many staff or management committee members being 'professionals by experience', or fulfilling professional roles in other aspects of their lives. In areas where there are separate fora for senior policy-makers and for practitioners, Women's Aid/women's voluntary sector representatives may be effectively excluded from active participation in policy development, unless representation is clearly built in. And while, in many areas, local Women's Aid representatives have a key input to training for which they are paid, in others Women's Aid staff, while often pleased to be able to offer training and support services to other agencies because of the importance for improving responses to women and children, are still unpaid and effectively undervalued.

The focus on multi-agency work has also supported the development of outreach services. While Women's Aid has always had an 'outreach' role to women and children not wishing or unable to access refuge services, this has been the focus of increased attention in recent years, partly as a result of the expansion of interest in domestic violence by a range of agencies and the service development opportunities this has created. A domestic violence initiative by the Allied Dunbar Charitable Trust in cooperation with the Women's Aid Federation of England in the early 1990s helped promote the development of outreach work in both urban and rural areas, as well as providing vital funding for a range of specialist training courses for all refuge-based services. Women's Aid rural outreach projects, for example in Devon and Hereford, funded jointly by local authorities and the Rural Development Commission, supported and encouraged the development of multi-agency work in those areas. Many

Women's Aid groups would like to extend their outreach services but this rests on local opportunities for creating a public identity and contact point within the community - operating out of a refuge can jeopardise confidentiality and safety. Specialist outreach projects and staff posts have now been established in at least 30 local groups in England, and outreach workers have identified improving public awareness through multi-agency work as a key element in developing more effective service responses to women in the community and for securing more resources for specialist outreach services for women.

Public awareness campaigns such as Zero Tolerance have been a feature of many multi-agency initiatives involving local authorities over the last 5 years and many of these have been supported by local Women's Aid groups, who have in some areas, for example, Cleveland, worked very hard to ensure that the Zero Tolerance campaign was supported by the development of appropriate agency policies and responses. Public awareness campaigns are crucial as part of promoting improved community responses to domestic violence but nevertheless some of these campaigns have to date unfortunately been short-term relatively low cost options for some local authorities wishing to be seen to be taking some action against domestic violence. Unless all agencies are able to provide effective responses to increased demand then they are being set up to fail, and women seeking help following public information campaigns may not get the active support they need. For Women's Aid groups this dilemma is not new - opportunities to publicise our service have always existed, the problem has been trying to meet the demand.

A feature of many multi-agency forums has been discussion of how to deal with abusers and the role of direct work with men. Many refuges now support the need for community intervention strategies that include re-education programmes for abusive men that actively address their beliefs about women, that acknowledge power and control issues, that focus on behaviour changes, and that have a vision of non-violent relationships and equality in gender relationships. However the resources for this must not be found at the expense of services for women and children. Equally, evidence of the effectiveness of such programmes is ambivalent - in Duluth success has been estimated in the reduction of female homicides by partners or in the estimated 40% of men who stop being physically violent, but these programmes do not necessarily end other forms of dominating and controlling behaviour. New initiatives by the probation service (see Stelman et al, chapter 15) which focus on active intervention which does not condone abuse, which are sensitive to power issues, and to the need to promote women and children's safety, are welcome, and are in some areas providing opportunities for more joint work with Women's Aid and other women's voluntary groups, and the development of parallel advocacy and support services for women.

While it has been argued (see for example Patel, Chapter 5 and Kelly, Chapter 6) that multi-agency working leads to a less critical or feminist approach to domestic violence, many Women's Aid activists do not feel that they have compromised their principles by active engagement with multi- agency work. Their passion, commitment and feminist perspective has not changed but they have learnt to be more diplomatic and strategic about getting other agencies to understand women's needs and experiences and the changes that are needed. Feminists and pro-feminists in other agencies within multi-agency fora also act as allies in supporting a Women's Aid survivor-focused perspective. Women's Aid representatives often still have to be a 'thorn in the side' of local and national government, keeping up the pressure for changes in policy and practice but have developed new skills and approaches to professional and feminist practice. Multi-agency work can be tiring and demoralising, and there are tensions within Women's Aid between our role as a pressure group for social change and as providers of woman-centred services, but our twin roles as service providers and advocates demand that we engage with it both critically and constructively.

Refuge development and multi-agency work

The last decade has seen a number of developments within the supported housing field which are changing the nature of refuge support services, with worrying implications for the role of Women's Aid and refuge-based services as independent sources of individual advocacy and support for abused women and children. Research into the provision and funding of refuge support services (Ball, 1994) identified these moves by some housing associations towards the development and direct management of refuges as putting at risk not only the valuable investment provided by local women supporters and volunteers within an independent and autonomous framework of advocacy, support and empowerment, but also as leading to a 'reductionist' approach to meeting abused women and children's needs solely in terms of housing, and the loss of the integrated approach of the women's voluntary sector to tackling and challenging violence against women and children.

In some areas new refuges are being developed and directly managed by housing associations as primarily a housing resource; in others new projects that were developed in 'partnership' with existing local Women's Aid groups are being forcibly taken over and staffing structures and roles 'downsized'. A number of factors have led to these developments: increased publicity and attention about the issue of domestic violence; a supported housing funding framework that encourages development by housing associations within a fiercely competitive market but within which there is a pressing imperative to reduce revenue funding; and the effects of 25 years of under-funding and lack of support for refuge services which in a few areas has led to burn out and disintegration of the core voluntary management committee.

The argument may be made that as long as the services are being provided to women and children, the means by which they are run and managed are irrelevant. Unfortunately, however, such developments not only have implications for the range of direct services to women and children - a focus primarily on housing-based services, and a de-emphasis on other crucial ancillary outreach and advocacy services, including sometimes children's advocacy and welfare services - but also for the development of effective multi-agency initiatives to tackle violence against women.

Feedback at Women's Aid conferences and training events from individual refuge staff (including those from housing association direct-managed refuges) across the country has indicated that participation in multi-agency initiatives is much less frequent, and often not allowed, that staff change more frequently, and that there is less 'expertise' in the absence of the 'value-added' independent management committees of committed volunteers, especially as housing associations are generalist housing providers and will not themselves necessarily contain relevant expert staff.

The important role played by independent activists and survivors within the refuge (or shelter) movement world-wide as institutional advocates has been a crucial factor in the development of effective multi-agency responses (see also Pence and Mahon, chapter 11, and Gardiner, chapter 13, this volume). It is worrying that this independent advocacy is being undermined by these recent developments. It is a vital principle that core support services for women are able to operate to a clear advocacy agenda, and are not compromised or undermined through management by statutory services (e.g. local authority run hostel-type refuges) or by bodies who have other key agendas. In one recent example, a refuge worker expressed her concerns that, following the 1996 Housing Act, her local authority housing services were routinely refusing to provide public move-on accommodation, and were referring to unsuitable accommodation in the private sector, which resulted in even greater pressures to return home to violent men. When she attempted to take up this issue with the local authority, she was warned off by the housing association management, who did not want to jeopardise their ongoing relationship with the council over other development and housing management opportunities.

These developments (sometimes supported by local authorities helping solve their own budgetary problems) and similar moves by councils attempting to move to direct provision of emergency and temporary accommodation, and reduce the provision of refuges, or amalgamate specialist refuge provision for black women with local generalist services, are ironic especially in areas where multi-agency initiatives are simultaneously beginning to develop.

While there are in Women's Aid, as in other services, a number of areas where re-evaluation of service responses and opportunities for new developments to meet identified needs, in particular in relation to outreach services, must be grasped, this must not be at the expense of independence and autonomy. Partnership with other 'bigger fish' - statutory bodies and bigger 'voluntary' organisations like housing associations - may, if we are not vigilant, gobble up the women's voluntary sector, and our feminist independent voice.

The challenge for developing effective multi-agency responses: changing the social policy framework

Despite the heightened awareness of domestic violence over the past decade, the increasing seriousness with which it is addressed, the important changes in agency policy and practice that are taking place, and the development of multi-agency work on domestic violence, there are still a number of issues of great concern to Women's Aid activists. One of the most frequent concerns expressed is the lack of effective protection for women and children and the impact of current legislation and social policy. Nationally, we still have an uncoordinated and contradictory legislative and policy framework which often fails to protect women and their children. (see Harwin and Barron, in Itzin and Hanmer (eds), 1999, forthcoming, for full discussion). We need a review of the civil and criminal law to audit all aspects of family law and its implementation by the courts to ensure victim/survivor safety and abuser accountability. The new Family Law Act 1996 may go some way towards improving protection but we need clearer regulations and practice guidance, as well as training of judges, magistrates and other professionals in domestic violence awareness and safety issues.

One problem is that domestic violence legislation tends to be dealt with in isolation from other legislation or policy changes affecting families. But domestic violence cannot be treated as a discrete issue: social security changes, divorce legislation, housing policies, child protection practices and changes in the criminal justice system all have enormous impact on the relative ease (or otherwise) with which women who are living or have lived in violent relationships can gradually begin to build new lives for themselves. Various pieces of recent legislation - such as the Children Act 1989, the Child Support Act 1991, and the establishment of the Social Fund in 1988 - can have potentially adverse effects on women in this situation. There is a desperate need for decent affordable housing, for a basic income, access to child-care facilities, job opportunities and retraining, to enable women leaving violent relationships to provide secure homes for themselves and their children. Attacks on single parent families, cuts in social security benefits, restrictive homelessness legislation, the gross shortage of social housing provision and punitive immigration laws are all obstacles to women trying to rebuild their lives independently of violent ex-partners.

Many aspects of the way relationship breakdown and arrangements for children are dealt with within the courts and family proceedings do remain of serious concern to activists and survivors, in particular the implementation of Section 8 of the Children Act 1989. Attempts to increase protective remedies under criminal and civil law, such as the Protection from Homelessness Act, 1997 and the Family Law Act, 1996 (Part IV), have been undermined by child contact arrangements under the Children Act. Making safe arrangements for children is a key element of the long-term safety strategy for women and children.

Recent research confirms regular reports from refuges that violent men often use contact arrangements with children as a means to continue to harass ex-wives and partners, or to try to persuade them to return. Hester and Radford (1996) found , in a sample of 53 families, that in 85% of cases, women and children experienced further violence and abuse. They also found, contrary to myths held by many solicitors, court welfare officers, social workers and judiciary, that most of the women wanted contact for the children's sake but wanted this contact to be safe. The implementation of National Standards on Court Welfare work has clarified the need to ensure that abused women are not forced into joint meetings with their abuser during court welfare investigations, but procedures within the courts are still placing women in direct contact with their abusers at the 'court directions' stage to make agreements on contact without the need for a court welfare report or order. There is also little cross-referencing between criminal and family proceedings in relation to the risks to women or children from domestic violence. In one recent case, a man on bail for threats to kill his wife and child, was able to apply for and receive a contact order, and then return to the criminal court to apply for bail conditions to be lifted in order to enforce the order. Only the last minute intervention of a probation officer prevented this.

The absence of routine screening for domestic violence or checks for corroborative evidence from relevant agencies in family proceedings raises questions for improving the role of all agencies in promoting the safety of women and children, and indicates a need for a better strategic relationship between criminal justice and social welfare law and practice to assess what information and evidence should be shared and cross-checked and how this can be done within the boundaries of safety and confidentiality. This remains a challenge for multi-agency initiatives.

Government responses

The government's perspective, which since 1986 has (rightly) seen domestic violence as a crime, has tended to gloss over the fact that it is also a major social problem with enormous repercussions for family life and relationships generally. Any serious approach must go far beyond a narrow focus on the criminal justice system.

In May 1997 the Labour government came to power, having

already made a number of pledges to tackle domestic violence in its manifesto and pre-election consultations with women's organisations. In particular, commitments were made to review the civil and criminal law, and to address the needs for proper funding of refuge support services, which the previous administration failed to do. The first action was to publicise the new provisions of Part IV of the Family Law Act 1996. The Department of Health funded a series of multi-agency seminars on Part IV, as well as publishing a new circular on its provisions. The Department of Health has also reviewed the connections between domestic violence and child protection, and developed a training pack for social services departments on domestic violence and children, 'Making and Impact'. The implementation of the Crime and Disorder Act 1998, which focuses on a 'multi-agency'-type approach to community safety, has also highlighted domestic violence.

The need for an effective national strategy on domestic violence has been highlighted by the Women's National Commission, as well as in the Global Platform for Action developed at the United Nations World Conference on Women in Beijing. A national strategy must cross-arbitrary bureaucratic divisions with a holistic approach that can promote safety and empowerment for the survivor/victim while making the offender accountable. 'Families Without Fear', the Women's Aid Agenda For Action, recommends the establishment of a national task force involving key government departments (Home Office, Health, Social Security, Education and Employment, and the Lord Chancellor's Department), and expert gender-sensitive representatives from relevant national statutory and voluntary agencies, such as the police, social services, health care, courts, probation, and Women's Aid.

Violence against women has been a priority for the new Ministry for Women and interdepartmental work on domestic violence is to continue, once again led by the Home Office. In June 1999, the government published 'Living Without Fear: an integrated approach to tackling violence against women', which makes clear the continued commitment to these issues, and contains examples of many positive initiatives being undertaken by government in partnership with statutory and voluntary bodies. Nevertheless, a number of important concerns remain.

A key issue is and always will be the provision of independent advocacy and support services for women and children: adequate refuge accommodation backed up by 24 hour helplines and outreach services which would enable any woman in any part of the country immediate access to support, advice, and emergency accommodation whenever she needs it, for herself and her children. Yet despite virtually unanimous recognition of the need for refuge support services (for example among nearly all the agencies responding to the Home Affairs Select Committee), there is as yet no national strategy to improve funding and support for refuge-based advocacy and support services. The 1992 Select Committee recommended: "the first priority for Government action on Domestic Violence should be the establishment of a central co-ordinated policy for refuge provision throughout the country". The current review of funding for all supported housing "Supporting People", may yet deliver this, but many local Women's Aid projects fear the outcome unless existing funding is protected and ring-fenced. "

Conclusion

Ultimately changes in community responses to domestic violence, to woman abuse, will be measured not by the number of multi-agency forums that have been established, nor by the number of public pronouncements by government and statutory bodies as to the seriousness of the issue, but by the quality and sensitivity of services that are (or are not) available to women and children who are at risk from violence from men they know or with whom they live. However the prevalence of domestic violence is such that formal services can never be enough to meet the potential need for support, and responses by individuals - as part of friendship networks, kinship support, workplace and neighbourhood communities - will always be crucial. We need therefore to continue to widen public awareness, and to promote community intervention that goes beyond formal agencies, but also challenges existing power structures within local communities and political life, with more support for informal networks that women often use as a first step (Pahl, 1985, Mooney, 1994). The focus for change must also of course stay firmly on the civil and criminal law, and on the responses of criminal justice, health, social services and welfare agencies.

We need a multi-layered approach. Education - the watchword of the new government - is however crucial and truly appropriate for this issue: education of young people and children to challenge and change interpersonal relationships and promote new models of conflict resolution and gender equality; local and national public awareness campaigns to enhance community responses, and the responses of individuals wherever they may be located, building support at every point that women can access for help; education for all individuals and agencies charged with a role in managing criminal justice or social welfare responsibilities on what it means to face dilemmas of living with abuse - about how ending violence is a complex process, which begins, for survivors and victims, with the recognition of abuse and its consequences, and how there are many different strategies that abused women use to try to prevent it, and to protect themselves and their children.

The needs of abused women and children - for support, information, advice, legal protection, emergency refuge, permanent accommodation, financial support and safe arrangements for the future - cross the boundaries of agency roles and services. The challenge is the development of a multi-agency approach that can:

- prioritise women and children's safety;
- support women's empowerment and choices;
- deliver specific and appropriate integrated services;
- offer effective legal protection within the civil and the criminal law;
- develop strategies for dealing with perpetrators; and
- raise community awareness of the issue.

The challenge is also to create more fundamental social changes that will prevent woman and child abuse in the longterm. Domestic violence has existed for a very long time and is rooted in very ingrained and deep social assumptions about relationships between men and women and our respective rights and abilities and this has implications for our methods of work and presents challenges to all professional and front line workers in criminal justice and welfare agencies.

Addressing the question of domestic violence, of woman abuse, means that we have to grapple with our own notions and expectations of family life, of intimate relationships, and with our own feelings and experiences of power and abuse. It brings into sharp focus contradictions within our society between abstract notions of human rights and very particular assumptions about the rights of men and the rights of women, and it presents a very personal challenge to all of us which we must confront at the same time as we attempt to improve laws and develop services, if we are really to ensure the safety and empowerment of abused women and children in their own homes.

References

Ball, M. (1994) *Funding Refuge Services*. Bristol: Women's Aid Federation of England.

Barron, J. (1990) *Not Worth the Paper? The effectiveness of legal protection for women and children experiencing domestic violence.* Bristol: Women's Aid Federation of England.

Barron, J. Harwin, N. and Singh, T. (1992) *Written Evidence to the House of Commons Home Affairs Committee Inquiry into Domestic Violence.* Bristol: Women's Aid Federation of England

Binney, V., Harkell, G. and Nixon, J. (1981) *Leaving Violent Men: A study of refuges and housing for abused women.* Bristol: Women's Aid Federation of England

Department of Health (1997) *Local Authority Circular: Part IV of the Family Law Act 1996. Family Homes and Domestic Violence.* London: Department of Health

Dobash, R.E. and Dobash, R.P (1992) *Women, Violence and Social Change*. London: Routledge

Dunhill, C (1989) *The Boys In Blue: Women's challenge to the police.* London: Virago

Hague, G. and Malos, E. (1998) *Domestic Violence: Action for change.* (2nd Ed) Cheltenham: New Clarion Press

Harwin, N. (1998) *Families without Fear: Women's Aid agenda for action on domestic violence.* Bristol: Women's Aid Federation of England

Hester, M. and Radford, L. (1996) *Domestic Violence and Child Contact Arrangements in England and Denmark.* Bristol: Policy Press

Harwin, N. and Barron, J. (forthcoming) 'Domestic violence and social policy: Perspectives from Women's Aid' in Itzin, C. and Hanmer, J. (eds) *Home Truths.* London: Routledge

Hague, G. and Malos, E. (1996) *Tackling Domestic Violence: A guide to developing multi-agency initiatives.* Bristol: The Policy Press

Hester, M. and Radford, L. (1996) *Domestic Violence and Child Contact Arrangements in England and Denmark* Bristol: Policy Press:

Home Office (1995) *Inter Agency Circular: Inter-agency Co-ordination to Tackle Domestic Violence.* London: Home Office and Welsh

Office

Home Office (1990) *Circular 60/90: Domestic Violence.* London: Home Office

House of Commons Home Affairs Select Committee (1993) *Report of Inquiry into Domestic Violence.* London: HMSO

Law Commission, (1992) *Family Law: Domestic Violence and the Occupation of the Family Home,* Report No 207. London: HMSO

Mooney, J. (1994) *The Hidden Figure: Domestic violence in north London.* London: Islington Police and Crime Prevention Unit

Mullender, A. and Morley, R. (1994) *Children Living with Domestic Violence: Putting men's abuse of women on the child care agenda.* London: Whiting and Birch

National Inter-Agency Working Party (1992) *Domestic Violence.* London: Victim Support

Smith, L. (1989) *Domestic Violence: An overview of the literature,* Home Office Research Studies 107, London: HMSO

UN Department of Information (1993) *Convention on the Elimination of Discrimination Against Women: Directive on Violence Against Women.* New York: United Nations

UN Department of Information (1995) *The Beijing Declaration and The Platform for Action.* New York: United Nations

Welsh Women's Aid (1989) *Report of the International Women's Aid Conference.* Cardiff: Welsh Women's Aid

Women's Aid (1997) *Annual Report.* Bristol: Women's Aid Federation of England

Women's Aid Federation of England (1996) *Report from Annual Survey of Refuges and Helpline Services* (unpublished)

'Women and children in Refuges' (1988) *You Can't Beat a Woman.* Bristol: Women's Aid Federation of England

'Women's Education Project' (1989) *Breaking Through: Women Surviving male violence.* Bristol: Women's Aid Federation of England

Women's National Commission and Equal Opportunities Commission (1996) *National Agenda for Action.* London: Department of Employment

The Women's Unit (1999) *Living Without Fear. An integrated approach to tackling violence against women.* London: Cabinet Office.

4
Domestic violence and inter-agency child protection work: An overview of recent developments

Thangam Debbonaire

Domestic violence as an inter-agency child protection issue

Domestic violence is widespread and affects women from all classes, races, religions and educational backgrounds. Incidence is difficult to measure, by the very nature of domestic violence. Offences often have no witnesses or other corroboration and many women for various reasons do not or can not tell researchers or others about their experiences. Mooney (1994) in a carefully constructed piece of research which took these factors into account, found that 30% of women respondents had experienced domestic violence 'more severe' than being pushed, grabbed or shaken.

Domestic violence has also been clearly recognised as having an impact on children, certainly in the short term and possibly in the longer term, although this is less well researched. Jaffe and colleagues (1991) detailed possible distress, confusion and stress for children who witness domestic violence. NCH Action for Children (1994) in a study with over one hundred women attending their family centres in the UK who had experienced domestic violence found that the vast majority of the mothers reported similar symptoms in their children to those identified by Jaffe. Many children had also been abused by the same man as their mothers.

In *Children Living with Domestic Violence* (1994), Mullender and Morley drew together a review of the available research on the effects of domestic violence on children. They also included chapters covering a whole range of related issues such as child contact (with abusive fathers), child deaths, refuge provision in the UK and abroad for children, and so on. This book has become a key resource in identifying needs and appropriate responses in this country. One reason for this is that it identifies clearly a wide range of policy implications, for example for social workers and court welfare officers, and begins to develop practical ideas for responses.

There are clear links between the abuse of women and the abuse of children (see Kelly, 1994 for a more thorough review and exploration of the links). Stark and Flitcraft (1988) and Bowker et al. (1988) found strong overlaps between the incidence of domestic violence and the incidence of child physical abuse in families. Although these findings cannot be generalised because of limitations in the methodologies and samples of participants, they confirm the experience of Women's Aid refuges and shelters around the world since their early days. In her review of the links between child abuse and woman abuse (in Mullender and Morley, 1994) Liz Kelly recommends that wherever the presence of one of domestic violence or child abuse is known about, the presence of the other should be investigated.

Recent research in the UK on the impact of changes in social work practice arising from the implementation of the Children Act 1989 has identified other ways that domestic violence has a significance for child protection work. Farmer and Owen (1995) found a link between the presence of domestic violence and 'poor outcomes' for child protection cases. They also confirmed a link between the abuse of women and the abuse of children.

Many women coming into refuges report that their children were the reason they either stayed or left their partner, and in some cases why they returned to him. This should not be interpreted as mothers placing their children at risk; rather it is usually mothers trying to make difficult decisions with poor choices. Many children love their father and miss him, even if they hate the violence and want it to stop. There is a great deal of pressure on women to stay with fathers rather than become single mothers, in press and policy discussions on children. However, many women are still experiencing the reverse pressure, usually from child protection workers, if they stay with their partner. Cathy Humphreys (1997) in a study of child protection practice in a UK local authority, found evidence that social workers were telling women that if they did not leave their partner or refuse to let him in the house, they would face possible removal of their children. Despite expecting the women in these cases to do this, Humphreys also found evidence that social workers tended not to work with the men themselves, or did so inappropriately.

Some of the limitations of current child protection processes have been noted by women in Women's Aid (staff and residents) for some time. Case conferences and other formal or informal meetings where the abusive partner is present do not allow a woman to participate safely and usefully. The non abusing parent is one of the primary resources in most child protection interventions and is the source of much information about the child's life. Therefore, involving the mother of any child who is the subject of a child protection investigation in this way without paying attention to their safety and ability to participate or not with their abuser present is at best of limited use and at worst dangerous. The emphasis in the Children Act on 'partnership with parents' seems to have meant blurring any differences between those two parents. In circumstances where one parent is afraid of the other this partnership often has the effect, at least from the woman's point of view, of being a partnership with the more powerful parent.

For many families, leaving a violent man means leaving home, possessions, moving to a new area and new school, moving away from friends and family. It is likely also to mean legal proceedings, dealing with benefit and housing applications and money problems. This is all in addition to dealing with the effects of living with violence. For many children, the relief at leaving violence is mixed with feelings of loss and separation. Many spend time in a refuge where there are specialist staff for children as well as women who can help deal with all of these. Others have to live in other temporary accommodation such as bed and breakfast, with all the attendant risks to health and safety (Greve and Currie, 1990) and education (Clark, 1993). Therefore, the very process of leaving a violent man may in itself bring children in to contact with child protection professionals or others such as education welfare officers.

The risk of homicide is also a child protection issue. Fortunately such cases are rare but the rate remains steady over the last ten years at around 100 women killed by their partner or ex-partner each year in England and Wales (Home Office, 1994). Clearly, this has great importance for the child's welfare as well as their safety.

Links between domestic violence and child deaths have also been identified (see O'Hara, 1994, for a review of this subject). Available evidence about failures to respond to domestic violence in time indicate that this failure contributed to the inability to protect the child in question (e.g. the Bridge Child Care Consultancy report on the death of Sukina Hammond). Supporting women experiencing domestic violence early on may be preventative child protection. This is of course impossible to prove or disprove but given that the support needed may be relatively inexpensive to provide compared to the cost of having to take a child into care, this seems to be a sensible child protection practice to consider.

Recognition of the significance of domestic violence in child protection work

Prior to the early 1990s, there does not seem to be much evidence of children's experiences of domestic violence being taken seriously as a public issue or as an important matter for child protection staff. However, within Women's Aid there has been from the start an awareness of how many children were leaving violent men obviously affected by the experiences. Women's Aid was also amongst the first agencies to begin raising the subject, then still very taboo, of child sexual abuse within the family. As such we have often been at the unpopular forefront of child protection work, dealing with problems and raising debates that many would rather not know about, for women and children throughout the country.

There appears to have been little if any consideration of the impact of domestic violence in either private law proceedings (residence and contact - which replaced custody and access) or public law (statutory child protection work) during the passage of the Children Act through Parliament. Additionally, the Department of Health circular *Working Together* which sets out the guidelines for inter-agency working on child protection, does not consider the impact of domestic violence sufficiently to guide social services departments and others in their responses to the issue.

The consequences of this lack may have been a lack of recognition in formal child protection procedures of the widespread presence and impact of domestic violence on children as well as women. Until recently, there also seems to have been a possible tendency to marginalise it in relation to the abuse of a child, partly of course because there are statutory obligations towards children which do not extend to women. This has certainly been the case in private law (Hester and Radford, 1996), where contact orders have often enabled violent men to regain access to their ex-partners where they have abused and threatened them and sometimes also the children. It may also be part of the explanation for Farmer and Owen's findings.

However, in the last three years, this has begun to shift visibly. A series of events has contributed to this development. Although these are welcome events, the policy developments they prompted have not always been the most effective and in some cases have been counter productive. It is important to learn the lessons from the mistakes as well as the successes.

In 1991 conferences were held in Hackney and Hammersmith on children's experiences of domestic violence. These ground breaking events took place within a week of each other and were probably the first of their kind. They were strongly influenced by the work of Women's Aid and included keynote speakers and workshop leaders from refuges and national Women's Aid. The reports from these conferences (Holder, Kelly and Singh, 1992; London Borough of Hackney, 1992) became two of the first UK publications on the subject.

In a policy change in a Scottish local authority in 1992, the social services department decided to include living with domestic violence as grounds for registering a child on the child protection register. Women's Aid groups throughout the country, whilst pleased that there was at last some recognition of the experiences of children living with domestic violence, were extremely anxious that this would not have the effect it was perhaps intended to have. During consultation workshops on the subject at both Scottish and English Women's Aid national conferences during that year, refuge staff and residents expressed the view that this move would simply deter women from seeking help even more, and was likely to place children in even greater danger. The policy was subsequently reviewed, but it started the move for social services to take formal steps to deal with domestic violence and the impact on children.

In 1994, as noted earlier, NCH Action for Children published a report of a piece of research they had undertaken in their family centres. Their findings reflected what had been learnt from refuge work in Women's Aid: that children are usually aware of the violence, often intervene or are abused themselves, suffer confusion and distress and often have their home and school lives greatly disrupted by the control of the abusive man.

In the spring of 1995, NCH Action for Children and NSPCC jointly organised a conference on the issue. This was also the occasion for the launch of the third UK publication on the subject within six months (Saunders et. al. 1995). This was a joint piece of work between ChildLine, NISW (National Institute for Social Work), WAFE (Women's Aid Federation of England) and Alex Saunders, who had started the process by approaching individuals in those organisations about publishing his report of a piece of research with adults who had lived with domestic violence as children. This formed one chapter of the book, with WAFE and ChildLine adding each of their organisations perspectives.

The NSPCC/NCH Action for Children conference was also an opportunity for two of the big national children's charities to add their weight (again with significant input from WAFE) to the pressure for change in responses to children experiencing domestic violence. Concerns were expressed at this conference that domestic violence might be being treated as simply the latest issue, to be discussed one year and forgotten the next. Others were also worried that the crucial work of Women's Aid might be forgotten as others took it on. Another concern was that the knowledge and expertise held in the refuge movement would be ignored or downplayed.

There is some evidence that the warnings were necessary, but were partially heeded. The issue remains live in both national children's charities as well as in social work at the time of writing. Both charities have included domestic violence in recent publications and research. Many social work departments or Area Child Protection Committees are putting on seminars for staff in various agencies dealing with children's experiences of domestic violence and child protection. However, the need to support Women's Aid refuge and other services, including the specialist services for children, has not always been acknowledged. Many refuges remain underfunded, despite the life saving work that they do, with a strong child protection focus. Those inter agency forums and others tackling the issues who exclude Women's Aid and other similar organisations do so at their own cost - refuges are in a unique position to monitor the impact of domestic violence policies and practices in other agencies on women and children, as well as offering them emergency accommodation, support and advice.

The aforementioned publication of Mullender and Morley's (1994) thorough and extensive review of the whole range of children's experiences of living with and leaving domestic violence in this country provided and still provides the most comprehensive analysis of the available research, practice and thinking on the subject.

In March 1995 the Social Services Inspectorate organised two conferences for social service directors and subsequently published a report of these conferences containing the papers presented and good practice guidelines for social service department responses to domestic violence (SSI, 1995). These conferences were organised with substantial input from Women's Aid at a national level, both before and at the conferences. The report highlights the impact of domestic violence on women and children, the role of social services for both women and children, ways of working with violent men and also the key role of Women's Aid in providing safety and other services. Amongst the recommendations for social work response were: developing and implementing policy and good practice guidelines locally; publishing and providing information for the public and staff; induction and specialised training for staff; and financing non statutory services and options for women and children including Women's Aid work with children.

The development of specialist work with and for children living in refuges in the late 1980s and since then has meant a steadily growing pool of knowledge of the short term impacts of domestic violence on children and more usefully, some of the ways that these can at least be alleviated. There has also been growing recognition of the skills and knowledge that the women doing this work have (Ball, 1992; Hague, Kelly, Malos and Mullender, 1996). Some of these children's workers are now becoming involved with inter-agency child protection work and are able to offer unique insights into the range of needs and experiences of these children. The presence of a National Children's Officer post in Women's Aid has allowed the organisation to reflect these developments at a regional and national level. For the first time, child protection professionals have been coming to Women's Aid for advice, training and consultancy as well as keynote speeches at major national and international conferences.

Within Women's Aid this has meant a welcome recognition of both the knowledge and skills of those involved in refuge work, many of whom are survivors of domestic violence themselves. However, it has also presented new challenges and opportunities to develop stronger child protection practices ourselves, often with the help of social service departments.

As domestic violence issues have continued to be raised and discussed by the range of professionals working in child protection, a demand has been created for help for those professionals in responding to clients experiencing violence in the home. Of particular concern has been how to balance the statutory duty to protect children with a commitment to protecting and supporting adult survivors of domestic violence. The publication of a guide for these professionals by NCH Action for Children (1997) provided the first comprehensive, simple and clear guide for health, police, housing and social services staff on how to manage the various practical duties and child protection responsibilities in the context of domestic violence, with separate chapters for working with perpetrators, work with children and work with adult survivors. It provides a valuable starting point for agencies and individual staff who want to improve their responses to survivors of domestic violence and as such builds on the earlier discussion about the links between the abuse of children and the abuse of women in Liz Kelly's chapter of Mullender and Morley (1994). However, there is still much more to do.

Implications this raises for developing domestic violence and child protection inter agency work

Above all, women experiencing domestic violence, like other mothers, fear losing their children. Many violent men threaten their partners that if they try to leave or even tell anyone about the violence, they will get the children removed. This means that women may be unwilling to talk to statutory child protection staff about their own or their children's experiences unless they feel that they can trust the staff and know what is being done with that information. A woman may also be terrified of her partner. Just one look from an abuser in a case conference, as in court, may be all that is needed to keep her from contributing anything useful.

Safety for women as well as children is a human rights issue and a child protection issue. A mixture of factors can limit the safety of women and children living with or leaving a violent man and no assumptions should ever be made that simply leaving or evicting the abuser will ensure safety. Indeed, the effect of child contact orders frequently ensures that the woman is as unsafe as before she left. Any agency or individual operating a policy of forcing a woman to leave or evict her partner by threatening her with removal of her children, needs to consider whether or not this is protecting the children and working in partnership with the non abusing parent. Non abusing parents are far more likely to cooperate with a child protection process and intervention if they do not feel that the process itself is endangering their own safety.

Gender in any case may be the most significant factor in many child protection cases. Where there is domestic violence this is clearly the case, but by considering the implications for these cases, there may also be necessary improvements to other child protection practices. Parents are not necessarily in complete agreement or equally responsible for a child's suffering. Assumptions about what is 'normal' behaviour for girls and for boys can influence decisions about diagnosis and interventions. Assumptions about 'mothering' and 'fathering' can mean that the mother is the focus of child protection work even where the father is the source of risk.

An underlying assumption of the Children Act and associated guidance is that parents are themselves a partnership. As noted, if one of those partners is terrified of the other, this is clearly not an equal partnership. Case conferences and other processes may need to be re-evaluated to ensure safe participation for all including the child and non abusing parent.

As inter-agency working has developed for both child protection work and domestic violence work, there has been a need to reflect on how these two networks operate and connect. Most stay separate for the important reason that child protection is a statutory responsibility and combining it with woman abuse almost inevitably sidelines woman abuse. Liaison between Area Child Protection Committees and Domestic Violence Fora therefore needs to be focused and clear so that there is no duplication of resources or work, and to try to ensure better consistency in responses to child protection and domestic violence within all relevant agencies.

Child protection workers are increasingly aware that children often disclose abuse to refuge children's workers once they are in the safe surroundings of a refuge. Additionally, children's workers are in a position to observe and interact with children in what is temporarily their home and can often place problems in the full context of whatever legal and other processes are also taking place that affect the child and mother. This means that ongoing and specific liaison between social workers and refuge children's workers is useful for all and in the best interests of the children concerned.

Some local authorities have identified children affected by domestic violence as 'children in need' as defined under section 17 of the Children Act. Coupled with moves towards more preventative and support work in child protection including creative use of section 17, this has allowed local authorities to use these funds to provide nursery or playgroup places for children living in refuges, child guidance or family support, funding for refuge children's workers, practical help such as money for clothes or in at least one case, money for food for a family who had no recourse to public funds because of uncertain immigration status.

As child protection professionals become increasingly aware of the presence of domestic violence in their case loads, some have tried to develop check lists of 'indicators' of domestic violence for use in assessment and investigation. It is easy to understand the wish for a set of behavioural or other characteristics to assist busy social workers conducting complicated investigations. However, the nature of domestic violence and of children and childhood seems to Women's Aid to be such that clear cut indicators do not exist. What can be said to exist is a set of experiences that are common amongst children leaving domestic violence and a set of common responses to those experiences. These may include distress, confusion and talking about being scared at home, for example. However, these responses seem to be affected by many diverse factors, such as family income, position in the family, the results of any criminal proceedings, housing and so on. Additionally, many of these behaviours have other causes, including adolescence.

From Women's Aid experience it would seem that such a list of behavioural indicators does not exist. The clearest indicator of domestic violence is still a woman or child saying that it is happening. The professional role here is to create the conditions and trust that make it possible for a woman or child to say this, and help to make this process positive and useful, rather than using a checklist of behaviours. Further research on children's experiences of domestic violence will hopefully reveal further the extent of the observable impact of domestic violence on children.

Good practice in inter agency child protection work relating to domestic violence

Thus, there are practical, theoretical and other issues to consider in developing good practice. These are a range that have emerged or developed in current work done by WAFE staff with child protection staff and ACPCs around the country, in training and consultancy work:

- Taking a visibly anti-violence stance as an agency, including posters and information about help with all forms of violence, including domestic, available and accessible in social service premises.
- Recognising non abusing parents as the most effective child protection resource and supporting them accordingly to make safe choices for themselves and their children, without making women responsible for their partner's violence or acting punitively if they do not make the choices professionals would have liked.
- Using women to chair case conferences - in some areas this has meant considerable thought about who is available to do this and questioning why there are still so few women chairs.
- Recognising the value of Women's Aid as a monitoring and child protection resource that is effective and good value for money and helps to keep non abusing family members together, which is entirely in keeping with the Children Act.
- Funding the children's work in refuges accordingly, possibly through use of section 17 'children in need' funds.
- Examining the possibility of domestic violence whenever child abuse is known about and considering the impact of this at every stage of investigation and intervention.
- Providing information about rights and services for women survivors of domestic violence to clients.
- Providing assistance with escaping a violent man, including cash or other practical help with travel and getting into a refuge.
- Understanding the role and function of Women's Aid and supporting this

- Making links with Domestic Violence Fora, in order to improve practice, share information about services and ensure no duplication of work.
- Training for front line staff and managers about the impact of domestic violence on woman and children, to inform practice with families. This has often been done by or with staff from local or national Women's Aid.

In Women's Aid there has always been a recognition that violence against women by known men affects children. Women's Aid children's workers and others have developed substantial expertise in working with children experiencing domestic violence and their mothers and helping them to rebuild their lives together (see Hague et al 1996, Debbonaire, 1994, Ball, 1990 and 1992; Scottish Women's Aid, 1995). Refuge workers are talking with children and young people who have lived with domestic violence every day. They have unique knowledge of the impact of these experiences, as the child sees it and makes sense of it (see, for example, Higgins, 1994 for a selection of accounts which a group of children who had been refuge residents gave of their experiences at home and in the refuge).

As other agencies take on the issue, the refuge movement welcomes their support and contribution. It is still vital that the unique work, role and knowledge of Women's Aid and allied services are recognised and valued in order to develop thorough understandings of the effects of domestic violence and leaving it on all involved and in so doing to ensure that the professional responses do improve the safety and wider welfare of children and women.

[Since this chapter was written, an important Reader, together with extensive training materials on domestic violence and children, has been published by the Department of Health in conjunction with Barnados and NSPCC, with input from Women's Aid (Hester, Pearson & Harwin, 1998). These materials, Making an Impact, *are now being widely used by social services.]*

References

Ball, M. (1990) *Children's Workers in Women's Aid Refuges: A report on the experience of nine refuges in England.* London: National Council for Voluntary Childcare Organisations

Ball, M., (1992) *An Evaluation of the National Children's Worker Post and a Report on Children's Work in Seven Refuges Funded by the BBC Children In Need Trust.* Bristol: WAFE/Children In Need (unpublished)

Ball, M. (1995) *Domestic Violence and Social Care: A Report on two conferences held by the Social Services Inspectorate.* London: Department of Health Social Services Inspectorate.

Bowker, L., Arbitell, M., and McFerron, R. (1988) 'On the relationship between wife beating and child abuse', in Yllö, K. and Bograd, M. (eds) *Feminist Perspectives on Wife Abuse.* California: Sage

Bridge Child Care Consultancy Service (1991) *Sukina: An evaluation of the circumstances leading to her death.* London: Bridge Child Care Consultancy Service

Clark, A. (1993) *Homeless Children and their Access to Schooling: A Bristol Case Study.* Bristol: SPACE Trust

Debbonaire, T (1994) 'Work with children in Women's Aid refuges and after' in Mullender, A. and Morley, R. (eds) *Children Living With Domestic Violence: Putting men's abuse of women on the child care agenda.* London: Whiting and Birch

Department of Health (1995) *Child Protection: Messages from Research.* London: HMSO

Farmer, E. and Owen, M. (1995) *Child Protection Practice: Private Risks and Public Remedies - Decision making, intervention and outcome in child protection work.* London: HMSO

Greve, J. and Currie, E. (1990) *Homeless in Britain,* Housing Research Findings, No. 10, February. York: Joseph Rowntree Memorial Trust

Hague, G., Kelly, L., Malos, E., and Mullender, A., (1996) *Children, Domestic Violence and Refuges: A study of needs and responses.* Bristol: WAFE.

Hester, M., Pearson, C. and Harwin, N. (1998) *Making an Impact.* London: Department of Health/Barnados

Hester, M. and Radford, L. (1996) *Domestic Violence and Child Contact arrangements in England and Denmark.* Bristol: Policy Press:

Higgins, G. (1994) 'Children's accounts' in Mullender, A. and Morley, R. (eds) *Children Living With Domestic Violence: Putting men's abuse of women on the child care agenda.* London: Whiting and Birch

Holder, R., Kelly, L. and Singh, T. (1995) *Suffering in Silence? Children and young people who witness domestic violence.* London: LBHF/ DVF

Home Office (1994) *Criminal Statistics: England and Wales 1993.* London: HMSO

Jaffe, P., Wolfe, D.A. and Wilson, S.K. (1991) *Children of Battered Women*. California: Sage

Kelly, L. (1994) 'The interconnectedness of domestic violence and child abuse: Challenges for research, policy and practice' in Mullender, A. and Morley, R. (eds) *Children Living With Domestic Violence: Putting men's abuse of women on the child care agenda*. London: Whiting and Birch

London Borough of Hackney (1992) *The Links Between Domestic Violence and Child Abuse: Developing services*. London: London Borough of Hackney

Mooney, J. (1994) *The Hidden Figure: Domestic violence in north London*. London: Islington Police and Crime Prevention Unit.

Mullender, A. and Morley, R. (eds) (1994) *Children Living With Domestic Violence: Putting men's abuse of women on the child care agenda*. London: Whiting and Birch

NCH Action for Children (1994) *The Hidden Victims: Children and domestic violence*. London: NCH Action for Children

O'Hara, M. (1994) 'Child deaths in contexts of domestic violence: Implications for professional practice' in Mullender, A. and Morley, R. (eds) *Children Living With Domestic Violence: Putting men's abuse of women on the child care agenda*. London: Whiting and Birch

Saunders, A., Keep, G. and Debbonaire, T. (1995), *It Hurts Me Too: Children's experiences of domestic violence and refuge life*. Bristol: WAFE/ChildLine/NISW

Scottish Women's Aid (1995) *Children, Equality and Respect: Children and young people's experience of domestic violence*. Edinburgh: SWA

Stark, E. & Flitcraft, A. (1988), 'Women and children at risk: A feminist perspective on child abuse' in *International Journal of Health Services,* 18(1), pp 97-118

5

The multi-agency approach to domestic violence: A panacea or obstacle to women's struggles for freedom from violence?

Pragna Patel

THERE IS a growing consensus amongst feminists, particularly at the activist level, that multi-agency or inter-agency forums initiated by the local police or local authorities provide a viable way forward in addressing domestic violence. Southall Black Sisters (SBS) has been troubled by the theory and practice of such forums from the very start of their promotion by the police and the Home Office when they were forced to acknowledge their failure regarding the challenges posed by domestic violence, racial violence and police/black relations. At the heart of our concern about the multi-agency approach is that it is being promoted as a substitute for real accountability from the police and other key state agencies.

Drawing largely on the experiences of SBS, I seek to show that the approach has wider political and economic ramifications not only for women but for all sections of society. Against the backdrop of the decline of the welfare state and the erosion of civil liberties, the promotion of multi-agency forums may undermine democracy and equality for all disadvantaged sections of society. The focus of this article is on the multi-agency approach within the policing of domestic violence, but many of the questions here may also have resonance for multi-agency approaches adopted by local authorities and other bodies in other contexts. In raising this critique, we hope to encourage a long overdue critical debate on the nature of multi-agency work within the women's movement.

The promotion of the multi-agency approach

Like many other social welfare initiatives, the multi-agency approach[1] is borrowed, with some modifications, from models developed by the police and other agencies in the USA, Canada and elsewhere. Multi-agency work in essence, is about the coming together of a range of state and voluntary sector agencies, professionals, and increasingly the business community, in formal arrangements within a specific locality to develop a common strategy or programme of action on a range of issues. Since the eighties, domestic violence, racial violence, drug abuse and juvenile crime have been singled out for multi-agency work. Such initiatives are likely to be led by the police or local authority and those led by voluntary groups will usually involve police and local authority participation.

In the last ten years or so, the multi-agency approach has been vigorously promoted by the state as the key mechanism in the policing of domestic violence. It has come to symbolise a 'positive shift' in police attitudes to domestic violence. In 1986, an internal Metropolitan Police report recommended implementation of the concept to stem the tide of criticism of police handling of rape and domestic violence. Since then, its validity has been endorsed by virtually every major enquiry that has been conducted (National Inter-agency Working Party, 1992). The result is now a consensus in its favour across the political parties and a range of statutory and voluntary organisations.

It needs to be stated at the outset that our scepticism about multi-agency work is not about the idea per se. We have long recognised the need for a coordinated strategy on domestic violence, particularly at the national level, where coordination of legislation and policies through the involvement of all the main government departments is crucial. Any such coordinated strategy would also serve to illuminate the interconnectedness of different power structures, including racial and patriarchal structures, which construct powerlessness and inequality within and between communities and between men and women in different communities.

Unfortunately the reality of the multi-agency approach as we see it is very different. At a national level, the recommendations of the Home Affairs Select Committee on Domestic Violence (1993a), came to be examined in more detail by an inter-departmental forum on domestic violence set up by the Home Office. The only outcome appears to be a circular encouraging multi-agency initiatives at the local level, whilst leaving untouched the many substantial recommendations made by Women's Aid and other groups, on safe and improved housing, full access to legal aid, reform of civil legislation and other proposals which are so necessary if all women and children are to secure safety and control over their lives. The document was circulated for consultation and approval amongst various agencies, but SBS refused to endorse the official strategy it proposed because it ignored the need for resources for all women and for a reform of immigration legislation which has a devastating impact on black and minority women fleeing domestic violence who have insecure immigration status.[2]

Whilst there has been some attempt to examine how the multi-agency approach works in practice (Hague, Malos and Dear, 1996), there is still a paucity of information available as to its long term success. It is arguable that many feminist groups who have attempted to engage in inter-agency work in order to influence the agenda and practices of a number of disparate agencies have little critical analysis of the political consequences of such involvement. The decision to be involved in such forums is born out of a perhaps understandable need to protect the gains that have been made. Statements such as 'what will happen if we are not involved'? and 'it is better to be inside than outside' have often been encountered by those of us who have questioned the formal participation of feminists in police initiated multi-agency projects. It is not a question of being 'inside' or 'outside' of the process, since the need for change has always involved strategies that combine internal and external challenges to state oppression. The central question, however, is whether such involvement seriously compromises political demands for democracy and accountability (see the discussion of police accountability through independent monitoring below).

Another related issue is the question of funding. The links between multi-agency work and funding from the state are becoming more obvious. A majority of the domestic violence projects funded by the Home Office in the early nineties, for instance, were conditional upon the formation of local multi-agency projects. SBS's own proposal – a research project to investigate the links between mental health and domestic violence amongst Asian women- was one of the projects approved for funding. However we eventually pulled out because one condition of funding was the formation of a local multi-agency initiative which we believed involved engineering a false consensus on the complexities of the politics of race, domestic violence and mental health with groups with which we had little in common. As with all government funded research, there was also a stipulation that any publicity about the project had to be first 'approved' by the Home Office. These conditions would have severely compromised our critical and autonomous voice on race, domestic violence and mental health, especially in relation to the state's failures and shortcomings.

Local authorities and the multi-agency initiatives.

It is worth noting how multi-agency initiatives have moulded local authority responses to domestic violence, changing the face of local state relations with policing. Such initiatives have become the main means by which local authorities have chosen to address a variety of social issues related to crime prevention and victim protection. Underpinning these initiatives is a shift in the ideological thinking of those local authorities controlled by Labour. The 'new labour realism' has translated into attempts at consensus building and the 'partnership' approach on social issues, in contrast to the approaches modelled on the old style Greater London Council radicalism which emphasised the need for local democracy and accountability through mechanisms of independent monitoring, including police monitoring units, and the politics of municipal socialism. These were not without their own problems, but allowed for some measure of autonomy in the voluntary sector.

Many of the multi-agency projects, including those that are held up as models of good practice, may be well intentioned attempts to do a good job in constraining circumstances. But we would argue that they appear unable to move beyond multi-agency jargon consisting of key phrases such as 'sharing information', 'partnership', 'openness', 'facilitating', 'networking' etc. which are meaningless in the absence of real changes to improve conditions of women both before and after fleeing violence. We do not see much evidence of multi-agency forums campaigning and lobbying central government to bring about changes in housing, immigration and other legislation which constrains local authority delivery of services. Even Labour controlled local authorities do not offer comprehensive housing options on re-housing due to homelessness or eviction actions against violent perpetrators holding joint tenancies. In this light, multi-agency forums amount to nothing more than a formal recognition of domestic violence, giving the appearance that 'change' is occurring in 'partnership' with many organisations including the police and women's groups. Questions remain as to the long term impact of multi-agency work in all localities and whether the benefits are conferred on all sections of the community in equal measure.[3]

It is the problematic notions of 'consensus', 'shared responsibility' and 'equal partnership' so central to multi-agency approach that need closer examination. We note with increasing concern that the very terminology of the multi-agency approach reflects the shift towards the 'new realism' or the new corporatism within local authority and police governance.[4] For instance, the growing acceptance of the police as a 'service' provider, rather than a 'force' – a term which more accurately connotes police monopoly of coercive powers – shows the tendencies of the multi-agency approach to deny issues of structural power and inequality. Multi-agency policing of domestic violence serves as a good illustration of the contradictions we face in drawing up an agenda for change.

Multi-agency policing: Paternalism, conspiracy or pragmatism?

The concept of multi-agency policing was first propounded[5] in response to a perceived lack of coordination between different state and other agencies concerned with the criminal justice system. The multi-agency approach was put forward as the solution to the crisis of inner cities - to bring about greater inter-dependency and consensus between agencies through the sharing of aims and objectives. This model of multi-agency policing has been labelled 'benevolent corporatism and paternalism' (Sampson et al, 1988). The problem with this approach, as has already been noted, is that it assumes rather than problematises the notion of 'consensus' and it fails to recognise the organic aspects of communities and the conflicts and divisions which exist within them. Our experiences at SBS confirm such criticism (see below).

On the other hand, a considerable critique of the multi-agency approach, especially in relation to policing of black communities, has been mounted amongst others by commentators such as Louise Christian (1981) and Paul Gordon (1987). They argue for example that the notion of 'community policing' of which the multi-agency approach is a variant, is essentially an attempt to revert to a mythical 'golden age' of policing by consent-where police enjoyed the support of the public. And initiatives such as police inter-agency projects with attendant liaison officers and consultative committees specifically set up to deal with the 'problems' of youths and blacks, serve a very useful function in the control and surveillance aspects of policing albeit in a less obviously oppressive manner. This 'soft' policing strategy complements and does not displace 'hard' reactive and highly militarised methods of policing. Such views have, in our view, been somewhat unfairly labelled 'conspiratorial' by critics such as Sampson et al, who argue that the thesis amounts to perceiving multi-agency policing as a 'police take-over', a means by which the police coopt other agencies and even the entire community, to pursue police-defined goals and objectives (Sampson et al, op cit).

Sampson and others examining both the theoretical underpinnings and the practical outcomes of multi-agency initiatives in relation to crime, reject both 'conspiratorial' and 'benevolent' theories as inadequate in explaining the very real tensions and conflicts that arise, as a result of power relations amongst state agencies and between state agencies and voluntary groups. They conclude that both theories are inadequate in explaining the processes at work on the ground and so advocate a more 'nuanced' approach to multi-agency work which takes into account differences in power relations. The problem here however, is that there is no attempt to define what a nuanced approach should look like, particularly in the face of conflicting interests based on differential power relations between different agencies, especially the police, and individuals. Nor is there an attempt to show how the multi-agency model can overcome the inherent contradictions of corporate policing or provide a basis for democratising a constitutionally undemocratic police force.[6]

Whilst we do not subscribe to a grand conspiratorial analysis of policing, our own experiences and those of others, notably in black communities, do bear out some of the policing imperatives outlined by Gordon and others – the widening of the net of social control, cooption of a number of state and other agencies and most importantly, the breaking down of political resistance thereby isolating and excluding radical voices within our communities (see, for example, the SBS experience outlined below). The development of multi-agency policing was perhaps a pragmatic approach to the crisis of legitimacy in policing generally. But we do not doubt that the need to engineer consensus and seek legitimisation for the coercive functions of the police remains a vital objective, particularly as the crisis of policing continues unabated in the light of a series of scandals of police corruption, miscarriages of justice and other police malpractice. It is difficult to disentangle the coercive and emergent 'welfare' functions of policing, but it is wrong to assume that those functions are distinct and separate.

The 'welfare' functions of policing embodied in the multi-agency approach, developed partly out of a need to respond to mounting criticism about police handling of child abuse, domestic violence and rape. Nevertheless they co-exist and interrelate with the coercive and control functions of policing. The question as to which aspect of policing is emphasised often depends on which section of the community is being policed or the social and political circumstances of a locality. The resultant often contradictory pull between policing by consent and policing by coercion is well typified in the confusion that exists as to whether the 'welfare' functions epitomised by domestic violence units is 'real' police work. Within rank and file police culture, the response to domestic violence does not correspond with the multi-agency rhetoric. DVUs and the like are often viewed as a distraction from the enforcement of law and order on the streets. The extension of the police multi-agency approach into the area of domestic violence, infused as it is with the language of equal responsibility and duties on the part of all participating agencies, seems to us the clearest example yet of the need to seek consensus,. But we would argue that the language also masks the fact that the police by their very nature are the dominant partners in such forums.

Policing of black communities:
What's it got to do with domestic violence?

Our starting point is that the multi-agency approach to policing domestic violence must be contextualised within overall shifts in policing that occurred in the 1980s and 1990s - the move towards corporatism and crime prevention. Nor can multi-agency initiatives be viewed in isolation from police responses to urban unrest brought about by racism, poverty and the alienation of certain sections of society from the political process. The history of policing in black communities is especially crucial to absorb if feminists are to avoid falling into the trap of uncritically accepting the police as legitimate agents of protection or as equal partners in combating domestic violence.

The full significance of the multi-agency approach can only be understood if viewed as an aspect of the development of the concept of community policing: a concept that eludes a precise definition and has come to have a wide elastic meaning[7] Similarly the multi-agency approach to policing also defies exact definition. In practice its implementation is largely left to local police discretion, although the need to build a consensus remains at the heart of its promotion.

Community/multi-agency policing was put into practice by Sir Kenneth Newman, Commissioner for London in the late seventies and early eighties, in the wake of confrontations between black youths and police in Brixton, Southall, Tottenham and other inner cities around the country. (This approach was also recommended by Lord Scarman in his enquiry into the Brixton disorders in 1981[8]). The main aim was to achieve consent for police operations amongst sections of black communities: youths who have and continue to be targets for 'over-policing'. At the same time in relation to racial violence - an area which has historically been 'under-policed' - the police have not been able to claim 'success' in the way that they do with regards to domestic violence. There is a significant silence about multi-agency initiatives on racial violence.

It is notable that community policing/multi-agency forums have not led to increased confidence in the police largely because the multi-agency approach has not succeeded in deflecting criticism or attention away from coercive policing operations and abuse of power[9]. Nor have they succeeded in establishing any consensus in black communities (except with community leaders) largely due to the absence of an honest and open consultation process concerning all aspects of policing or independent scrutiny of their work, especially the more coercive operations.[10] In our experience this is also true of the community consultative forums in Ealing where, as elsewhere, they largely perform a rubber stamping exercise for police operations.

Multi-agency policing and domestic violence

Another influence in the development of the multi-agency approach was the growing criticism from feminists and others about police responses to rape and domestic violence. These developments led to the Metropolitan Police Force Order, numerous force policies and various Home Office circulars setting out new tasks and directions for the police. Research on domestic violence and policing from Canada and the US also fed into the developments here.

The background and history of initiatives on domestic violence taken by the police is well documented by many feminist researchers (Morley, 1993). The 1986 Metropolitan Police Internal Working Party Report was the first police endorsement of the multi-agency approach to domestic violence. Although, like most police reviews, it was never made public, leaked copies of the report showed that its two central recommendations to all police divisions in London were the adoption of pro-arrest policies and multi-agency initiatives in local areas. The growth and development of DVUs which became the main vehicles for multi-agency initiatives are therefore consistent with Scarman's recommendation on policing by consent. It is more than a striking coincidence for instance that all DVUs and multi-agency domestic violence projects have been led by or have involved community liaison officers.

The first DVUs in Brixton and Tottenham

A cursory glance at the work of DVUs throughout London show how the need for effective criminal justice responses have become subsumed under the need for liaison with local agencies which in turn has spread (and displaced) responsibility for police accountability onto civil society and even individuals themselves. Whilst recognising the ongoing debate on the merits or otherwise of mandatory arrest policies, the problem with the current emphasis on the multi-agency approach is that valid criticism of the criminal justice system as a legitimate option of redress for women has been seriously undermined.

Tottenham Police Station saw the first DVU, where two female officers first attempted to institute and develop better recording procedures and a local multi-agency forum involving relevant local statutory and voluntary agencies. Their aim was 'to educate the police and the public that domestic violence is a serious problem and not just a police problem...to get everyone together to discuss ideas, pool resources and find out what each group does and can offer women...' (*The Job,* 11th December, 1987). The multi-agency forum was 'an opportunity to exchange information, to bring the police and other agencies closer together, to bridge the gaps that existed between police and other agencies, and to reach a consensus on how to deal with the problem'. The minutes of the forum state that the rationale for participating was to let all organisations know what each other was doing and 'to build up trust for the police'[11]

It is interesting to note that in those early days the two officers at the Tottenham DVU were critical of the 1987 Force Order in not recommending the disciplining of rank and file officers who fail in their response to domestic violence. But their call for such measures of accountability have never been institutionalised by the Metropolitan Police as a whole. Instead the Metropolitan Police directives placed emphasis on consensus building with groups who had hitherto remained hostile to the police. This underlying imperative was revealed by the community liaison officer in charge of the Brixton DVU in 1988. 'From a community liaison point of view, if you look at it totally cynically, it has been absolutely marvellous. It has brought and drawn us together with organisations in the community, particularly women and feminist groups. They have always been anti-us and it has broken down all sorts of barriers...A female officer has been invited to be on the management committee of the local Women's Aid which is unheard of'.[12] The same officer claimed success for the Brixton DVU in another way. At the same time as providing a service to women, it was also able to perform an intelligence gathering function. Women were drawn into their confidence and the information gained was used to carry out a number of drug raids in the locality.

Not surprisingly, many black women are particularly reluctant to involve the police for fear of enhancing the criminalisation of black men. This dilemma is not easily resolved and is the focus of ongoing debate between black feminists and anti-racist activists within black communities. The debate is one that ought to transcend the 'minority issue' ghetto within which it is so often perceived by the wider feminist movement. It is about the inevitable manifestations of policing and its different but simultaneous authoritarian tendencies, raising profound questions about the nature or framework of relations that ought to be developed by feminists with the police, without compromising the right to seek formal and political accountability in the face of the denial of civil rights of certain sections of the community. It has been argued that multi-agency policing actually works at an informal level, but as research on multi-agency initiatives shows: 'Within informal multi-agency forums it is not uncommon to encounter excessive breaches of confidentiality in information exchanges, together with unacceptable working practices which, because of their informality, are also unaccountable' (Pearson et al, 1988).

The story of police multi-agency forums on domestic violence elsewhere in the country, is all too familiar. Whilst some forces have emphasised and perhaps implemented pro-arrest policies, many have merely established multi-agency forums. This has left untouched the need for more thorough going reforms of the entire criminal justice system itself. Instead, the emphasis remains on committing scarce resources to awareness training and information dissemination, which in some cases duplicates previous work. In practice, these programmes amount to a patronising conceptualisation of citizenship, creating not a culture of rights but a culture of passivity and ignorance. What is absent is any understanding of civil justice and democracy based on informed choices and participation in civil society, which can only be encouraged by an effective machinery for accountability through an independent complaints and disciplinary system, mechanisms for independent monitoring of police powers, and greater powers for local authorities to oversee and control overall police operations.

All too often the police feel that the mere setting up of a multi-agency forum is all that is necessary to show that there is a 'shift' in their thinking and practice. Whilst some divisions may be better in recording domestic violence and in providing information, that cannot be taken as a safe indicator of a more responsive police force. Nor can involvement in multi-agency work be taken as being indicative of openness and accountability between the police and agencies within the voluntary sector. Indeed, our experience bears out the fact that any attempt to voice criticism of police in such forums has met with a resolute denial that there are problems. The need for consensus overrides any serious attempt to make the police answerable in public. The position of all other agencies in such forums becomes untenable, since it becomes difficult to disengage from an entity to which one belongs and for which one is expected to shoulder equal responsibility. Our experience at a multi-agency forum in Haringey which we attended revealed that even critical voices in such forums are likely to succumb to acts of self censorship for the sake of unity.[13]

The death of Vandana Patel

The death of Vandana Patel, so tragically killed within the supposed safety of the DVU at Stoke Newington Police Station on 29th April 1991, and the failure by the police to institute a public enquiry into the matter, should have alerted all of us as to the difficulty of working with the police in multi-agency forums that are largely exercises in image or news management as opposed to serious attempts to give women equal access to the criminal justice system. It is instructive to note that whilst the Vandana Patel incident precipitated an internal Metropolitan Police review into all procedures on domestic violence, no apology to her family was forthcoming and attempts were made to justify police actions, seeking to legitimise the view that 'reconciliation between the two parties was a viable option for the police to pursue (*Guardian,* 30th April, 1991).

Subsequently, a series of seminars billed as an attempt to 'consult' and work in 'equal partnership' with all agencies and professionals with an interest in domestic violence were organised throughout London. Despite the rhetoric of 'equal partnership', Scotland Yard has admitted that the final report will not be available for comment to the participating groups or to the public at large.[14] Such practices confirm our view that the 'multi-agency' exercise, like all police operations, is far from transparent and gives lie to the claim that the 'equal partnership' approach is working. We are called upon merely to sanction police policies and their pre-determined agendas. If this is the case at the highest levels, how much more likely is the deficiency of the multi-agency model at the local level?

That there is a growing consensus amongst Women's Aid groups as to the viability of the multi-agency initiatives cannot be doubted. Criticism of the police is now muted. There is a general consensus that the police have cleaned up their act through DVUs and other initiatives.[15] But the reality is that most DVUs are more to do with diverting women to the civil justice system instead of focusing on the failures of the criminal justice system in meeting women's complex and changing needs in the face of domestic violence. A WPC in Wembley DVU proudly summed up this paradox at the Metropolitan Police Seminars: 'In my experience, we have had far more success in helping women with civil remedies, helping women getting injunctions with powers of arrest.'[16]

Local experiences In West London

The first attempt by Southall Police to set up a multi-agency forum was in February 1987. SBS attended two meetings along with other invited groups such as the local victim support groups, probation services, psychiatric nurses and social workers. The terms of reference were set by the police. Their stated aim was to build up a profile of 'problem families' whose behaviour was seen to characterise domestic violence. To this end all agencies were asked to pass on their case files on domestic violence to the police. No indication was given as to how information contained in the files would be utilised. It became obvious that we were being asked to take on the task of 'social control' over such families, and our involvement within the group became untenable (SBS, 1989)

This experience in Southall displayed all the tendencies which have been highlighted by commentators such as Gordon (op cit). It exemplifies the contradictions of corporate policing: the need to build a consensus, but also to utilise information gained for purposes that are entirely within police control and consistent with their goals. This has had to be acknowledged even by those who have sought to criticise the view that multi-agency policing is about social control. '...There is considerable blurring of roles between agencies, and this in turn leads sometimes to a breaching of confidentiality and the naming of problem families on the estate at forum meetings' (Sampson et al, op cit).

In 1988, Southall Police asked the consultative group in Ealing to coordinate the domestic violence working panel known as the 'The Violence in the Home Committee'. The panel, set up by the Southall Division the previous year, applied to the then Racial Equality Unit at Ealing Council for a grant. Its remit was widely drawn to include children who suffer violence in the home as well as the 'occasional battered husband'![17] Such display of ignorance about the gendered nature of domestic violence, its causes and consequences has been one of the reasons for our continuous reluctance at SBS to be involved in such forums.

Elsewhere in Ealing, we saw the emergence of a number of initiatives including a DVU at Ealing Police Station. When SBS met the two WPC's deployed at the DVU, they reinforced our view that, although well meaning, their main aim was to supply women with the information necessary to seek protection through a range of agencies other than the criminal justice system itself. The multi-agency aspect of their work never really took off, partly because we refused to formalise our relationship. We preferred instead to liaise on a case by case basis, allowing ourselves maximum autonomy to raise difficult questions and to challenge police failures.

The practice of Ealing DVU, like others, gives the appearance that the police have 'shifted', but in fact the criminal justice system remains untouched, feeding into the myth that women are 'reluctant' to press charges. The limits to the claim to new found 'enlightenment' are shown in comments made by an officer in West London who, when challenged by SBS on behalf of a local woman for failure to arrest a perpetrator despite her wish to pursue the matter through the criminal law, retorted that their aim was to operate a 'positive intervention policy' not a 'positive arrest policy'. This attitude ties in neatly with the national view on crime prevention that shifts responsibility from the state to the local community and the family itself.[18]

Our criticism of the police and the criminal justice system, centring on the routine failure of accountability to women, has been strengthened by the experiences of those who come to our door complaining of abuse from their partners and from the police to whom they turn as custodians of their safety. Some recent examples of women who have been denied redress by the police have highlighted the necessity of an urgent re-assessment of the claim that multi-agency policing of domestic violence is a 'success'.[19]

Such cases are not exceptional. Routine police failure and malpractice seen by SBS cannot be summed up simply as strange 'peculiarities' not repeated elsewhere, nor can police failure and abuse of power be explained away as a case of a few 'bad apples' within the police force which can be overcome by training and awareness.

The 'carrot and the stick': Questions of accountability and democracy

A frequent response to SBS's deliberate policy to submit formal complaints where there has been police inaction is that it is 'better to reward officers for getting it right than beat them with a stick for getting it wrong.' This is a worrying response given that the police have extraordinary powers to maintain law and order in the streets and in the home. The assumption behind such a statement is that we can expect the police to get things routinely wrong in domestic violence cases, begging the question as to whether such an attitude would be palatable to society at large in other areas of crime. We were met with a similar response when proposing an independent police complaints procedure at the Home Affairs Select Committee's inquiry into domestic violence in 1992. A representative of the Metropolitan Police Commissioner replied that the 'carrot approach is better than the stick'. The question of police accountability cannot be framed as one of either rewarding or punishing police failure and malpractice. The real issue is how far the police are willing to make themselves, their policies and their procedures open to public scrutiny. Not surprisingly this central question eludes the police and the Home Office, and the vigorous promotion of multi-agency projects is one means by which it has been avoided.

We are aware that we are probably unique amongst women's groups in having a policy of encouraging users of our centre to submit formal complaints in every instance of domestic violence where there has been police failure to take effective action within their powers. We have become a thorn in the side of our local police who are often exasperated by the need to deploy scarce police resources and staff to investigate what they consider to be problems that are largely 'trivial' and to do with entrenched 'attitudes' in the force. To date, not a single complaint made by us or our users has been upheld. But this has not deterred us for two important reasons. First, the process affords women themselves a glimpse of how the machinery of police accountability works or fails to work, especially its disabling effects in seeking redress and justice. Secondly, the lack of an effective independent complaints system allows us as feminists to situate our demands within the wider movement for police accountability, thereby contributing to a wider analysis on policing.

The questions that our cases raise pose a serious challenge to those who advocate multi-agency participation. It is difficult to work with the police on an equal footing without recognising that the emphasis on consensus building actually coopts criticism and bypasses the need for police accountability. Whilst there may be some accountability within a multi-agency forum, it is a self sealing and limited form of accountability, largely restricted to the professionals involved, without extending to the 'victims' or the public, which actually weakens demands for political accountability. For example, we are often asked by Southall Police and other police divisions to build strong links with their local community liaison officers to resolve the difficulties our clients experience with the police. But the problem is that there is nothing in place to ensure the women in their homes have similar lines of communication and accountability. Instead, our experiences show that they are fobbed off when they are not subject to harassment and assault. The wider public who do not have 'cosy' links' with the police are entitled to the same immediate attention and service that we as an organisation are offered. Just as importantly, we demand that debates on police operations and policies take place in public forums. These are not inconsequential demands for feminists to take on board, since it allows us to influence debates on democracy, accountability and citizenship.

The excuse of multi-culturalism

In Southall, as in other minority communities, the police have from time to time invoked language difficulties and cultural and religious differences as reasons for non intervention in response to Asian women's demands for protection against domestic violence. Cultural traditions are excuses which are in fact borne from 'liaisons' with certain male 'community' leaders who are called upon to define traditional and religious customs and practices of the community. Specific police rationales for non-intervention have ranged from 'not wanting to offend Asian men', (although this is never a factor when enacting immigration raids or carrying out extensive stop and search practices) to recognising that 'older Asian women have a higher tolerance level'.[20] This classic multi-cultural view - predicated on notions of fixed and homogeneous (as opposed to dynamic and changing) concepts of minority community culture and religion - dictates social welfare policies towards Asian and other minority women not just within the police force but also extensively across the welfare and legal systems. The many failures of such a perspective include its inability to take into account the vested patriarchal power and interests that most community leaders have in the institution of the family from which flow demands for non intervention in the family affairs of minority communities.

The dangers of such homogeneous constructions of minority communities lie in the relativist or differential approaches adopted by the police and other state agencies to the needs and demands of Asian women. Asian/minority women are treated differently merely because they experience violence in a different cultural context. We have always been at pains to point out that all women experience violence in a cultural context and that differences of culture and religion should not lead to denial of civil rights for minority women. The fallacy of such muddled multi-cultural thinking is not of course limited to Southall Police, Morley and Mullender for example, in the course of their research into the development of police initiatives on domestic violence in London, observed that officers elsewhere frequently said that 'the Asian community prefer to deal with marital conflicts through conciliation processes within the community and that cultural differences should be respected.' The dangers of multi-culturalism are particularly acute for minority women in places such as East London and towns and cities in Northern England where there is dominant religious and traditional leadership but no counteracting, progressive voices like that of SBS. It is especially in such circumstances, where there is a lack of effective outside pressure and scrutiny, that the police, and community leaders to a limited extent, are able to set the agenda of what issues are to be policed and how.[20]

We strongly suspect that the need to 'respect' cultural differences in the resolution of marital violence was a strong factor in the police response to Vandana Patel.[21]

It is our view that the multi-agency approach, with its emphasis on consensus building and cooption, accommodates a multi-cultural perspective. Precisely because the multi-agency policing model gives centrality to liaison with so called 'community' leaders and representatives, other more radical voices are easily ignored and de-legitimised. One of our strongest criticisms is that the police and the entire criminal justice system, notwithstanding the multi-agency project, actually disempower women from minority communities in very specific ways.

Ultimately, the multi-cultural perspective has a de-politicising and undemocratic effect. At its best it is a laudable attempt to promote racial tolerance and respect for cultural diversity, but at its worst it challenges neither the structural basis of racism nor inequality. Indeed it by-passes the need for local democracy because it relies on community leaders who are self styled, un-elected and historically have no interest in social justice or women's equality.

Our critique of multi-culturalism also leads us to reject the training 'solution' advocated by multi-agency projects to increase racial awareness (often collapsed into cultural awareness) and awareness on domestic violence. We remain highly sceptical as to the merits of awareness training to improve police response to domestic violence, having witnessed the spectacular failure of racial awareness training, particularly fashionable in the 1980s, which did nothing to challenge institutional racism because racism was perceived as a question of individual prejudice (Sivanandan, 1985). Similarly the indifference and sexist police response to domestic violence requires more than 'awareness' training. Structures and practices breed and perpetuate the 'operational culture' in which the police operate, and that cannot be dislodged by awareness training on its own. A change in attitudes will require a more sweeping transformation in policing and prosecuting institutions, involving mechanisms for independent monitoring and investigation of complaints. In the absence of such radical reforms all that occurs is that 'changed' individual officers are returned to unchanged and often unchallengeable sexist and racist environments.

Conclusion

We have encountered arguments that in areas where there is no tradition of radical activity on domestic violence, or where domestic violence is a taboo subject, multi-agency initiatives can bring about an increase in social awareness and a decrease in social acceptance of violence against women. SBS recognises the need to assess the value of multi-agency work within such contexts. However this does not take away the force of our critique, especially given the important strides already made by the women's movement in gaining widespread recognition of domestic violence. The new challenge is to meet the rising expectations generated amongst all women in relation to domestic violence. It is in this context that our critique on multi-agency takes on importance. In the absence of an adequate alternative to the police, we need to rely on them for protection for which they have been given powers. But at the same time we need to be wary of recent developments, to see through the diversionary and undemocratic effects of multi-agency initiatives promoted by the state as substitutes for enhancing substantive rights or access to resources which make a material difference to women's' lives.

For those of us from black communities, multi-agency initiatives have not stemmed police racism, oppressive stop and search practices or deaths in custody,. The police have not displayed any real willingness to unmask their essentially political agenda, which is to police the crisis of cities through policies designed to build consensus and with the effect of deflecting demands for police accountability and stifling the emergence of effective local democratic control.

SBS has attempted to understand the nature of multi-agency policing initiatives on domestic violence by viewing their development in the context of the trends in policing generally and through the prism of citizenship and democratic rights. Jones, Newburn and Smith (Jones et al, 1994) have highlighted the main indicators of democracy as being equity, information, redress, delivery of service, responsiveness and distribution of power. They tentatively suggest that insofar as domestic violence units and other specialist units have been set up due to pressure from various women's lobbies and from internal shifts in police culture, there is a degree of democratisation and so a movement towards equalisation of the playing field or the odds.

We would strongly dispute that the multi-agency initiatives, of which DVUs are a part, are about levelling the playing fields. Our cases provide ample evidence of the lack of equality and concentration of power firmly in the hands of the police. Whilst some shift is noticeable, for example better police recording and information dissemination (although much of this is about the civil justice system and the services provided by agencies other than the police), we cannot agree that such developments in the long run are about greater and not less democratisation. Even studies on multi-agency policing commissioned by the Home Office concede the point that whilst there may be some impact on localities, it is unequal (Sampson et al, op cit). Jefferson and Grimshaw make the point that under the current structure, working class people, ethnic minorities and women do not receive equal amount of police protection and /or are subject to an unequal amount of police coercion (Jones et al, op cit).

The impact of multi-agency policing cannot simply be viewed in terms of one section of society. It needs to be considered for its ramifications on different classes and groups of people within and between minority and majority communities. Significant amongst the central questions that remain unanswered is whether multi-agency forums can help to bring about the transformation of women from 'victims' to 'citizens'. Against the backdrop of creeping state centralisation on the one hand, and a view of society on the right and left which seeks to reinforce the stability of the 'family' and promote 'individual responsibility', it is difficult to see how the multi-agency approach can buck the trend towards less democracy.

Sadly the critical edge within the wider women's movement in respect of multi-agency policing has been lacking, with the consequence that there is an increasing separation between the groups who have developed good relations with the police formally and informally, and those who have not. Amongst the groups who are marginalised by this process of slow, albeit unconspiratorial, cooption are black and minority groups working with men and women in the face of police and state coercion and oppression. This then has profound consequences for the possibility of political alliances to challenge inequality. Demands for equality for all sections of society are weakened or fragmented as only sectional interests are articulated and defended.

There is an urgent need to debate and develop clear feminist perspectives on the multi-agency project. We need to develop an inclusive feminism which integrates the insights from the black and civil rights movements. We cannot afford to compartmentalise our thinking or graft different perspectives onto our own in a mechanical way. All experiences and knowledge are partial but it is only by understanding the totality of such insights that we can learn something about the true nature of oppression and the need to resist collectively without marginalising or compromising other disadvantaged voices or rights.

Acknowledgements

My thanks to Hannana Siddiqui, Meena Patel, Bill Dixon and Graham Smith for helpful comments, discussion of the issues and information/cases. I am immensely grateful to Raju Bhatt for his critical eye, patience and unflinching support, and to my daughter Radha for forcing me to take long breaks which have been great fun. Finally thanks are also due to the editors of this collection for their comments, patience and above all for allowing me to go way beyond the original word limit.

Notes

1. Multi-agency and inter-agency are terms which are often used interchangeable. The terms commonly have no distinct or separate meaning.
2. Metropolitan Police Working Party, 1986.
3. This is especially significant when viewed in the light of the history of multi-agency projects on a range of other issues. For

instance Alice Sampson and other raise this question in assessing the impact of multi-agency projects in other geographical areas and conclude that it is not always clear that multi-agency initiatives bestow general benefits on a locality as a whole (for example, Sampson et al, 1988).

4. See for instance Adam Crawford (1994) who analyses the multi-agency approach and crime prevention through the concept of corporatism.

5. The concept was promoted by John Alderson, Chief Constable and principal architect of community policing, serving in the Devon and Cornwall Constabulary between 1973 and 1982.

6. The 'System equips [the police] with wide powers of compulsion and intrusion ... They enjoy a unique dominance within the institutional structures of law enforcement. In a liberal society, this calls for vigilant external control. Yet the police in England are subject to fewer constitutional, legal and political restraints than in virtually any other western democracy. This paradox is the signal feature of the problem of police governance'. Although Laurence Lusgarten (1986) makes this point in the context of the criminal justice function of the police, given their constitutional position, the police refuse all attempts to be subject to external democratic control in the context of the multi-agency situation.

7. '"Community Policing" is a conveniently elastic term which is often loosely used to accommodate virtually any policing of which its proponents approve' Weatheritt M. (1987).

8. Lord Scarman's findings on the Brixton Disorders (1986) led him to make the key recommendation to set up police liaison committees or consultative committees throughout the country. This recommendation was later enshrined in the Police and Criminal Evidence Act, 1984 (PACE). However, the legal framework for liaison committees was carefully circumscribed so that it did not dent police autonomy or power in operational or decision-making matters.

9. Witness for example, the increasing alienation felt by Afro-Caribbean and South Asian youth manifested in the new wave of confrontation with the Police in Brixton (1995) Bradford (1995) and Birmingham (1996).

10. Research into multi-agency initiatives in localities, including those with a high black population, reveals that multi-agency fora can actually exacerbate pre-existing tensions and conflicts between police and blacks because the police 'fail to consult, disclose, or even give advance warnings about their coercive operations' (Sampson, op cit).

11. Minutes of Tottenham multi-agency domestic violence meeting. 11/10/1988.
12. Interview with an officer at Brixton Domestic Violence Unit by Rebecca Morley 11/1/91.
13. At a multi-agency meeting in Haringey into which SBS was invited, all agencies involved including local women's groups refused to accept SBS's view that domestic violence units are failing to provide an adequate criminal justice response to domestic violence. Indeed they became very defensive of the police generally. Subsequent minutes of the same meeting contained unanimous criticism of SBS's address, suggesting that our experiences were unique to our locality and not replicated in Haringey.
14. Telephone conversation between an SBS member and Scotland Yard in 1996.
15. See evidence given by a number of women's groups both written and oral, to the Home Affairs Select Committee (1993b).
16. Workshop, Metropolitan Police Multi Agency Seminar on Domestic Violence at Bushey, Hertfordshire, 16th June 1992
17. One member of the committee, in support of the need to include battered husbands commented: 'some men are married to wives bigger than them' (Ealing Consultative Group 1988).
18. Betsy Stanko (1995) has for example made the important point that crime prevention rhetoric has shifted police responsibility to meet women's demands for protection and placed in onto the women themselves.
19. In one case in 1993, a young Asian woman badly beaten by her father, with injuries warranting examination by a police doctor, was told by a detective constable that she should take out a private summons against her father from her local magistrates court which would be 'just as effective as criminal proceedings'. Our client went to the court, only to be advised by a concerned clerk that she would be at a considerable disadvantage as she was not legally represented. She was urged to return to the police station to demand action. She was then simply shunted about from one police station to another without success, despite the fact that there was a DVU at one of the stations to which she was referred. Her father was eventually charged and convicted of actual bodily harm, despite the reluctance of the police and the Crown Prosecution Service. Later with the help of SBS, she filed a complaint about the initial police response. As appears to be the norm, she came under intense pressure from the police to drop the complaint and to resolve the matter informally.

In 1993, in another case of an Asian women whose husband had subjected her to violence and threatened to have her locked up in a mental institution, the police actually assaulted, arrested and detained her when she called them for help. She spoke no English, but instead of providing an interpreter, the police spoke to her husband and then forcibly dragged her off without her shoes to the police station after threatening to handcuff her. At the police station she was searched and locked in a cell without explanation. Some hours later she was released without assistance. She has not made a formal complaint to the police for fear of reprisals.

20. Views expressed at the first multi-agency forum established in 1987 and more recently at the multi-agency forum-Ealing Community Safety Partnership in 1994.

21. It is well known that the police came to an informal 'arrangement' with a local Asian women's refuge that the estranged parties would meet to resolve their 'differences'. There is no evidence to suggest that Vandana Patel was given proper advice or a choice as to whether or not she wanted to meet her husband, although he had pressed hard for such a meeting. The substitution of cultural diversity for equality, together with a routine trivialisation of domestic violence despite Force Orders and Home Office Circulars, ensured that Vandana Patel had no control over her own life. In less extreme forms, this is an experience echoed by Asian women up and down the country. The police justification that followed Vandana Patel's death not only validated mediation as a legitimate option for the DVU to pursue, but also signalled a message to Asian women that mediation is the only legitimate option open to them.

References

Christian, C. (1981) *Policing by Coercion.* London: GLC

National Inter-agency Working Party (1992) *Domestic Violence.* London: Victim Support

Crawford, A. (1994) 'The partnership approach to community crime prevention: Corporatism at the local level', *Social and Legal Studies, 3*

Downes, R. *Unravelling Criminal Justice.* London: Macmillan

Gordon, P, (1987) 'Community policing: Towards a police state' in Scraton, P. (ed) *Law, Order and the Authoritarian State.* Buckingham: Open University Press

Hague, G., Malos, E. and Dear, W. (1996) *Multi-Agency Work and*

Domestic Violence: A national study of inter-agency initiatives. Bristol: Policy Press

Home Affairs Select Committee (1993a) *Domestic Violence,* Vol 1. London: HMSO

Home Affairs Select Committee (1993b) *Domestic Violence,* Vol 11. London: HMSO

Jones, T., Newburn, T. and Smith, D.J. (1994) 'New policing responses to crime against women and children' in *Democracy and Policing.* London: Policy Studies Institute

Lusgarten, L. (1986) *The Governance of Police.* London: Sweet & Maxwell

Morley, R and Mullender, A. (1994) *Preventing Domestic Violence to Women.* Police Research Group, Crime Prevention Unit Series, Paper 48. London: Home Office Police Department

Morley, R. (1993) 'Recent responses to "domestic violence" against women: A feminist critique' in Page, R. and Baldock, J. (eds) *Social Policy Review 5.* Nottingham: Social Policy Association

National Inter-Agency Working Party (1992) *Domestic Violence.* London: Victim Support

Pearson, G., Blagg, H., Smith, D., Sampson, A. and Stubbs, P. (1988) 'Crime, locality and the multi-agency approach', *British Journal of Criminology, 28(4)*

Scarman, L.G. (1986) *The Brixton Disorders, 10-12 April 1981: Report of an Enquiry by Lord Scarman.* (cmnd 8422). London: HMSO

Sivanandan, A. (1985) 'Racial awareness training and the Degradation of black struggle', *Race and Class,* 26(4)

Scraton, P. (ed) *Law, Order and the Authoritarian State.* Buckingham: Open University Press

Southall Black Sisters (1989) 'Two struggles: Challenging male violence and the police' in Dunhill, C. (ed) *The Boys in Blue: Women's challenge to the police.* London: Virago

Stanko, E. (1995) 'Desperately seeking safety: Problematising policing and protection'. Paper delivered at the British Criminology Conference, Loughborough

Wetheritt, M. (1987) 'Community policing now' in Wilmott, P. (ed) *Policing and the Community.* London: Policy Studies Institute

Wilmott, P. (ed) (1987) *Policing and the Community.* London: Policy Studies Institute

6
What happened to the 'F' and 'P' words ? Feminist reflections on inter-agency forums and the concept of partnership

Liz Kelly

Domestic violence is a complex problem requiring the combined and coordinated efforts of people from different professional backgrounds and the community. No one agency can deal with the problem. Time and time again, horrific cases reported in the media indicate the necessity for an inter-agency approach ... There is an urgent need to develop an interdisciplinary approach involving practitioners from all disciplines in problem solving and solution building. This includes any means of assisting practitioners to work together to improve responses to domestic violence, to coordinate service delivery and avoid overlaps and gaps. (Dublin Women's Aid, 1995).

This extract encapsulates the rationale behind inter-agency initiatives on domestic violence. The document it is taken from proposes a National Inter-agency Working Group in the 26 counties, and a conference took place in Dublin in November 1995 as part of this initiative.

In this chapter I want to take a critical look at the concepts of 'inter-agency' approaches and 'partnership' from a feminist perspective: the possibilities and dangers in these currently fashionable approaches. In doing this I am not locating feminism only in women's organisations which have explicitly addressed violence; but more broadly to encompass both individuals and organisations in a variety of locations which use feminism as both an explanatory framework and a practice tool. Nor am I drawing on one particular example, but ten years of involvement as an active member of several groupings[1], conducting evaluations of a several domestic violence projects which include inter-agency elements[2], and as an engaged observer of recent policy and practice. I am drawing on the accumulation of knowledge and experience in these reflections.

Before looking at how inter-agency work is conventionally understood, it is worth remembering that many women's organisations have always been 'multi-agency', drawing their membership from women who work (paid and unpaid) in a variety of statutory and voluntary settings. It is not unusual, for example, for refuge, rape crisis and campaign groups to have within their membership lawyers, social workers, local councillors, play and youth workers, nurses and doctors, counsellors, teachers, community workers and even the occasional police woman, probation officer, bank manager, business woman and magistrate. As with 'equal opportunities' before it, the concepts of 'inter-agency' and 'partnership' provide a formal legitimacy for ways of working which women's organisations have long been practising. I note this fact for a number of reasons. My fear is that in the process of social change the multiple and varied contributions of the women's movement to it are either forgotten or misrepresented. I also worry that, as has been far too often the case in relation to equal opportunities, the attempt to find new, more democratic and accountable ways of working will be replaced by formulaic systems. These often create as many problems as they solve; since they come to be seen and treated as solutions rather than strategies in the struggle to create different kinds of organisations and responses.

Equal or unequal partners?

Reflecting on the meaning of 'partnership' in the context of domestic violence is especially poignant. The violence women suffer arises within, and out of, particular forms of partnership, where the exercise of power and control by one partner against the other becomes routine, and has been historically accepted and even legitimated. The implied equality of status in the term 'partnership' should, for feminists at least, be treated with considerable caution.

Nor does the concept have a good pedigree in the other sphere where it is commonly used - business and commerce. The notions of some partners being more 'equal' than others abound here, even to point of this being recognised in the language of 'senior' and 'sleeping' partners. Many of the attempts to disguise and/or make surface rather than fundamental changes in the power relations between owners, managers and workers use variants on the notion of partnership.

If these concepts, and the practices which flow from them, are to be of any benefit for women's organisations and for women currently suffering domestic violence we must be alert to these histories and meanings, and have a clarity about the limits and possibilities of creating different forms of cooperation between agencies.

More than 'buzz' words?

'Inter-agency' and 'partnership' approaches have become the buzz words (sound bites?) of 1990s social policy. Their appearance in the written and spoken word acts as a marker of legitimacy, but they are seldom explored in detail or defined in practice. There are a multitude of ways of 'working together' ranging from occasional meetings through to the creation and implementation of agreed protocols. Much of what currently takes place in Britain and Ireland with respect to violence against women falls in between these two possibilities, with little consistency in structure or overall framework for the work. At the very least feminists ought to be involved in discussing how inter-agency work best benefits women and which of the models available offer the most and the least.

The Dublin Women's Aid document notes the fundamental justification for inter-agency work: that women seek help from, and require the assistance of, a number of agencies. Research since the mid 1970s has consistently revealed the failure of agencies in both addressing violence directly and providing appropriate responses. Increasing awareness of violence against women and creating consistency of respectful and helpful responses is clearly in women's interests.

Beyond that basic starting point, however, minimal consensus exists either within many inter-agency groupings, or across them, about what this 'partnership' consists of. Even at the level of definition, it is unclear whether members begin from a shared definition of either the problem or the task of the group. Some members see their first priority being improving responses to women and children living with domestic violence and its consequences, others as ensuring that their agency is not singled out for criticism, others fulfilling some current local or national requirement for developing partnership approaches. Few have set themselves the basic goal of reducing the local prevalence of domestic violence, or even the more attainable reduction in the number of domestic homicides.

These varying orientations are seldom made explicit at the outset, and thus a spurious consensus sometimes emerges based on lowest common denominator politics and policies. It is here that one of the main dangers lurks, namely a loss of perspective and orientation such that the targets groupings set for themselves are often at the most minimal level, and the very real differences between members can be glossed over.

The 'p' word

In much of the commentary on inter-agency approaches (very little of which, at least in Britain, focuses directly on violence against women) the role of the 'lead agency' has been of central concern. Who initiates cooperative links, who sets the overall agenda, and who (if anyone) maintains the vision and drive over time have all been identified as significant in determining the forms, content and outcome of initiatives. That leadership may also involve the exercise of power and control has been avoided in all but a few commentaries, and who occupies these locations has seldom been the subject of intense scrutiny. The exceptions to this rule are several papers from the Home Office addressing crime prevention (Liddle and Gelsthorpe 1994; Sampson et al 1988).

Both groups of researchers point to the importance of status, resources and confidence in the emergence of 'leaders', and to the salience of gender and race. Each of these factors puts women's organisations at a disadvantage, and their cumulative and compounding impacts make the position of 'lead agency' unlikely for many local refuge and campaigning groups. This inequality, combined with a feminist analysis of domestic violence, means that many women's organisations and individual feminists come to inter-agency work with an immense amount of knowledge and expertise, but minimal formal and/or institutional power and acute discomfort with the ways power is routinely exercised by powerful agencies and individuals. Unless power - the 'p' word - is explicitly addressed, leadership in inter-agency groupings will follow traditional lines; small women's organisations whose funding and standing in the community is fragile cannot alone create change in large hierarchical organisations.

The experience of 'working together' in both child protection and crime prevention work is instructive here. In both contexts the tendency for the police to become the 'lead agency' has been repeatedly noted. In both contexts the fact the police are a male dominated, hierarchical institution has also been noted as contributing to this pattern (see Campbell, 1988, 1995 and Sampson et al, 1988). Police officers are used to using power routinely, and extremely unused to either analysing it, or ceding it to those who have less status than they do. The resonances with the structures and dynamics of many heterosexual relationships should not go unnoted.

What appears to make a difference are local histories of organising: for example, if the emergence of inter-agency initiatives is an organic outgrowth of ongoing work (such as in Leeds or Hammersmith and Fulham). Where strong networks of feminists have been forged, a different agenda and style of working is more likely to emerge. This is both because the impetus for 'working together' often begins in women's organisations, and because pre-existing feminist networking between and within agencies provides a strong membership base for the initiative. These contexts are also the ones in which the question of who is included and excluded will be asked, and where connections with other forms of violence which women and children experience are made. Equally, local histories where mistrust, limited communication and poor/bad practice have been the order of the day are unlikely to be fertile ground for inter-agency work.

A basic requirement, therefore, if the needs and experiences of women and children, rather than agencies, are to drive inter-agency work is the creation of alliances between women's organisations and feminists in other agencies. Such coalitions are themselves powerful, but are based not on conventional sources of power, but on a common framework and sense of purpose.

The 'f' word

It is not an accident that the inter-agency initiatives where some form of leadership has been possible for women's organisations are the ones where the 'f' word - feminism - continues to be used unashamedly. In the 1990s it is not fashionable to call oneself a feminist - but without the last quarter of a century of feminist activism, research and theorising, violence against women would not be an issue of public and professional concern. Rather than this being a matter of pride, however, the reverse is too often the order of the day - with both women's organisations and individual women seeking what they perceive as acceptability by distancing themselves from 'extreme' positions. This can take many forms, but one of the most obvious (and insidious) is the disappearance of feminism from how groups define themselves, and the perspective they bring to the work.

Equally, while the Women's Aid federations and many refuges consistently attempt to offer a feminist analysis, feminist activity against male violence has always included a much wider range of organisations. To leave this broad range out of multi-agency work betrays both the origins of our movement to end violence against women and the courageous women who are struggling to maintain and extend feminist perspectives. Even Women's Aid itself, although now recognised by the government in its inter-agency circular and by other organisations as the lead agency in tackling domestic violence, is often marginalised or isolated in multi-agency initiatives, as discussed in other chapters in this book. Where this happens, the result can be lowest common denominator politics and policies - where minimal challenge and change occurs. It is in these contexts that calls for gender neutrality in how domestic violence is defined and understood are accepted as valid, rather than thoroughly discussed and the intended and unintended consequences explored. It is in these circumstances that the issues of women as abusers and violence in lesbian and gay relationships are used to undermine, rather than confirm and extend, feminist analysis (Kelly, 1996).

Working closely - in 'partnership' - with much more powerful agencies, including those which fund local women's organisations, understandably creates concerns. On the one hand are concerns not to 'rock the boat', appearing cooperative, on the other are concerns about cooption, having less space and opportunity to voice critical comments. But there are many examples of feminist groups which have maintained their critical perspective, yet are respected. As service providers and advocates for abused women and children, local Women's Aid, black women's domestic violence projects and others continually offer challenges and critiques. Campaigning organisations like Justice for Women work with lawyers, the media and other agencies from an unapologetic radical feminist agenda, and have undertaken some of the most effective feminist campaigns in the 1990s (Bindle, Cook and Kelly, 1995). Southall Black Sisters have combined effective support work with women and campaigning for over a decade. They have successfully resisted a number of attempts to cut their funding, whilst never shying away from being critical of other agencies, including their own funders.

Our power in attempting to create change for all women comes from the potency of this experience and our analysis. If inter-agency work is to benefit women (rather than provide legitimacy to agencies) it must be rooted in this perspective. Rather than seeing it as (at last) a form of recognition of our work, we should be approaching it as yet another challenge to develop new ways of working.

What would make a difference

What, in my view, makes a difference is working with a model of inter-agency work that begins from developing alliances between feminists in different locations, and which takes as its starting point a feminist perspective on why violence against women occurs and what will be required to end it. In making this argument I am taking issue with the conclusions Mark Liddle and Lorraine Gelsthorpe draw from their study of inter-agency crime prevention work (Liddle and Gelsthorpe, 1994). While not discounting grass roots organising, they conclude that, to create change, membership of inter-agency groups should be drawn from middle and higher management levels in agencies, since these individuals have the power to make and change policy and practice. They are also the people who are used to using formal and institutional power, and who are extremely skilled at 'foot-dragging'. In the context of violence against women effective inter-agency groups require a core of committed feminists who bring with them commitment and vision: commitment to trying to find ways to create change which will involve challenging limited movement within the inter-agency forum, and possibly also their own agency/group, and visions of the kinds of short and longer term changes which are needed.

During a study visit to London, Ontario I had the opportunity to explore how such models could develop. Lorraine Greeves, Director of the recently established Centre for Research on Violence Against Women and Children, stressed the importance of having gender and power at the centre of any attempts to create change. She attributed the 'success' of London (in building a range of high quality services for women and children, in being policy innovators, and in inter-agency work) to a particular combination of factors:

- a strong and sustained network of feminists who were both visionary and strategic;
- the city being something of a 'perfect laboratory', medium sized with unified statutory agency boundaries;
- the involvement of academics and the strategic use of research to prompt and underpin change;
- diversity amongst agencies which enabled debate and discussion once the change process began;
- commitment to the coordinating committee, and within that working with conflict as well as consensus as routes to change.

The study visit also raised some doubts about the extent of change within some statutory agencies, so I am not presenting London, Ontario as the model. That said, however, The London Co-ordinating Committee to End Woman abuse (LCCEWA) offers some important lessons for the development of work in Britain. In its name and objectives it has become more, rather than less, explicitly feminist over the years and has moved from a focus on domestic violence to encompass all forms of woman abuse. Groups working on rape and sexual assault, incest and sexual abuse and sexual harassment are full members. LCCEWA's aims and objectives specify that direct services to women "must be based on feminist philosophy". Both the goals and 'community accountability principles' (standards of practice to which all members can be held accountable to) reflect this too.

Whilst domestic violence still drives the LCCEWA the potential for a more integrated model has been laid. A number of the local activists stressed that they had reached the limits of what it was possible to achieve through a consensus model, and they supported a move towards developing binding protocols

London Co-ordinating Committee to End Woman Abuse

Goals

- Promote co-ordination between criminal and family [civil] justice, mental health, medical and social services.

- Evaluate the effectiveness of community responses in reducing woman abuse.

- Ensure a consistent approach to woman abuse amongst member organisations.

- Actively promote community education on the issue of woman abuse.

- Increase awareness amongst professionals of the effects of violence against women.

- Provide a centralised intake and referral point for the collection and dissemination of information about woman abuse.

Standards of practice

- The safety of abused women and their children is the fundamental priority of intervention.

- Service delivery must extend beyond traditional concepts to include advocacy and political change.

- Services to abused women, their children and men must work within a co-ordinated framework.

- Women's choices and expertise related to their own situations must be respected. At the same time service workers have a responsibility to:

  i) create conditions where a woman is given the opportunity to make informed choices;

  ii) create reasonable boundaries and safety provisions.

- The needs of abused women and their children are paramount not the needs of her family, service provider, religious group(s) or the state.

- Service agencies must be responsible for critically reflecting on how their organisations' hierarchical structures and the service providers related positions of power may negatively impact the desired mutuality of the working relationship with the client.

- Services must recognise 'symptoms' in abused women and their children as common adaptations to intolerable social and interpersonal situations of violence.

- Service providers must not collude with tactics of control used by abusers.

- A de-institutionalised, non-medical approach to intervention is to be employed along with the necessary and appropriate use of medical and psychiatric services.

- Services must recognise abuse as criminal activity and promote the application of the full measures of the law against the perpetrator.

- Services must be universally accessible and will respond sensitively and appropriately to the needs of:

  - diverse multicultural/multilingual communities;

  - First Nations people;

  - lesbians and gay men;

  - persons with physical disabilities;

  - persons with developmental disabilities;

  - older persons;

  - persons with HIV positive testing;

  - persons with low literacy skills.

which would be monitored (similar to those in Duluth, Minnesota and Hamilton, New Zealand).

What became increasingly clear during the visit was that the creation of a feminist framework to which all member agencies (including the police and crown prosecutors) formally ascribed could not have been achieved without a strong coalition of women's organisations and individual feminists. This did not mean agreement with each other about everything, or even that individuals liked one another, but that they came together for a common cause, supported one another in public and attempted to resolve conflicts in private. There was also a sophisticated awareness that it was possible to recognise and use the 'moderate' and 'extreme' labels which different groups had been ascribed to move issues forward, to extend provision and to create securer funding bases for existing services. Their bottom line was that they would not cede the issues of domestic violence or violence against women more broadly to other agencies, and that to maintain the impetus for change they had to learn how to act strategically and together.

There are glimpses of what inter-agency initiatives would look like which do not shy away from either feminism or an analysis of power in Britain. (Some examples are discussed elsewhere in this book) Building on these examples, and integrating all forms of woman abuse into such explicit collective agendas is the challenge we face for the rest of this decade.

Notes

1. I was involved in establishing one of the first inter-agency initiatives in Norwich in the mid 1980s. It brought together all the local women's groups working on violence and other voluntary and statutory agencies (see Norwich Consultants on Sexual Violence, 1988)
2. The Home Office funded Domestic Violence Matters crisis intervention project in Islington and a Rowntree funded evaluation of the Domestic Violence Intervention Project in West London with Sheila Burton and Linda Regan at the Child and Woman Abuse Studies Unit, University of North London.

References

Bindle, J., Cook, K. and Kelly, L. (1995) 'Trials and tribulations: Justice for Women A feminist campaign for the 1990s' in Griffin, G. (ed) *Feminist Activism in the 1990*. London: Taylor and Francis

Campbell, B. (1988) *Unofficial Secrets*. London: Virago

Campbell, B. (1995) 'A question of priorities' *Community Care*, 24-30 August, pp18-19

Dublin Women's Aid (1995) Discussion Document on an Inter-Agency Approach to Domestic Violence. Unpublished

Kelly, L. (1996) 'When does the speaking profit us? Reflections on the challenges of developing Feminist perspectives on abuse and violence by women' in Hester, M., Kelly, L. and Radford, J. (eds) *Women, Violence and Male Power*. Buckingham: Open University Press

Liddle, M. and Gelsthorpe, L. (1994) *Crime Prevention and Inter-Agency Co-operation*. Home Office Police Research Group, Crime Prevention Unit Series, Paper 53

London Co-ordinating Committee to End Woman Abuse (1992) *An Integrated Community Response to Prevent Violence against Women in Intimate Relationships*. London (Ontario): LCCEWA

Norwich Consultants on Sexual Violence (1988) 'Claiming Our status as experts: Community organising' *Feminist Review*, 28, 144-149

Sampson, A. et al (1988) 'Crime, localities and the multi-agency approach' , *British Journal of Criminology*, 28(4), pp478-493

7
Equalities issues in multi-agency work

Charlene Henry, Ann Webster and Gill Hague,

This interview was conducted in the summer of 1996, with Charlene Henry, Chair of the Derby Domestic Violence Action Group (DDVAG) at the time and Project Manager, Hadhari Nari project, Derby, and with Ann Webster, Equalities Officer, Derby City Council and the then Treasurer of DDVAG.

DDVAG was a local inter-agency domestic violence group based in Derby. It conducted preventative, educational and awareness-raising work and attempted to meet gaps in services. At the time of the interview, it was engaged in a great deal of domestic violence training and public education work and ran both a night advice-line for people experiencing domestic violence and a programme for male perpetrators. DDVAG has been instrumental in assisting in setting up other inter-agency groups in the country and was also a catalyst for the establishment of a local authority strategy domestic violence group and a county-wide forum.

The organisation had a very committed management committee and employed a coordinator, Bimmy Rai, and other workers. Both the management committee and the coordinator were particularly active in equalities issues. Since the interview, DDVAG developed its equality work further. The group ceased to exist in 1998.

DDVAG participated in the study of multi-agency domestic violence initiatives conducted by Ellen Malos, Wendy Dear and Gill Hague of the Domestic Violence Research Group at the University of Bristol, and this interview was conducted and transcribed by Gill Hague.

GH: *What part do you feel equalities work should play in multi-agency work?*

CH: I feel it is essential that equalities work must be on the agenda. Without equalities work in an inter-agency group, I feel it is a non-starter. From day one, for an inter-agency forum and for its steering committee if it has one, we need to have equal representation of black people, disabled women, lesbians, and so on.

 The community is made up of all sorts of people - disabled people, people of all ages - and, as we all know, domestic violence effects all sorts of different people across the board. So I feel it's essential that inter-agency groups take this on, otherwise they are not meeting all needs. A domestic violence forum is not a single service provider or one agency. Its an inter-agency group and that says to me that we need to include the whole community or at least all the groups that are part of the community.

AW: It must be an integral part of everything - not an 'add-on'. It should be part of the whole culture of the group.

GH: *Equalities work is quite well-developed in DDVAG. Can you talk a bit about the general issue of equalities?*

CH: Generally DDVAG seems to be far more developed on equalities work than lots of other inter-agency groups that I've come into contact with. In some areas we have moved slowly, such as sexuality issues. We do give advice to other agencies and we've tried to go out and deal with issues as best we can. In terms of sexuality, we need to develop that and deal with it more thoroughly, although we've made a beginning. In terms of other areas - race issues, disability - we try our best outwardly, and we have done a lot.

 Personally speaking, as a black woman I feel there are still race issues that need to be addressed especially on the management committee, and also among forum members. I feel it is essential that we now provide equalities training both to the committee and to the members. And it needs to be done holistically right across the board. Even if we've developed work in some areas, we need to look at those again. We need to look at it as a whole rather than just the bits we're not so good at - to continue to evolve an overall equalities strategy.

AW: We've made a good head-start with *practical* things on

equalities, such as the large-print, the tapes, the translation, but there is still a lot of education needs within the group - on sensitivity issues really. Sometimes people make comments and they are not really meant to offend others, but they do. And although this is not intentional, at the end of the day it does leave some people hurting. We so desperately need some awareness training and equality training so that everyone is more conscious of things they do and say - not just in the group but outside. Because we reach out now to all communities and at all levels.

GH: *Can we move on to specific, concrete things. I'd like, if its OK with you, to deal with structural and organisational things first - how you structure and run the project - and then what you do in terms of the work afterwards? It would be great if you could describe the concrete things that DDVAG has done to give other groups some 'tips'.*

AW: Recruitment and selection we are very very careful on. We've adopted the City Council's Equalities Policy for monitoring applications. When we short-listed for the coordinator's post, every application was carefully monitored for equal opportunities. The person specification was very carefully drawn up in these respects. Everyone was given careful reasons for why they were short-listed or not. The short-list was scrutinised again on a deeper level from an equalities perspective - its really important to scrutinise very very carefully for equalities - it can't be done superficially. We also advertised very widely in all different communities, we targeted a very wide list - using all sorts of community organisations and outlets. Interview panels are always representative and there's always questions about equality issues .

We try and look at all equalities issues in everything we do, including class issues and age. We do need to look more at sexuality issues - its not that we haven't had the will to do it but we're only just getting to grips with race and disability which we've done more work on. We've got a long way to go with that. We need general equalities training - and then specific e.g. disability equality, sexuality equality. That's so important. Because its OK having a paper policy and people being expected to abide by it. But sometimes they don't know *why* they have to abide by it - they need help and support to understand it. And it can be tough on them too.

For us to get anywhere, its important to have people from the specific groups to address and bring up their own specific experiences of working on the issue. For example, I have to say this, I notice that in the conferences you have organised on equalities issues and inter-agency working, you have black women including Cherry speaking, but what about disabled women? If disabled people aren't there, they are not represented, their views don't get heard and the issue is overlooked and forgotten.

There's a long way to go on race issues, but I'm afraid there's even further on disability issues. People always seem to forget. For example, people always forget disabled people's statistics when they're monitoring. So the issue is how we can get everyone taking it on instead of just a few of the same people always harping on about it. I can only think that training would help to get people thinking for *themselves* about it - not saying what they think they should say - or what is the 'right' thing to say. But everyone taking it on so they 'own' it for themselves - not being told. It's a good way to put it, to say that everyone should *own* equalities as a joint thing, not just for those in equality target groups.

There has been criticism that we need more black women on the groups. We need more disabled people too - there are 13% disabled people in Derby. What we need on the group is people with the skills and expertise of their particular specialism to be representative of the community in all its facets. We also have survivors of domestic violence involved but attending as professionals.

CH: Membership and representation are so important. On the membership issue, we have always advertised widely and asked people to become members from as wide a base as possible. And we keep re-doing it to reach out. We do have disabled members represented, members from the gay community, black members etc. But this is not formal representation.

There are not enough black groups involved - that's very apparent at forum meetings. Personally to me, it very apparent that I'm one of very few black members, and we think that perhaps having certain special places reserved on the forum and the committee could help. And, by that, I mean not just in a narrow sense but more widely. We could say we want a certain minimum of voluntary sector groups involved, for example, or particularly strong representation of Women's Aid and women's agencies. Voluntary sector agencies are officially represented on DDVAG but Woman's Aid is often the only voluntary sector group involved in reality. There are black women, disabled people, people of a range of ages and class backgrounds on the steering committee though, which is where the power is. We are also approaching Lesbian Line, Derby Friend etc. So we are making moves in these directions.

GH: *So its important for minority communities not just to be represented, but to be in positions of power?*

CH: Yes, I'm the chair. Its very unusual for a black woman to be chair of a forum of this size. Sometimes, though, I wonder if it's just because it looks good to have a black woman from Woman's Aid in the chair. But, overall, we are all committed to having a real mixture of people in positions of power. There is representation of disabled women. Ann is the treasurer, for example, and is very proactive in the disability community. So we have made good progress, but there is still a lot of problems - I wouldn't want to make it look as if we've got it all sussed.

On the good side, equalities issues are always number 1 on our agenda - part of our structure. They are never a separate issue tacked on - does that make sense? For instance, if we are talking about training, then equalities is an integral part of that. If we talk about service provision, then equalities is part of that. But when you actually come down to the nitty gritty, the running of the meetings for example, when certain people speak, they are 'heard' more than others.

There are so many little things - its evident to me all the time - I can't really put it into words - I feel it. I don't know if we'll ever be able to address all these hurtful things. But we are now embarking on equalities training. And certainly, on the committee, a positive is that things are picked up all the time - because there are black and disabled members - we might slip up on sexuality issues sometimes but we always try. On the down side, challenging all these issues all the time is hard and you get tired and drained. But perhaps we can talk more about that later.

AW: I'll just reiterate, here, that, while it is important to have representatives at all levels, the most important thing is having people from 'equalities groups', however you want to put it, in positions of power, where they can influence things and change things (at the same time that everyone needs to take equalities on as a joint enterprise).

And we have equal opportunities policies in place of course. You need to have your policies and you need to *review* them regularly.

GH: *To move on to the work you actually do - regarding equalities - can you describe this a bit to give other organisations ideas for ways forward.*

CH: Yes - its almost automatic to us now to include equalities in everything, we do, and it seems strange to us to find that not everyone else does. Translation etc. - that's what you do first of all. To publicise the forum and produce publicity and information and training materials - everything needs to be in community languages, everything in large print, on tapes. We distribute these materials all across the community. We keep the tapes here for anyone who needs them.

And that's an automatic part of all grant applications. It's part and parcel of everything we do and I find it difficult to believe that other people don't do it automatically - or at all sometimes.

AW: In the Nightline, we need more volunteers from different communities - the leaflets are OK but they only reach some people. We need to do more networking across all communities, reaching out. Trying new ways all the time. If one way doesn't work, we come up with new ways. We have to try to address each community's different needs.

You can do research as an inter-agency group into different needs. But what we are interested in is putting things into practice - translating it into practical things. Otherwise there is no point doing it. You need to do a bit at a time and keep trying new things. You can't do it all at once if you are going to do it properly.

GH: *Cherry has touched on the issue of translations and using large print etc. but as the treasurer of DDVAG and the City Council Equalities Officer, can you expand on it a bit?*

AW: For me in my role at the City Council and here, I don't think its sufficient reason for people to say 'we'd like to do equalities work but we haven't got the money" because everyone should be including equalities in mainstream budgets like we do. There's no way that I would turn around and say 'we haven't got any money for large print or for translations?" But so many people do and it really sickens me. I can understand if its an old project, but for a brand new project, it should never be an issue.

    We automatically translate into large print, community languages and onto tapes. We will put things on braille if people want, but things are changing now with computer technology. We did do some research on these needs. And we include it all automatically in all grant applications. And, as regards translation, it's not OK just to translate word for word - it needs to be culturally sensitive - you always need to check that carefully.

CH: Members of the steering committee, with the relevant expertise check the appropriateness of all translations, check that they are culturally sensitive, sensitive to disability and sexuality issues etc.

GH: *You do a lot of training, don't you - and all your domestic violence training includes equality issues?*

AW: Yes, we always include an equalities dimension - always. Because of the specific nature of some of the issues on equalities, we have a separate section on those as well as dealing with it all the way through. Some people don't seem to link equalities and domestic violence together. They don't seem to understand the connection. So it's letting outside agencies and training courses know that our commitment to equalities is integral to everything about us. We include age issues, HIV and AIDS - all sorts of perspectives on equalities.

    Equalities still get forgotten by other agencies: for example, using venues not accessible to wheelchair users. And some agencies are quite offensive if you bring it up, as though it doesn't matter. We all agree with freedom of speech but not freedom of speech if it offends others.

CH: All the programmes and trainers have been trained on equalities. Equal opportunities is an integral part. But it also has a separate specialist section to focus on it. Some agencies don't want this special section. There can be a problem of always the same officers doing the equalities part. But our training packs are designed individually to meet the special needs of each agency.

Now, we need to move on to look at specialist training for specific groups - maybe going out into the community and presenting ourselves and saying what we can offer. For example, providing culturally sensitive training, say, for African-Caribbean women or the Chinese community, providing specialist training is not just for professionals - its more than that - more about awareness - a way of spreading the word.

AW: We try to reach out in all sorts of ways. For example, we advertise that all our refuges are fully accessible. But its a constant struggle to get people to realise that they're for everybody. Just because the publicity mentions black women and children and disabled women and children, they think we must only take those women! They don't seem to understand that it's for everybody, do they.

Domestic violence issues and services are for everyone and you need to let everyone know this.

So we advertise all this widely and also we've got minicom services for deaf callers. And we have volunteers on the Nightline who speak a variety of languages and so on.

GH: *So, in summary, you take on equalities at all levels of the structure and organisation of the project, in representation across the board, in selection and recruitment, in all aspects of the work that you do, in trying to meet the needs of different communities, identify those needs and responding to them, in terms of making equalities an integral part of everything you do. And you also try and respond to instances of discrimination, don't you, both within the group and outside?*

CH: Yes. There's been occasions when there has been quite blatant discrimination between members - we've sometimes had to hold special meetings - we don't just leave it. We take things up and challenge each other at all times.

I am unhappy about certain issues but I'm not sure how they can be resolved. But I never accept these situations. To me that would be colluding with racism in this case. But it can be very difficult. We take on all areas of discrimination and equalities all the time like this.

We are all proactive in our own communities. Ann is very active in the disability movement for example. We're all very active in different movements, groups in the community outside DDVAG and we are able to channel all this experience into DDVAG. I think that's where we're quite unique in some ways. We're proactive in the community, challenging things, taking on issues.

GH: *Can you say a little about the difficulties in doing all this work or what holds you back?*

AW: Time. Time is the thing. Because not everybody comes from the same background. OK, the local authority has done work on equalities but some of the smaller voluntary or private agencies might not even know what equalities means or have an equal opportunities policy. So that's why we always include something as basic as 'what is equal opportunities". But there is so much to do. So what holds us back is time and people's different levels of awareness - trying to meet everyone's different needs. And also trying to monitor all the member agencies to see if they adhere to equal opps. You can just see straight away that so many of them don't - and you think 'where do we even begin here!"

GH: *So where do you begin - where does any forum begin?*

AW: Making sure you have the right people in positions of power in the organisation who can give support to each other but who also push things forward. If our group was made up of white, able-bodied women, I don't think it would have developed like it has. And those of us who are there are all strong women - but we all cry on each other's shoulders if it all gets too much. If it wasn't for all our 'customers" if you like, everyone we're doing it for - it gives you the strength to keep on doing it all.

You've got to have the right people and at the right level of assertiveness to say 'come on - we're not doing it properly this way, let's try that way" etc. They've really got to know their stuff and be able to speak out and say things.

CH: It's a very difficult thing in general being a chair of an inter-agency group anyway. So, for me, it's particularly difficult doing it as a black women, given the added oppression black women sometimes face, and also as someone from the voluntary sector - from Women's Aid and the refuge movement which doesn't have any power really compared with the statutory bodies. You can imagine what I come up against.

For me, the biggest thing is being invisible - being ignored. Other professionals will go and talk to white members, automatically. I keep on challenging. It's very wearing but I haven't got an answer for what else I can do except to keep on challenging and keep on working on that struggle. And we've still got a long way to go.

It's not just DDVAG that is affected - it's everywhere. The reason why DDVAG has these uncomfortable times is because we're in existence and that's how difficult it is if a group is trying to evolve in this way. If we weren't involved - (the black and disabled members etc) - it would just revert to being a cosy little group like so many others. If we weren't there - if we leave - I feel equalities would just backslide. And with any area of equalities, it's not just having representatives of certain communities, it's having representatives who are aware and conscious about the issues - who have thought about it in a 'political' way and are prepared to challenge. So then we can all improve our awareness together.

GH: *You've talked a bit about the strain of keeping on doing that - how sometimes it would just be nice not to have to do it, just to be able to sit back and let someone else do it - but you never can. Is that right?*

CH: Yes - I know. We never can. For me, it's this double burden - I've got to be the chair, I've got to ensure that women's needs are met, that the voices of women experiencing violence are heard. I go along to meetings and all that is in my head - and also the importance of putting forward a Women's Aid view and a feminist view empowering women - and then a black women's view as well - challenging racism. It's hard to do it all at once. I'm never relaxed at meetings, trying to keep everything in perspective at the same time. But it is important to me as a person to do it - that's where the drive comes from.

It's tiring and its a strain often, but I feel that if I don't do it no one else will (apart from Ann and a few others) so its exhausting. You have to keep pushing all the time. And that's one reason why we need to develop the sexuality side of equalities more. There isn't a lesbian or a gay man representing those interests and the rest of us try but we don't do it well enough.

AW: Within the forum and DDVAG, things have improved on a general level, there is more awareness now. Others do now take the issues up and that does warm me when that happens. Because it can be so tiring when you keep going over and over the same issues – over and over (e.g. remembering about disability) – but it *still* keeps happening. And you think 'what else can I d*o*" - you lose heart sometimes when mistakes still keep being made, when people who should know better are insensitive yet *again*.

And in the end it's down to about four of us to do all the work. We have considered having an equalities group, but it would be all the same people.

GH: *So how do you overcome these difficulties? Do you have specific support structures in place on equalities to support members of equality groups because of the difficulties and stresses that they face in trying to get the issues taken on?*

CH: We need to do more on that. People taking on these equality issues need support and help to do it. You need to take care of yourself. Those of us carrying out this work support each other all the time (I have an external supervisor but that's through Hadhari Nari where I'm project manager, not DDVAG).

GH: *We've talked before about the importance of domestic violence forums providing support to members, perhaps providing specialist support (e.g. for black or lesbian members) or a specialist consultant (e.g. on disability).*

CH: Yes, they are excellent ideas - we need to work more on that. We tend to all go and get our own support rather than coordinating it, but perhaps we could .... We'll have to think more about that.

GH: *Because equalities work is such a difficult thing for everyone, isn't it - a challenge for everyone - not only those representing different communities but for those being challenged as well. It's hard for everyone - but exciting. There perhaps needs to be more support for everyone to move forward together?*

CH: Yes, that's an excellent point and it can come out of engaging in equalities training together - moving on from there.

GH: *What about the idea of an Equalities Advisory Group - not in order to hive off equalities issues but rather to keep an eye on the group or forum, to monitor everything done, to advise etc., to check everything?*

CH: That's a more complex version of what we do here, where everything is checked for equalities by the whole group. It's one way forward because they can concentrate on the equalities issues but then there's a danger of everyone else leaving it all to them.

GH: *So Equalities Advisory of Monitoring Groups can be useful? And proper policies and procedures on equal opportunities? What other lessons can we learn?*

CH: One of the most important lesson to learn for me is for domestic violence forums to look at equal representation from the beginning. To make quite certain that all communities and groups are represented - race, gender, sexuality, class, disability - equalities in general. And also voluntary and statutory - the women's organisations which are the ones struggling to change things for women. It does matter that these are on board - the key agencies need to have a say - especially Women's Aid. You need to have a good group balance and representation, so that the appropriate groups and people are involved across all communities and not forgotten about, so that there is support for members and training.

And also that some sort of grievance procedure and other policies are in place to support you - you've got to have something to fall back on, to back you up so you're not isolated or alone. At their best, policies and procedures can do that - can provide a framework of support while you get on with moving forward on equalities.

GH: *Is there any final point you'd like to make?*

AW: I would love a year's secondment to really go into equalities issues in depth - on a different level! Because normally - it's the lack of time. I'm not using that as an excuse because that's as bad as the money excuse but it's such a big issue and you need the time and energy to develop it because while you're not, you're selling some people short.

You need to change everyone's thinking, develop the new good practice. And you need to tell everyone about the good practice. Spreading the information is so important. It's no good having leaflets on the shelf if no one knows they are there. So you need to advertise your services - tell everyone about domestic violence and about equalities - tell everyone about the issues across all communities.

We need to tell the world, don't we.

8

Creating an unholy alliance: Inter-agency developments on domestic violence in Hammersmith and Fulham

Robyn Holder

Keep in mind always the present you are constructing. It is the future you want. Alice Walker

In the course of 20 or more years of active campaigning against domestic violence in Britain a revolution has occurred. This is a revolution not only of real action on the ground, but also of social and political perspective.

In 1975 a woman suffering a catalogue of blows, abuse and humiliation had little alternative but to stay put. In place of this desert of support services, a network of some 300 refuges and advocacy groups have been created from (and virtually with) nothing. At that time what was happening at home between husband and wife was a private matter. Over 20 years later it is an issue of widespread public concern. In 1975 not one large service, welfare or criminal justice agency deemed domestic violence as demanding serious consideration. By the late 1990s, the publicly stated policy position of the majority is that domestic violence is both unacceptable and criminal.

In 1975 the silence and ignorance surrounding violence in the family was profound. Now it is being aired in all media from prime-time 'soaps' to local radio stations and newspapers. Back then virtually no information was available on what domestic violence actually was let alone on what could be done about it. By 1997 much resource material in a range of languages, styles and descriptions is accessible across the country. These days there is stated commitment from small and large agencies to accept joint responsibility for devising responses to the problem, whereas the only groups interested previously were women's refuges. A comparative examination of the submissions to the 1975 Parliamentary Select Committee on Violence in Marriage to those of the 1992/3 Select Committee show how dramatic these changes actually are (Parliamentary Select Committee, 1975; House of Commons Home Affairs Committee, 1993).

Inter-agency work is a product of these changes, and should even be regarded as one of the principal achievements of domestic violence campaign history. These changes and the current level and extent of activity across the UK to tackle domestic violence - on a single or inter-agency basis as well as within communities - have arisen largely from the single-minded determination of the women's refuge movement, and the Women's Aid Federations in particular, to drag the issue from the shadows of the family home into the full glare of the public domain.

Of course, it almost goes without saying that, the more things change the more they stay the same. As a whole, the Women's Aid refuges have moved from a position of no funding to chronic under-funding. Those local authorities which have sought to take on the issue of domestic violence, particularly on rehousing, find themselves unable to meet the level of demand. Encouragement of women to seek civil legal remedies is undermined by restrictions in access to legal aid. And the more pro-active responses of some police forces are circumscribed by the limitations of the law in practice.

Certainly what has not changed in these 20 years - nor indeed the past 200 or so - is the pain, fear and loneliness of the women and children who live with domestic violence. Similarly, those men who do abuse still believe, at some level, that they have the right to control the members of 'their' household and to expect servicing from their partners or wives. And moreover, that it is acceptable to use intimidation, threat, abuse and violence to achieve these things. The rot that seeps out of this mess is that women continue to blame themselves, abusive men abjure responsibility, and a considerable proportion of people who work in both statutory and community agencies hold, with varying degrees of discomfort, similar opinions.

So, if inter-agency work can be considered an achievement of the movement in the UK, it needs also to acknowledge the extent of deep change still required.

What is inter-agency working?

The practice of agencies - whether large or small, statutory or community - working together to address a commonly defined problem is well known and frequently utilised. There are, however, a number of different perspectives on it. For some it is about direct service provision - the creation of a 'project'. And for others it is about getting together in some as-yet-to-be-defined collaboration. What is new in the UK is the extent to which inter-agency working is currently being upheld and employed as a policy and developmental tool for a range of social issues - from child abuse to community development, and from inner city regeneration to juvenile delinquency.

The terms inter-agency, multi-agency and partnership working tend to be used interchangeably. They have commonly tended to refer to formal structures and processes which involve the key statutory organisations plus some community groups and more infrequently private sector agencies all working in a specific locality. They usually try to put into practice the idea of the work being about an equal partnership. Most inter-agency structures in, for example, community safety or crime prevention, have broad terms of reference and are not specific to violent crime against women. It is around these more formal structures that issues of leadership, identity, durability and evaluation are commonly discussed (Home Office, 1990).

Feminist and community networking also has a long practice histories and often comprises the cutting edge for more formal inter-agency developments. It is a form that is particularly important for ethnic minority communities. Indeed, it is probably a key method of survival for many marginalised peoples within society. The concepts of self-help, advocacy and of empowerment that characterise informal networking are also cornerstones of the women's refuge movement. The effectiveness of networking rests very much on its informality and upon a common philosophical approach based upon a shared set of experiences. Such networking is usually practically based and issue specific, or casework related. The lack of recognition accorded to it has on occasion been welcomed as non-interference and, at others, decried.

Much inter-agency work on domestic violence draws both its strength and its limitations from both of these formal and informal practices.

Inter-agency work and domestic violence

Some have criticised inter-agency activity as a form of benevolent corporatism and paternalism where 'good managers' and 'respectable' community leaders get together for 'the good of the community' at large. Others basically see inter-agency work as a means whereby the police in particular or 'the state' in general co-opt other agencies to pursue their own ends, with particular threats to civil liberties or to ideological purity (Sampson et al, 1988).

Many others, however, find these criticisms far too simplistic (Liddle and Gelsthorpe, 1994). The real situation for inter-agency work on domestic violence is both more fluid and more fragmented. Other influential factors are that:

- Power differentials exist between and within agencies that relate to differing resources, functions and duties, access to decision-making, and to gender and race dynamics; these can be played out as struggles for perspective, prestige and priority.
- There are different perceptions of the problem to hand and therefore of tasks and priorities making 'ownership' of issues and responses crucial but variable; the question of who domestic violence as an issue is perceived to 'belong' to also means that the power dynamics are by no means a simple assumption of government BIG/BAD and community SMALL/GOOD.
- Despite their differences agencies share a range of uncertainties; some of which are externally driven (eg. spending constraints), and others are driven from the inside (eg. competing priorities);
- There are deep structural and functional differences between agencies which of course are reflected in their philosophies and can emerge as conflict and tension in meetings and then reappear 'on the ground' and vice versa, although recent Home Office research suggests that quite the reverse can occur as well (Liddle and Gelsthorpe, 1994).
- Similarly predictable, 'turf-based' professional tensions can feature, and there are inevitably competing ideologies and analyses of crime in general and domestic violence in particular.
- The question of accountability is more multi-layered than at first sight.

And finally there is also the fact that domestic violence is itself both a complex and often controversial issue.

Some of the earliest inter-agency domestic violence groups came into being around 1989/90 in isolated spurts across the country. No one really knew what they were doing, all had a variety of motivations and often agency representatives believed everyone else was wrong-headed about domestic violence except, of course, themselves.

The Hammersmith & Fulham Domestic Violence Forum

The Hammersmith & Fulham Domestic Violence Forum (HFDVF), set up in December 1989 in West London, evolved gradually and reflects many of these dynamics. There was no inaugural meeting of senior or even middle managers of the large agencies, and certainly no strategic plan nor guiding vision. In fact the initial impulse for inter-agency work was as much negative as positive; and had as much to do with police accountability as with domestic violence.

At informal meetings during 1989 women from both the Women's Aid refuges, the local Law Centre, and the Council's Community Safety Unit (CSU)[2] discussed recent domestic violence initiatives from the Metropolitan Police. Officers in the Force's first Domestic Violence Unit in Tottenham, North London, had organised and were servicing a multi-agency group. The preference in Hammersmith & Fulham was that any such local grouping not be led by police. Whilst relations between the Council and the local voluntary sector were, at the time relatively cordial, those with police were strained. The remit of the (then) Council, Community and Police Committee of the local authority spoke of police accountability through collaboration but there was little history of trust for this to take place immediately. Other activities compounded the suspicion.

Late in 1988 the Council had commissioned the Polytechnic (now University) of North London to conduct a study into service provision in the borough for women experiencing domestic violence. Additionally, following a rather off-hand invitation from a senior officer for feedback on police action on domestic violence, CSU convened a group in early 1989 to facilitate this. The PNL study and the policing review were to parallel each other (McGibbon et al, 1989). The local Chief Superintendents were barely cooperative with the former whilst the Community Liaison Officer actually boycotted the latter.

The umbrella organisation for the local voluntary sector, Hammersmith and Fulham Association of Community Organisations (HFACO), agreed to convene the first meeting of agencies as a general discussion about domestic violence. The choice of HFACO as convenor and chair came to symbolise the primacy of the voluntary sector as service providers for and advocates about domestic violence. It acted both to neutralise tensions between the council and the police, and to add weight to the balance of power between the voluntary and statutory sector agencies[3]. Reflecting now on the process of inter-agency working it is debatable whether it would have made much difference if the police had led developments[4]. However, at the time it did matter.

From this rather negatively focused beginning, the realisation dawned that an on-going dialogue between agencies might provide opportunities for all manner of action. Certainly the feeling that came to prevail was to 'give it a go'.

The development of the HFDVF was very organic and related to local circumstances and resources. It has passed through five distinct phases. From the beginning the inter-agency group was perceived as 'a good thing' and better to be in rather than outside of. It began by asking basic questions - *what are we all doing now about domestic violence* and *should we continue to meet to discuss this?* This led to an exchange of information on what each agency was doing, making individual contacts, listening to invited speakers from other areas and discussing the feasibility of certain activities in the borough.

This first year could have justly been called a 'talking shop'. It is unfortunate, however, that this term is used so often to discredit the direct exchanges which form such a fundamental prerequisite to realistic and effective inter-agency working. In these discussions people gained a sense of others' values, beliefs and experience, and of who each other were as individuals as well as agency representatives. Participants had the opportunity to air perspectives on domestic violence, why it occurs and what it means as well as what could be done about it. Cautious and guarded as those early discussions were, continued later with colleagues or with other agency representatives, they became more and more relaxed over time. These exchanges strongly influenced the tenor and tone of local inter-agency work over succeeding years.

In this first phase of exploration, or 'storming' as in classic descriptions of group dynamics[5], the Forum quickly came to an awareness of its own limitations. Local police made a suggestion that the group set up a multi-agency 'drop-in' for women staffed by representatives on rota. Whilst this sounded like a good idea in the abstract and sought to address an agreed gap in provision, the representatives were in fact a mixture of people from direct service providers to policy people, and all were facing tremendous work pressures in their own agencies. Aside from a number of other issues, the drop-in idea was simply not practical at this time.[6]

The decision-making on this issue prompted the group to face the stark question of its purpose and role, and led to its second phase of 'norming'. The proposition that it should disband galvanised the group to agree its role, purpose and identity via written Terms of Reference, a new title as Forum with logo and letterhead. The Terms of Reference provided the Forum with a framework of guiding principles and broad objectives for action.[7]

During this 1990/91 period of normalisation, the discussions held within the Forum enabled a range of perspectives to be heard.[8] Over time and from this willingness to listen, debate and incorporate grew a general acceptance of the view that domestic violence was primarily an issue of men's abuse of women, and was an abuse of power. Invited speakers covered topics such as the work of the Crown Prosecution Service, and a Black women's refuge. The Forum also undertook active recruitment of black and ethnic minority groups, and made a submission to the Royal Commission on Criminal Justice. Two other initiatives passed almost without comment but reflected an unheard of openness compared with previous years and an indication of the extent of consensus reached between disparate agencies. First, the council and the police agreed to regularly submit statistical information on domestic violence, and second agencies committed themselves to adopting a Code of Principles of Good Practice when dealing with clients.

The third, fourth and fifth phases of the Forum were performance oriented and purposeful with specific objectives for work being set. In 1992/93 a process was established that came to be utilised in future years. External facilitators divided the Forum into small groups to brainstorm what issues people wanted addressed. Then, in the larger group, these were prioritised. There was a surprising degree of unanimity and realism in the agreed objectives. Finally, individuals volunteered themselves onto Task Groups to achieve each target. After eighteen months the Forum had:

- updated the Terms of Reference,
- produced a Directory of Services,
- organised a seminar on children and young people who witness domestic violence,
- produced a report entitled *Suffering in Silence?* on the issues of child witnesses, (Holder, et al, 1992) and
- begun a major training of trainers initiative - Project PETRA.

Each Task Group was responsible for ensuring its work proceeded in accordance with the Forum's wishes, finding funding if necessary, and achieving its objective. Each group was therefore time limited, self-supporting, and had a mix of voluntary and statutory representatives. The benefits of this way of working are that action is as truly 'multi-agency' as it can get, that things happen only if people want them to happen, project funding in small amounts is easier to find than larger sums, and work only proceeds at the level of input that individuals have the capacity or willingness to give. In this method, targets can take longer to achieve (though not always) and certain individuals and agencies can bear much of the load.

The fourth phase of the Forum in 1994/95 was hampered by the lack of a stable voluntary sector chair, but featured a new way of operating. Most previous activity had been agency-focused, and people now wished to increase public involvement as well as sustain their own flagging interest. The two objectives agreed for the year were, therefore, to increase public involvement[9] in making domestic violence unacceptable in Hammersmith & Fulham, and to raise awareness of the existence and role of the Forum.

To achieve these objectives and maximise opportunities the Forum linked its activities to existing initiatives - the United Nations International Year of the Family and the London-wide Zero Tolerance campaign. Under the campaign heading, *Promoting Violence Free Families*, the Forum produced a resource pack for practitioners, a leaflet aimed at the public, an emergency help card, and a series of lunch time workshops with refreshments and deliberately provocative topics. Certainly a much wider audience attended these workshops although they were usually practitioners rather than the public! Additionally the Violence Free Family campaign enabled the Forum to raise issues about other forms of abuse notably elder and child abuse.

It was only in this phase that the Forum agreed an overarching 'vision statement' for its work being:

to work towards an end to all forms of domestic violence especially that directed at women and children.

In the fifth phase, the Forum managed to adapt to some significant changes in participants, notably from the local authority and the police, over 1996/97. It was restructured to become a sub-committee of the borough's Community Safety Board. This structural shift brought advantages and disadvantages to the Forum both of which relate to the fact that the Forum's activities came more directly into the mainstream, and into closer oversight by the chief officers of the main statutory agencies. A major emphasis on formalising some inter-locking criminal justice procedures by working to establish a 'Duluth-style' intervention system has also taken place.

Key functions of the forum

The role of the HFDVF relates to the activities it sets itself. Once it decided not to become a direct service provider the Forum's principal functions have been to stimulate policy and practice improvements, and to address gaps in provision that are more effectively done in concert than singly. Whilst fora in other areas have become service providers and achieved an independence separate from their constituent parts, Hammersmith & Fulham chose to remain flexible allowing it to:

1. share information and contacts, encourage openness about agency practice, and stimulate self-criticism and reflection;
2. facilitate networking and casework liaison and referral;
3. provide a focus for developing shared action, priorities and the implementation of project ideas;
4. support (or not) and influence the establishment of new projects;
5. share different perceptions of 'the problem', different roles in addressing it, and debate 'the issue';
6. present a concerned 'front' to agencies, and act as an umbrella and lobby grouping of agencies on a controversial subject

thereby providing strength in numbers;

7. provide access into agencies traditionally distant from providers, eg, the police and the council;
8. raise and maintain the profile of domestic violence as a key issue but one that was marginal to the work of most;
9. provide individuals within agencies with a mechanism with which to pressurise their own agencies, and also provide them with an umbrella if they were isolated in their work on domestic violence;
10. share small resources for a shared need, and combine energy on specific projects and activities;
11. coordinate services, identify gaps, avoid duplication and competition and achieve 'added value'; and
12. develop new resources and protect existing ones.

Factors in the Success of the Hammersmith & Fulham Forum

The Hammersmith & Fulham Forum is one of the longest established and most productive groupings in Britain. What constitutes 'success' varies for its participants. For example:

HWA is part of a national network of WAFE refuges and women come to us from all over London. The DVF enables HWA to work with other agencies at a borough level to improve local facilities for survivors. Not all women experiencing abuse want to use a refuge. The DVF is able to look at the range of local services and options, to identify gaps and to take action to bridge them. The Forum has been a development resource to HWA in terms of (a) space to think about issues outside the refuge and the pressures of daily life, (b) skills to be shared within the Forum, and (c) the focused sub-groups of committed women. The DVF has been a place to break down distrust between agencies such as the police and Women's Aid, and break down prejudices about refuges held by many agencies. (Beryl Foster, Hammersmith South Women's Aid, HWA)

The best thing about the DVF was getting to know the real people behind the organisations and realising we were mostly working for and towards the same things. The best thing we did was to sit around a table and get to know each other, and find out what we

really do and what our limits were. We were practical for women.
(Stephanie Knight, Metropolitan Police)

Locally the DVF has been a model of collaborative working between statutory and voluntary agencies, breaking down barriers of poor communication and stereotypes, and within a harsh financial climate. Nationally, it has won recognition, especially for developing issues of children's safety in violent relationships. (David Cutler, Hammersmith & Fulham CSU)

A number of factors have contributed to its productivity and longevity.

- *Hammersmith Women's Aid*[10] is itself one of the longest running and most respected refuges in the country. It is remarkable in that it has maintained an active commitment to the politics of collective working and equal opportunities, a passion for justice for women and children, an involvement in local issues related to domestic violence, and a clear attention to meeting the needs of survivors of domestic violence for nearly 20 years. It has a stable and experienced work team whose political maturity allowed considerable risk-taking on inter-agency development. It is HWA's persistent and constructive profiling of domestic violence over the years that brought it eventually to the top of the local agenda. The collective committed time to the Forum as an agreed part of their work. It was Women's Aid whose interventions and experience ensured that the inter-agency priority was on promoting the safety of women and children.
- *Specialist units* within the local authority and the police gave those outside of these agencies points of contact and access into traditionally closed institutions. Officers in these units facilitated access to senior managers and elected members, collaborated on strategies to persuade and influence, levered resources, and interpreted policy and practice. Additionally they formed supportive alliances with each other, acted as change agents, worked to have their agencies act corporately, and moved their organisations to place an unusually high and consistent priority on domestic violence as a crime and social issue. With a relatively high degree of autonomy within their organisations, these specialist units stabilised and supported the Forum. The Council's Community Safety Unit in particular performed a key coordinating, strategising

and resourcing role.

- *Taking opportunities* for institutional change when they occurred. The signal for change in the larger organisations was created by the issue of the Metropolitan Police Force Order on Domestic Violence in 1987, by the Council/PNL research in 1989, and the Association of Chief Probation Officers Position Paper on Domestic Violence in 1992. These documents acted both as catalysts and tools for change which were utilised by officers within each agency and by activists outside of them. Each agency had enough senior managers and/or elected members sufficiently committed (for whatever reason) to improving services or at least not to block changes. Utilising opportunities included adapting initiatives such as the UN Year of the Family to profile domestic violence with a different audience. Being opportunistic was also important as a method of choosing what issues the Forum could be effective on and what it would undoubtedly lose in energy and morale by fighting.

- *The role of individuals* has been crucial.[11] These are people within groups and organisations who would not ordinarily see common cause let alone actually like each other! Workers and officers with more work than they knew what to do with committed their professional, personal and political experience to creating effective and woman-oriented inter-agency targets. Most remained open to criticism and to learning from each other whilst continuing to participate in collective action. Individuals took great leaps of faith with other agency representatives and within their own organisation, and often had to argue against their own organisational culture and priorities for domestic violence to be taken seriously. However, it is equally important to note, and not as a criticism, that not everyone committed the same amount of effort or time to the Forum all of the time.

- *Attention to the process of inter-agency working* in Hammersmith & Fulham emphasised the importance of individual contribution within the group whole. The starting point was that we all had something to learn and something to teach. Mutual respect meant acknowledging the difference of experience and of perspective whilst still seeking a consensus about what domestic violence was and what was the vision for the work. Collaborative working meant prompting views from those who were silent, and still pushing for clarity of thought rather than comfortable opinions.

Arguments did take place and were necessary. It was often effective to rethink and re-argue for particular ways of seeing and doing things. Starting deliberately from where people were 'at' and building from there is not devolution to 'the lowest common denominator' (Hague et al, 1995). As the focus of the Forum's work was local then it had to speak and act with a relevance to local circumstances.

- *A positive attitude* greatly assisted the inter-agency process. In addition to working with an assumption that each could and would contribute, another starting point was to assume that everyone wanted to see continual improvement in their own service, to communicate better, and even to see an end to domestic violence. That is, that people came with the best of intentions. In practice, after listening to a particular problem the next step was to ask '*what are the range of options to address this?*' In a sense we became responsible for the problems in each others' service—though of course, individuals took this on at varying levels! A positive attitude also meant keeping meetings and activities interesting, maintaining that objectives could be achieved (without being unrealistic), and coming to a clearer perception of strategy.

- *Maximising the use of available resources* was a key function of the Forum. The process of agreeing priorities and how to achieve them and of establishing Task Groups essentially decided how available resources would be spent and how much to fundraise for. Even such a small thing as an emergency help card - which is of enormous usefulness to practitioners and women alike - felt like an inventive achievement when a number of people contributed to it. Maximising resources often means the smallest of amounts and includes things like time and energy. In Hammersmith & Fulham maximising resources also meant finding ways of ameliorating the worst effects of the cuts to services.

Reflections on inter-agency development

The battered women's movement in the UK has always been part of a wider social movement for women's liberation. And yet it has also always been the most prosaic of revolutionary groups. Not least because the lives of the women and children it set out to assist, to liberate from violence and abuse, de*manded* practical interventions such as rehousing and legal protection. In so doing it tacitly accepted the notion of the enabling state as one means of redressing violent injustices and imbalances of power with agencies. In this, the movement was also influenced by left and Labour politics that emphasise the role of the welfare state in transforming peoples lives (Dobash and Dobash, 1992). Whilst this pragmatism is a strength of the movement it does not always sit comfortably.

Engaging with state agencies has always been problematic for many feminist groups. From an ideological point of view the state and its agents are instruments of class, sex and race oppression, and not neutral mediators among competing social interests and interest groups. But feminists have also always recognised the enormous impact the state has on women's lives - particularly those on low incomes, elderly and young women, ethnic minority women, and those with disabilities. Understanding both the role and responsibility - in reality and the ideal - of statutory agencies in relation to women and children who have experienced violence has always suggested that it is a necessity for women's groups to engage in institutional change (Women's Research Centre, Vancouver, 1988).

The refuge movement has long campaigned for statutory agencies in particular to accept responsibility for tackling domestic violence. Whilst it has been a long time coming, it can be counted as one of the startling successes of the movement that there is currently so much inter-agency activity across the country. It is inevitable that a range of perspectives on the problem and how to respond to it should now be on the agenda. One of the consequent problems for the movement is of control of this activity or at least influence over it. As a movement that has been as much about social revolution as the development of direct services, the worry for some is whether the demands of institutional change have overcome the grander vision (Dobash and Dobash, 1992). Overthrowing the patriarchy has never been part of the plan for local authorities and the police!

For statutory organisations such as local and health authorities, the police and probation, and professionals such as solicitors and doctors the idea of participating in inter-agency fora on domestic violence is fraught with problems. First and foremost is the one of stimulating demands that cannot be met. In a political climate where cutbacks are part of normal business this is an ever-present anxiety. Second, and less easily articulated is a fear of challenges - to established practice, to professional competence, to their own attempts at internal reform, and to the belief systems of individuals and agencies.

Collaboration on commonly identified problems is one way that these organisations are attempting to meet the enormous changes to their structures, functions and resource base foist upon them by central government. This is being done with varying degrees of good grace and effectiveness. Domestic violence is, for these agencies, a thorny issue that refuses to be 'solved'. It is, in fact, one that many feel is so intractable, so deeply rooted in the structure and function of male/female relationships as to demand measures from every social policy level. As the 1990s has been a decade of extraordinary restructuring and restricting of public services, inter-agency activity has at times seemed like action in defence not only of the means and mechanisms whereby women and children can manage or escape the violence that circumscribes their lives, but in defence of an interventionist welfare state per se.

Whether or not she remains with her abusive partner, a woman experiencing domestic violence has manifold needs. For those who do make the difficult decision to leave, any intervention has to be supportive, swift and secure as this is the time of peak danger (Straus and Gelles, 1988). The concentration of services required when the urgency for safety is so acute points to the fact that no one agency could, or indeed should, meet all her needs. Added to the fact that it takes between 5-12 separate contacts before a woman seeking help finds a sympathetic and appropriate response (McGibbon et al, 1989) the case for agencies working together becomes imperative.

Conclusion

Inter-agency work should be viewed as just one mechanism for addressing domestic violence, and as a complement to single agency action. It cannot provide answers to all problems but its possibilities have only begun to be explored.

The work can be problem or task oriented, service specific or more general, it can be formal or informal, it can involve statutory agencies or need not; and it can be time limited to achieve a certain review or task, or it can be open-ended. The process of development within a locality is ever evolving and must determine these features.

Inter-agency work can create an umbrella under which action is guided and strategy coordinated. It can bring into the open the full range of problems experienced by those suffering domestic violence, plus those with which agencies grapple in response. Inter-agency working is at its best when, following deliberation of the issues, agencies can collectively prioritise and agree a course of action. But whilst the motivation may be to coordinate services and to improve communication amongst agencies, it is vital that the effect of inter-agency work is not simply to coordinate bad services and to communicate myths and stereotypes.

Inter-agency cooperation is more than simply knowing about and tolerating what each other is doing. And inter-agency collaboration or intervention is more than actively planning to influence and direct each others' practices towards a common goal. Either way, it is the nature of revolutions to occur in unexpected ways. And in unexpected places - for it is sometimes assumed that all the changes must take place within statutory and professional agencies. To engage in inter-agency activity inevitably does impact on the ways of thinking and ways of operating in women's and community groups as well. Sometimes the changes required of this sector can be just as awkward to carry through. The dilemmas involved should not be regarded as barriers. Rather they should be seen, in an evocative Chinese phrase, as 'dangerous opportunities'.

To engage in inter-agency work on domestic violence requires heart, courage and risk taking. Risks to one's assumptions about other people and organisations, risks to one's own beliefs about the world and how it operates, and risks to one's own sense of rightness, professionalism and competence. Making alliances with unlikely people and agencies is also risky. It is in these alliances, however 'unholy', that much rich potential lies.

If the point of inter-agency work lies in its potential for institutional change, the point of institutional change has to be to make the lives of women and children safer. For some, however, the real struggle against domestic violence will always lie in direct challenges to male power. Coordination, raised awareness, communication and improved service delivery are no small aims but a social and political revolution they do not make. Maybe ...

Notes

1. Robyn Holder worked from 1988 to 1995 in the Community Safety Unit of the London Borough of Hammersmith & Fulham.

She is co-founder of the training and consultancy partnership, *AWARENESS IN PRACTICE*. She wishes to thank Peta Sissons, Beryl Foster, Stephanie Knight, David Cutler and Yvonne Korn for their insight and comments in the drafting of this chapter. The views remain the author's own.

2. The Council's Community Safety Unit was initially known by the title of the committee to which it reported, the Council, Community & Police Unit.

3. Unfortunately the grant to HFACO from the local authority was cut in 1993/94 and the organisation was wound up. Since that time the Forum has had a number of interim chairpersons prior to reaffirming that the post holder should be selected from the voluntary sector. It proved difficult to find a volunteer for the position as most voluntary sector representatives were very overworked. Eventually Sharon Beecham from Fulham Parents & Children (FULPAC) agreed to take the Chair.

4. Most of the Metropolitan Police officers who staffed or supervised the domestic violence units in Hammersmith & Fulham were and are very committed to the women and children seeking their help. Their preparedness, after a time, to trust others in the Forum and to go against their organisational culture where necessary greatly influenced the stability and cohesion of the group. The units themselves have become essential elements in local service provision.

5. Tuckman (quoted in M. Argyle's *Social Interaction*, 1969) described a group progressing through four stages, namely, forming, storming, norming and performing. Randall and Southgate in *Cooperative and Community Group Dynamics*, (1980) expand on this by suggesting that a group's four stages can be constructive or destructive in nurturing, energising, peaking and relaxing.

6. It should be noted though that the drop-in did actually go ahead with police and social services, and eventually with Women's Aid as well. The decision by the Forum not to become a direct service provider had other consequences, specifically about servicing and funding. Discussions about fund raising for an independent secretariat have always come up against a number of arguments. These are: that access to the limited sources of funding should be prioritised for direct service; that agency representatives may be inclined to leave activities to a paid worker rather than all having input; the Council was prepared to continue the support; plus the sheer hell of fundraising. The Forum remains an unconstituted body with no bank account of its own. The Terms of Reference say

that serving the Forum should rotate between the statutory agencies given their larger resources and capacity. In reality the Forum has always been serviced by the Council's Community Safety Unit. Servicing means organising meetings, taking minutes, answering correspondence, liaising with the Forum's Chair, being a contact point, sounding out ideas with agencies, keeping an oversight of the Forum's history and direction, influencing strategy, keeping up-to-date on national and international developments, feeding this back, and also assisting the Task Groups.

7. The guiding principles of the Forum are that: (a) domestic violence is a crime and is unacceptable in our community; (b) services available to a woman should be offered in a non-judgemental way and should aim to maximise her choices; (c) mutual respect, trust, professionalism, and a desire for sensitive and appropriate service delivery are essential to our collaboration, and (d) respect for the accountability of each agency's representative to their own management and group. (Hammersmith & Fulham Domestic Violence Forum Terms of Reference 1991).

8. To this date, there is no formal membership of the Forum. People simply have to agree to abide by the Terms of Reference and be providers in Hammersmith & Fulham (the exception being groups which have to organise London-wide such as the Chinese Women's Refuge Group). For individual representatives to have a commitment to act on the issue of domestic violence is, in many ways, sufficient. There is a core attendance of about 10-12 people (on a mailing list of about 50) with higher attendance for interesting speakers or controversial topics.

9. For discussion about developing an integrated community response to domestic violence see Liz Kelly's *Abuse of Women and Children: A feminist response, (1994).*

10. When the Forum first began in 1989 there were two separate Women's Aid Refuges in the borough. In 1994, Hammersmith Women's Aid was reconstituted to run as one organisation, the two houses as Hammersmith South and Hammersmith North.

11. These were individuals from the Women's Aid refuges, local Housing Associations, the Law Centre and the Women's Mental Health Group, Domestic Violence Officers from the police, probation officers, workers from the Domestic Violence Intervention Project, and officers from the Council's Community Safety Unit, Housing and Social Services Departments, and Equalities Unit.

References

Argyle, M. (1969) *Social Interaction*, London Tavistock Publications

Dobash, R.E and Dobash, R.P (1992) *Women, Violence and Social Change*. London: Routledge

Hague, G., Malos, E. and Dear, W (1995), *Against Domestic Violence: Inter-agency initiatives,*. Working Paper 127. Bristol: SAUS, University of Bristol

Hague, G., Malos, E. and Dear, W. (1996) *Multi-agency Work and Domestic Violence: A national study of inter-agency initiatives.* Bristol: Policy Press

Holder, R., Kelly, L. and Singh, T. (1992) *Suffering in Silence? Children and young people who witness domestic violence.* London: LBHF/DVF

Holder, R. (1996) 'Creating unholy alliances: Policy developments on domestic violence in the UK' in *Making a Difference: Proceedings of a national conference,* Perth, Australia

Home Office (1990) *Partnerships in Crime Prevention.* London: Home Office

Parliamentary Select Committee on Violence in Marriage (1975) *Report from the Select Committee on Violence in Marriage, Together with the Proceedings of the Committee,* Vols.1-2. London: HMSO.

House of Commons Home Affairs Committee (1993) *Report of Inquiry into Domestic Violence.* London: HMSO

Kelly, L (1994) *Abuse of Women & Children: A feminist response,* London: University of North London.

Liddle, M. & L Gelsthorpe, L. (1994) *Inter-agency Crime Prevention: Organising Local Delivery,* Crime Prevention Unit (No.52), *Crime Prevention & Inter-agency Cooperation* (CPU No 53), and *Inter-agency Crime Prevention: further issues* (CPU supplement to Nos 52 & 53). London: Home Office

London Borough of Hammersmith & Fulham (1990) *Policing Domestic Violence in Hammersmith & Fulham.* London: LB Hammersmith & Fulham

McGibbon, A., Cooper, L. and Kelly, L. (1989) *What Support? Service delivery to women experiencing domestic violence in Hammersmith & Fulham.* London: LB Hammersmith & Fulham

Sampson, A. et.al. (1988) 'Crime, localities and the multi-agency approach', *British Journal of Criminology*, 28(4), pp478-493

Straus, M. and Gelles, R. (1988) *Intimate Violence: The causes and consequences of abuse in the American family.* New York: Simon & Schuster

Women's Research Centre (Vancouver), (1988) *In Women's Interest: Feminist activism and institutional change.* Vancouver: WRC

9
Leeds Inter-Agency Project (Women & Violence): A radical approach?

Andrea Tara-Chand

Inter-agency work operates within the context of existing services - it works with the traditional attitudes and approaches of service providers, agencies or organisations. The attitudes of these agencies have often been unsympathetic and unhelpful to women survivors of domestic violence. The challenge to inter-agency work, therefore, is precisely that of encouraging a new approach whilst working within traditional 'old' responses, supporting and initiating new developments and interventions that are meaningful to women's safety. I would suggest that meaningful interventions in themselves are a challenge to traditional notions of women's role in heterosexual family life, which has historically given little consideration to women's safety. It is this challenge, I would argue, that identifies a radical approach as it shifts the emphasis from an individualised, 'liberal' approach which responds to issues of 'individual' safety to an approach that identifies domestic violence as a more complex issue that mirrors women's position in society as a whole.

In this chapter, I will explore one model of inter-agency work on domestic violence: the work developed in Leeds through the Leeds Inter-Agency Project (Women & Violence) - LIAP. This is by no means the only model - it is rather the only one about which I have enough knowledge to make comment. The chapter cannot be an objective study as I have played a part in sculpting the shape of the project. I will therefore reflect personal views and opinions. It is however, generally well documented that the organisation considers the philosophy and values that inform the work to be at least as important as the work itself (see Leeds Inter-Agency Project, 1992, Information Pack and Terms of Reference). It is this aspect that places the work outside the traditional frame, whilst recognising that this traditional frame cannot be ignored and in effect may require re-shaping. The commitment of the project, therefore, is very clearly to work with agencies within traditional structures and at the same time to maintain an outsider/non-traditional perspective.

A number of models of inter-agency work on domestic violence exist globally and also in the UK (Hague & Malos, 1998) and some of these are based upon a feminist approach that challenges the idea of women's diminished rights within traditional relationships (see for example Russell, 1982) . The challenge, as expressed by LIAP, is to view the family or domestic situation from a gender perspective i.e. from the perspective of the woman (Leeds Inter-Agency Project, 1991). In this way the unequal position of women and men is used to express the concerns of those who are abused and controlled within families in which domestic violence is an issue. Overwhelmingly they are children and women (West Yorkshire Police, 1993). It is this understanding that LIAP places centrally in all aspects of its work. It is in this way seeking to change ideas and notions of gender neutrality within professional dialogue of 'the family'. The notion of neutrality distorts the reality of who is being violent to whom, thus preventing more appropriate support or protection interventions being made available to survivors of violence.

If this approach is followed, recognition of power differences between men and women is acknowledged as an integral part of understanding what domestic violence is. This understanding has itself led to a variety of approaches nationally (see eg Dominy & Radford, 1996), and some initiatives have developed responses to change abusive male behaviours in anticipation that this will prevent further abuse of women. The Leeds Inter-Agency Project has however taken another route. It seeks to develop responses that build the confidence of women. The concept of 'empowerment' of women therefore informs the model. Although I am unable to explain here the concept of 'empowerment' in detail, it will, I hope, be explained through describing the work.

Project ethos

Violence can include physical, sexual and emotional/ psychological abuse, degradation, verbal abuse and the denial of money to women and/or keeping women isolated. (Leeds Inter-Agency Project, 1991, ch1, p1)

This definition of domestic violence echoes the philosophy of organisations that have worked for over 20 years to support women who have experienced violence from men they know. Feminist refuges, nationally represented by the Women's Aid Federation of England and the other Women's Aid Federations, have recognised and raised awareness of the issue of women's loss of dignity and sense of self as a result of emotional and psychological abuse. A well recognised approach to responding to women therefore acknowledges women's need for the opportunity to discuss experiences of emotional abuse with each other as one way of challenging the debilitating effect of enforced silence by perpetrators of abuse.

Radical inter-agency projects have also picked up this theme. The Leeds project aims to use training of workers within agencies to raise awareness of the issue of silence and begin the process of equipping front line workers and managers of organisations with the knowledge required to begin talking about violence against women by men they know in ways that are supportive to women and identify violence as the responsibility of the perpetrator. Training and policy work identifies basic 'good practice' (forgive the jargon) that costs little other than a change of attitude from a cynical to a supportive approach.

The idea that there is a moral duty for organisations to support women who live with emotionally abusive men and/or male family members and children is a difficult ideal to achieve. In reality support for women severely physically assaulted is more readily available as physical abuse is seen as a violation and is identified as 'real' abuse. Additionally, it can also be identified as a crime in those situations where physical injury has been sustained by the woman. This is, however, not the case in relation to emotional and psychological abuse, regardless of the level of severity and depravation involved. Indeed, responses have included denial of the existence of emotional and sexual abuse, minimising of physical abuse and lack of recognition of women's right to have control over their activities, time and wishes. LIAP has therefore embarked on a comprehensive two day training programme for workers from a variety of agencies or organisations. The definition of violence outlined above is raised in all formal documents, and all agency representatives on all groups established by LIAP are asked to endorse 'principles of dignity and equality' in all aspects of work undertaken on the issue. In these ways it is hoped to begin the process of understanding that violence towards women is unacceptable. The project's Information Pack goes on to state that:

> *violence against women by known men is a serious social and criminal problem. It is critical to develop all work within a clear understanding of principles of dignity and equality and to show an active opposition to all forms of discrimination.* (Leeds Inter-Agency Project, 1991, ch3, p1)

It has to be recorded that opposition to all forms of discrimination has been developed as a direct result of the work and struggles of black and minority ethnic women, black and Asian women's refuges in the UK and the writing of radical black authors globally, including the work of Amina Mama and Southall Black Sisters. Having gained much from the pioneering work of community based women's organisations, the challenge to the radical approach in developing inter-agency work on domestic violence is the incorporation of this ideology into the work of the organisations with which they work. In Leeds this involves over 200 local organisations. How then is Leeds attempting to achieve this?

From philosophy to practice

The LIAP Information Pack identifies the project's aim:

> *to improve protection and support services to women who are abused by men known to them and to ensure that the needs of children of abused women are integrated into the provision of services.* (Leeds Inter-Agency Project, 1991, ch3, p1)

However, it is also stated that the project 'was established to help and support agencies to develop 'good practice' and in some instances to demonstrate 'good practice' towards abused women. The philosophy or ethos of empowerment of women forms the basis of this good practice.

A number of key strands have become apparent over the past five years. *Women focused policy or practice guidelines* on delivery of services have been important in achieving, to some degree at least, support for work on violence. These have been achieved in a number of agencies including housing, education, the probation service, the police and social services, and they inform the strategic plan of the Community Mental Health Trust. The LIAP is also represented on strategic city wide community and crime prevention bodies in an attempt to integrate women's safety into the thinking and planning for the city overall.

Training is another strand or theme that has been very important. Training has been used frequently as a vehicle for raising a woman centred perspective. Over 600 workers from a variety of agencies (all working in one area of the city) have been trained through the LIAP's two day multi-agency training programme. Additionally, specialist programmes have been developed and offered to a number of organisations including; social services, education, probation service managers, magistrates and West Yorkshire police (domestic violence specialist units). The training model used always incorporates a focus on abuse of male power and use of multiple forms of abuse to control and undermine women. The categories are broadly derived from the structure of torture used in prisoner of war (POW) camps to keep POW's disempowered, and they encourage a consistent and supportive approach to women across a range of organisations.

The provision of *direct services to women and children* is another theme that has arisen repeatedly. LIAP has become involved either in providing direct services to women[1] or supporting existing organisations to provide 'empowering' group work to women who have experienced emotional, physical or sexual violence from a man they know. This area of work has developed out of a realisation that women often need support before they can make the initial contact with agencies for protection or support. As a result, specific areas are being developed. The focus in some areas is on linking understanding of personal experiences of abuse and violence with the wider societal lack of protection for all women. This is being developed primarily through organised groupwork. Guide-lines for establishing and running groups are being produced in order that the work can be developed more widely in the city, the aim being that knowledge can be shared and incorporated into existing work. An adapted version of the Violence Against Women by Known Men training has been run in a mental health day care centre for women survivors of violence, with before and after support for women and workers. Advice and information sessions have been established for Asian and African-Caribbean women with varying levels of success. This incorporates information sharing and basic counselling/support. Much of this work is linked to issues of community loyalty, black women's rights as immigrants in this country and coping with the effects of white supremacist attitudes. Additionally, the project has established a volunteer programme called *HALT (Help & Advice & the Law Team) Domestic Violence!*) to support women using the civil and criminal courts. The aim here is to bridge the advice and information/outreach roles with specialist knowledge of civil and criminal court processes. It has therefore been vital that the scheme is linked directly into the multi-agency work being developed with professionals. The scheme has proven to be very successful with over 300 calls being received in the first year.

A small service providing a *violence advice worker / counsellor* has also been piloted in two general practice surgeries over a three year period. The aim was to bring multi-agency knowledge and support into this primary health care environment. The project faced numerous problems which it is not possible to explore in this chapter. However, it is relevant to state that finding doctors surgeries sympathetic to single gender work was itself a major problem, despite the fact that it is well recognised that many women go to their doctors for support early in the process of seeking help.

The care and sensitivity required to develop this area, has required a range of skills and expertise that have been gained primarily from 'outsider' (non-mainstream) women's voluntary sector organisations such as Rape Crisis Centres. It is however worth noting that easily available models of counselling/advice/ outreach work relate predominantly to work with white European women and able bodied women. In view of this fact, specific work with women who are physically disabled and also work on educating agencies on the needs of disabled women was established in 1996. The production of a training programme for agencies and guide-lines for work with black minority ethnic women is also in process.

Some issues of considerable importance to establishing direct services within the inter-agency context have been identified. I consider them significant enough to raise here, primarily because LIAP has always stated that it will not become involved in 'case work' i.e. work with individual women, unless it is to demonstrate future good practice. The aim of the project is to provide the tools for existing services to use to improve work with women. Additionally, the project has always been clear that it does not wish to duplicate existing services but rather to coordinate and rationalise existing provision. A few points are listed below:

- Direct work with women should only be developed to progress agency knowledge and understanding and inform future policy.
- Support and 'debrief' for workers undertaking 'face to face' work with women is built in at all stages. This must include counselling supervision as well as line management supervision in those situations where counselling is part of the service provided.
- Locating the work with voluntary sector organisations for the longer term has proved difficult due to insufficient resourcing of the groups.[2]

Conclusion

The Leeds Inter-Agency Project (Women & Violence) is by far the largest and widest initiative on women's safety from domestic violence in the UK. It has grown within a five year period from one worker to 9.5 full time equivalent posts (13 workers in all). It has been important that all workers accept the ethos of the organisation in order that there is agreement on the overall direction. To achieve this, all workers take part in the 2 day multi-agency training programme, and there is an expectation that developments are widely agreed by all workers and endorsed by the steering group of representatives from 13 organisations.

I would argue that the LIAP has achieved a fair degree of success in maintaining a radical approach. It straddles the voluntary and statutory sectors. 'Outsider' and 'insider' (both mainstream and fringe) organisations work together to oversee the direction of the project. Both are represented on all bodies established by the LIAP and all representatives are expected to endorse and agree LIAP's definition of violence. However, inter-agency projects, such as LIAP, will always be faced with difficult decisions about how far they can pursue a radical political line because they are not campaigning organisations in the accepted sense of the word. Bridging extreme perspectives is exhausting and requires constant re-evaluation. The work is often unrewarding and developments are largely dependent on the individual women and men working in organisations who have made a commitment to supporting radical ideals such as those expounded by the LIAP. It is their dedication and work that enable progress to be made as much as local political support and cooperation.

Notes

1. Direct services are only provided in those situations where no statutory or voluntary sector organisations are providing the service e.g. the HALT Domestic Violence scheme.
2. It has not been possible to progress approaches to voluntary organisations despite the offer of worker support to develop the work. This has been due to the groups feeling that additional responsibility would overstretch the organisation.

References

Dominy, N. and Radford, L. (1996) *Domestic Violence in Surrey: Developing an effective inter-agency response.* Kingston: Surrey County Council and Roehampton Institute.

Hague, G. and Malos, E. (1998) *Domestic Violence: Action for change.* (2nd Ed) Cheltenham: New Clarion Press.

Leeds Inter-Agency Project (Women & Violence) (1991) *Violence Against Women by Known Men Multi-Agency Training Pack.* Leeds: LIAP.

Leeds Inter-Agency Project (Women & Violence) (1992), *Information Pack.* Leeds: LIAP

Russell, D. (1982) *Rape in Marriage.* New York: Collier.

West Yorkshire Police (1993) *Domestic Violence Survey.* Leeds: West Yorkshire Police.

10
Sharing the responsibility: Reaching joint agreements on domestic violence policy

Annie Moelwyn- Hughes

Introduction

Sharing the Responsibility is a central theme of the Multi-agency Strategy on Domestic Violence in Central Scotland. This recognises that no one agency has sole responsibility for responding to domestic violence. It reflects the view that some agencies and departments may be reluctant on their own to shoulder responsibility for a problem which is considered difficult to deal with, that some agencies see domestic violence as outside their main function and priorities, and that all agencies have a role to play in responding to the needs of women who have experienced violence.

The aims of the Strategy are to develop a common policy, and foundation for the development of good practice in responding to those affected by domestic violence. It focuses on male violence to women by partners or ex-partners, and is based on a common ethos which can be agreed by all relevant agencies.

The Strategy addresses the action required by statutory and voluntary organisations. This includes the Police, Social Work, Housing, Education, the Health Sector, Women's Aid and various voluntary and community groups.

A further purpose of the Strategy is to develop a more consistent and uniform approach to providing services to women.

This will be achieved by providing a clear course of action for the development of an effective service on domestic violence taking account of the needs of women who require help, the gaps in provision, the barriers to development of the service and how these might be overcome.

In addition to developing the basis for a common approach across the above agencies, the Strategy encompasses a comprehensive approach. This has sought to combine proposals for service development with strategies for raising awareness, for prevention and for influencing a change in the culture which reinforces and supports male violence to women. The development of this approach within one year has meant that the Strategy has not been able to fully address issues relating to the response of the civil and criminal justice system to domestic violence. It is envisaged that this will be undertaken at a later stage

The Strategy focuses on responding to the problem of male violence to women by a partner or ex-partner. The definition of violence adopted in the Strategy includes physical, sexual, psychological, emotional and economic violence. The term 'violence' is sometimes interchanged with 'abuse'.

Background

The initial ideas for development of a common policy and approach came from a multi-agency seminar on domestic violence held in 1994, entitled 'Sharing the Responsibility'. This has been important to the task of reaching and sustaining joint agreements on policy and practice. It is difficult for the sponsoring organisations not to subscribe to the underlying approach, because of the emphasis given to it by the public seminar in the form of its recommendations.

The key points from the Seminar included:

- give priority to women's needs and preferences
- ensure client-led agency provision
- achieve a predominance of multi-agency work
- develop of common policies, procedures and good practice guidance, based on a common ethos
- establish a domestic violence forum
- appoint a coordinator

While there was considerable public commitment to the idea of developing a multi-agency policy, it took a further year before this was translated into practical action and the appointment of a coordinator. After several months working behind the scenes, a meeting was held between the inter-agency group who had organised the conference and the Chief Officers of the Regional Council, the Police, three District Councils and the Health Board. They agreed to jointly fund a one-year project and to appoint a Development Worker.[1] Subsequently the Scottish Office also provided a grant to the Project. It was nine months later before a Development Worker was appointed. A Steering Group was formed which is composed of representatives of six local statutory organisations listed above together with three Women's Aid Groups and the Development Worker.

Defining the problem to be addressed

Over the last 25 years attention has been drawn to the problem of male violence to women and to the difficulties experienced by women in gaining help from statutory organisations. These difficulties have been well documented elsewhere.

Public awareness of male violence to women has been greatly increased in Scotland by the work of Scottish Women's Aid, the Zero Tolerance Campaign and the Scottish Office television campaign. Violence to women has been identified as a social problem of significant proportion, yet despite this there is no national policy or guidance in this area, unlike other areas of social need. The responsibility for responding to domestic violence has been left to local organisations. A variety of inter-agency initiatives have now been developed in the UK resulting in some improvement in services. Overall the response of agencies to domestic violence is still far from satisfactory and has been developed on an incremental basis.

In general statutory organisations find domestic violence difficult to deal with. The nature of domestic violence is complex, women will often require a continuum of services from several agencies. Many managers and service providers do not have a clear understanding of the nature of men's violence, the sources of conflict leading to abuse, and its effect on the women and children who experience it. There is a lack of clear guidance for practitioners on how to respond to the problem, a dearth of policies setting out what is expected, and the need to clarify the role of practitioners and the responsibilities of agencies.

No particular agency has responsibility for responding to domestic violence; there is largely separate provision by a number of agencies; the response of agencies tends to reflect agency roles and responsibilities rather than the needs of women seeking help. Instead of common values and shared understandings, competing models exist with resulting confusion about what intervention is appropriate. There is need for a clear framework for the development of services.

A framework for service development

There are four fundamental problems to be overcome in developing a policy on domestic violence, these are:

- a lack of detailed knowledge and understanding of the nature and effects of violence, the needs of women and their children
- a low level of knowledge about the services required and what is available
- fragmentation of service provision across the relevant agencies
- lack of a coordinated response to the problem

In developing a multi-agency policy on domestic violence in Central Scotland we set out to design a coherent policy which adopts an holistic approach to domestic violence. The aim is to meet the needs of women who experience violence, create a model for the development of a needs-led woman-centred service, develop the means of overcoming the fragmentation of services and lack of coordination, and develop strategies to prevent violence and publicise the work.

The framework of the local strategy combines an understanding of the problem to be addressed, mechanisms for planning, service development and coordination and a structure for enabling and achieving change. The policy has five elements, these are:

- a needs-led approach
- building agreements around a shared vision
- the process of enabling and achieving change
- knowledge, attitudes and behaviour change
- improving quality of services

Community integration

The proposals for strategic change outlined above are important in ensuring that good quality services are planned and provided in a way that meets the needs of women seeking help. There is a need for a community-based structure which reflects women's social networks and their need to access services locally, and ensures the identification of unmet needs and that practical improvements to services will be achieved at a local level.

There is a need for the development of local domestic violence fora to enable practitioners from all agencies, voluntary and community groups, representatives of the private sector and women who have experienced violence to meet together for the purpose of raising awareness, exchange of information and ideas, identifying local needs, and working together on solutions to address the problems identified, and to influence changes in policy and practice.

Setting the direction for multi-agency work

The concept of a multi-agency coordinated approach to domestic violence is under-developed within the statutory and voluntary sector in the UK. Many women who have experienced domestic violence find difficulty in obtaining the help they require. The fundamental barriers to service development which have been identified need to be addressed in a coherent policy and the characteristics of an effective service need to be established. In order to provide a service which adequately meets the needs of women and their children, a multi-agency approach is required.

The model of service development proposed for Central Scotland relies on multi-agency collaboration and coordination as the core focus for planning and delivering services in Housing, Social Work, Education Services, Health, the Police, Women's Aid and within the voluntary sector. This requires the development of different ways of collaborative working and securing the necessary climate for a multi-agency approach.

In pursuing a more consistent approach emphasis is given to ensuring that all the relevant agencies through a planning and coordinating group are enabled to develop basic policy, guidance, best practice and recording and monitoring the service provided which is common to all agencies and in keeping with the philosophy of a multi-agency approach.

The basis for reaching agreements

In order to develop a common policy and approach and agree a way forward for all agencies, Steering Group members have a responsibility to represent and promote the agreed approach to their organisations. To do this group members need to be in full agreement, share common goals and to support the proposals.

The agreements are reached by a relatively small number of people, that is eight members of the Steering Group. The development worker also contributes to the discussion around agreements, as well as commenting on key points, acting as a facilitator for the group in clarifying statements, and drawing together common themes from diverse points of view, redrafting statements or encouraging others to do so.

There is a relatively small number of people involved in this process due to a decision that each statutory agency would have one representative on the Steering Group. Each Women's Aid group has a place on the Steering Group. The focus of the group is on strategic and not practice development. In order to achieve a common approach the policy and ethos need to be developed and adopted by all agencies before further development of practice. The time-scale of one year during the time of local government re-organisation has meant that more practical tasks which would have involved a wider group could not be undertaken, e.g. a directory of services for agencies, accessible information about services for women, a domestic violence forum.

The small number of people involved is both a help and a hindrance. It is a help because it is easier to agree common goals and direction amongst a smaller group who have a clear responsibility to represent the project to their organisations; it is a hindrance because, apart from Women's Aid, few people on the group are currently engaged in day-to-day work with women who are abused. Social Work, Education, Accident & Emergency and Community Health services are not represented directly on the group. There is a danger that the discussion becomes too abstract and places a greater reliance on Women's Aid to provide practical information relating to women's experience.

The process of reaching agreement

Agreements about the aims and goals of the project, principles and values, policy, practice guidance, action plans were reached in a number of different group settings. These settings are Steering Group meetings, sub-groups composed of three or four members of the Steering Group, and multi-agency working groups drawing on the expertise of practitioners. The sub-group and working group meetings were usually chaired and facilitated by the Development Worker. Conclusions of the sub-groups and working groups were always referred back to the Steering Group. Sometimes these proposals were adopted with minor alterations and sometimes there was a lengthy debate before agreement was reached.

The agenda for discussion leading to proposals about policy and practice was drawn up in four different ways:

1. A draft statement prepared by the Development Worker as a starting point for group discussion, to be amended and extended as the group decides;
2. A group discussion facilitated in order to draw up an agenda of topics to be included, and to encourage members of the group to work in pairs in writing sections of the paper;
3. Facilitated group discussion to draw up an agenda which would inform a paper written by the Development Worker, the paper was then circulated to the group for comment;
4. The Strategy and policy framework were drawn up by the Development Worker for comment and discussion, finally reaching agreement by the Steering Group.

Factors which help to sustain the work

Some of the factors which help to sustain the work are coincidental. They concern the commitment of the group and the role of key members. If the situation were to change they would be difficult to control. The key factors are:

1. Having a majority of group members who share the goals and the vision. Through discussion they can sometimes put pressure on other members to reach agreement, especially when minority views do not carry much support
2. Having a Chair of the group who with the Development

Worker shares and strongly supports the overall vision and the means of achieving it;

3. The involvement of committed senior managers on the group whose views in some situations may carry more weight in group discussion.

4. The ability to get to know members individually through informal discussion between meetings. Once a good rapport has been established this can provide an opportunity to consult them about proposals to be brought to meetings, and to find out what support individuals will give about particularly difficult issues due to emerge in a Steering Group meeting.

5. The coordinators in-depth knowledge of the subject, where there is disagreement. When strong advice is given backed up by evidence it will often be followed.

6. Having a sense of humour.

Factors which can impede reaching agreements in multi-agency work

Some of the difficulties which are common to all multi-agency work were encountered in this project. They relate to membership and roles of the group members.

Multi-agency work functions best when members of the group have similar levels of seniority and responsibility within their organisation, although this is difficult to achieve since the decision about who is represented on the group rests with the parent organisations.. Those in a more senior position are more likely to be able to work by group consensus and for group decisions to be adopted by parent organisations without having to refer to a more senior or chief officer. Senior officers are more likely to have a direct link with senior management teams, and to have opportunity to inform them of decisions made.

There is a need to consider the roles and contribution of group members in relation to their professional background. Ideally members of the group should have some understanding and insight into domestic violence practice issues relevant to the organisation they represent. There is also a need for the group to have access to officers with experience of policy and strategic development.

There is a need to assess the particular skills and knowledge of group members, and to identify the gaps. This is done with a view to sharing information about the contribution of group members, valuing the range of skills and knowledge, giving consideration to the need for skills development and inviting new members who can provide additional areas of expertise.

Breaks, changes in membership or in roles within the group have an impact on decision-making which can cause discontinuity. Some changes are inevitable as a result of changing roles of officers in their organisations. The effects of this can be alleviated by allowing time to hand over a particular role to other group members, or by allowing time to hand over representation on the group to a new member. It can take several meetings before a new group member is fully conversant with the project, and of what is expected of them within their organisation. This will affect the contribution they can make to discussion. Particular difficulties in relation to discontinuity are noticeable when changes in membership are sudden as for example in the case of a local emergency.

Time is an important factor. It takes longer to reach collective decisions and members underestimate the time needed to work effectively as a group. It has been difficult to persuade members of the group to commit sufficient time to the project. This includes difficulty in attending meetings, or arriving late and leaving early, reading papers and preparing for meetings, responding to requests to comment on papers between meetings. It is difficult to plan how long discussion will take on a particular item. For example in the later stages of the project there was a protracted discussion about whether to include a section on the process of consultation in the Strategy. There was a need to reach a consensus on this matter before proceeding with other business. Thus the timetable for that meeting was not met. This situation frequently occurred.

Existing working relationships between group members also have an impact on the group. Some members may have experience of working together on other inter-agency initiatives and this may have an impact on communication within the group, both positive and negative. Some members who know each other well may form a clique especially if they share a common agenda. This may not be in the interest of the main group.

There is a reluctance to acknowledge other peoples skills and expertise; recognising and valuing other people is an important tool in multi-agency work.

There is some inevitable caution and prejudice about other agencies, which can take a long time to break down. There is a reluctance for individuals to acknowledge when their own understanding of domestic violence is limited. It is difficult to find time to raise awareness of domestic violence and the policy issues amongst group members.

There are difficulties for Women's Aid representatives on a strategic planning group. They provide no financial support to the project and are perceived by some as unequal partners, especially with regard to financial and organisational matters. They have to develop new skills and to challenge officers of statutory bodies. This can be difficult if they rely on them for funding. There is need for a much greater recognition of contribution of Women's Aid to the group. They bring their experience and knowledge gained from working with women who have been or are being abused, which is sometimes under-valued. They are a constant reminder to other members of why the group exists and the needs to be addressed. They should be seen as having equal standing. There is a need for Women's Aid representatives to be confident about articulating their strengths, and the fact that the development of policy and practice would not have credibility without them.

There are ways of overcoming these difficulties by building up trust and looking at how the group can work more effectively together. It is difficult to fit this into a busy timetable when there is already a full agenda and pressure to deliver a Strategy. This involves recognising that multi-agency groups need to give themselves time to develop as a group, to develop group work skills, to take responsibility for the work of the group jointly and not just to see it in terms of their own organisation. It is important also to clarify the roles, responsibilities and expectations of each member and of the coordinator, to seek to have time allocated in their individual work programme and job description.. When we tried to raise these issues early in the life of the group some members considered we were reaching for an ideal and should just get on with the job. These issues do have an impact on how well a group can function.

The Chair of a multi-agency group has an important role to play. The question arises about whether to have a rotating or single chair, and the impact that either of these situations might have on keeping the balance, and power sharing between agencies. At the outset of the project emphasis was given to the need for the Chair of the Group to rotate between agencies, although the Women's Aid representatives were not included in this rotation. There was a reluctance to ascribe this role to a member of one particular agency. A number of factors influenced the shift from a rotating to a single chair. These include the need for continuity, to be more familiar with the work of the project in order to chair meetings effectively, to carry some responsibility for imposing discipline on the group, to provide support to the coordinator and to be someone with whom she could discuss difficulties that had arisen or were foreseen.

The formulation of the Domestic Violence Policy has coincided with Local Government re-organisation. This has had an impact on decision-making. Throughout the year there has been uncertainty about the form of new policies, and internal and joint planning structures of the new councils. The changes in local government finance have also created difficulties for obtaining funds for implementation of the Strategy. The greatest difficulty throughout this period has been the lack of opportunity to develop strong links with senior managers in the Education and Social Work Services and to engage in discussion with them about the aims and implementation of the Strategy and about the need for a coherent policy on domestic violence.

While re-organisation has created some difficulties in developing a multi-agency Strategy, it should also be seen as an opportunity for incorporating a new policy on domestic violence at a time when new policies, structures and planning arrangements are being introduced by the Local Councils. It is an opportunity to incorporate domestic violence policy as a priority.

The value of reaching and sustaining joint agreements

Agreement has been reached in all the papers for dissemination relating to the Strategy. This includes the Principles and Values, Best Practice Guidance, Training Programme, Participation by Women in the Planning Process, and the Proposals for Action. The Strategy includes sections on definitions, focusing on male violence to women, a policy framework elaborating on problems to be addressed and the organisation and structure required for implementation.

On the whole the development of a multi-agency strategy which is agreed across agencies has been an enriching experience. This has been achieved without compromising the underlying philosophy about supporting women in making decisions about their lives.

Reaching joint decisions has added to rather than detracted from the views of particular individuals or organisations. Through this process we have achieved production of a policy which is thought to serve the interests of women more fully than if a policy had been developed by any one of the organisations participating in the project.

The relevance and acceptance of the policy has still to be tested when we consult with the statutory and voluntary organisations, and the subsequent implementation of the Strategy. The difficulty will be in gaining acceptance from people who have not been exposed to the debate and discussion and awareness raising that has taken place in the multi-agency Steering Group during the year of development.

Continuity is an important factor in the degree to which the agreements reached can be sustained. There is a need to understand this as part of a process which starts with the concepts of the Strategy through to its implementation.

Where gaps exist in this process they will have an impact on sustaining the vision and momentum for implementing the Strategy. Only a small number of the core group who were committed to the original ideas for a multi-agency strategy, now remain on the Steering Group. There is also a need for continuity between strategy formulation and its implementation. During the second half of the project much emphasis was given to the need to sustain the momentum of the work achieved while formulating the Strategy, and the need to move directly into its implementation. Despite this the formulation and implementation have been perceived by some agencies as two distinct phases. Perhaps the best way of overcoming this kind of division is for domestic violence projects to have a longer life through long-term funding.

Note

1. The organisations who are currently partners in this Strategy are Central Scotland Police, Forth Valley Health Board, Stirling Council, Clackmannan Council, Falkirk Council, Stirling Women's Aid, Clackmannan Women's Aid and Falkirk Women's Aid. Central Regional Council were also partners in the project prior to local government re-organisation.

11
Duluth: A coordinated community response to domestic violence

Ellen Pence and Martha McMahon

How the Duluth Project Started

We want to describe the 'Duluth Model' of criminal justice intervention in domestic violence cases. The Duluth Domestic Abuse Intervention Project (DAIP) is a pioneer in coordinated community responses to woman assault. But it is often misrepresented as a 'batterers treatment model', a 'mandatory arrest project', or a 'no drop prosecution program'. Instead, the Duluth project should be seen as a system of networks, agreements, processes and applied principles created by the local shelter movement, criminal justice agencies, and human service programs that were developed in a small northern Minnesota city over a fifteen year period. It is still a project in the making:

> *If I were to say what is at the heart of our efforts here it would be our willingness to try to improve the community's intervention strategy. We try out things. If it works to protect women or to keep men from using violence again we keep it. If it doesn't or it backfires and makes things worse, we jettison it.* (Police Sergeant interviewed in Duluth, 1996)

Here's how the Duluth project started. In 1978 Cindy Landfried, who had been brutally abused by her husband for 3 years, shot and killed him. A locally convened grand jury decided not to indict the nineteen year old woman for murder. Cindy's case led to intense public debate on the responsibility of community services to intervene and stop domestic violence. At the time of the shooting, shelter activists from across the United States were meeting to find a city that would introduce a proactive domestic assault intervention plan. Duluth's shelter workers convinced the group that Duluth would be the best site for an experimental project. The experimental project would introduce multiple inter-agency agreements which linked all the intervening agencies in a community to a common philosophical approach. At the same time, it would also introduce ways for the different agencies to cooperate and so improve the community's ability to hold offenders accountable for their violence. The guiding goal was *safety*: the *safety* of women who were beaten by their partners. The first step was to get funds for and organise an autonomous, non-profit agency and small coordinating staff dedicated exclusively to the work of coordinating the project. Staff were to be selected with the approval of the shelter but would not work for the shelter nor any other participating agency.

The activists organising the Duluth DAIP in 1980 had little to build on. There was no role-model of 'reform coordinator'. Practitioners in the different agencies in Duluth allowed (sometimes reluctantly) the DAIP to fill that role. Today, of course, the question of *who* will organise inter-agency reform efforts has become a far more contentious one as actors from within the legal system, for example, take up the banner of reform and inter-agency reform councils.

How making victims' safety the central goal changes a lot of things

The DAIP's work was (and is) complex. Below we will try to describe this work by outlining eight activities. The DAIP took these as the essential elements in reorganising the community's legal and human service intervention so as to make victim safety the central goal.

Victim safety challenges conventional ways of responding to crime. For example, the legal system is designed to respond to a specific crime committed on a specific day. So much of what occurs in handling a case is geared towards gathering evidence about that specific incident. The work is geared towards prosecution with the goal of conviction. One constantly hears people in the judicial system talk about whether or not they have a good case or a weak case. Behind the scenes, a weak case is often referred as a 'shit' case. A shit case is one that will likely never result in a conviction because the evidence is weak, typically because the victim is not in a position to testify against her attacker. Nobody really wants a 'shit' case. Most domestic assault cases drop out of the legal process without a conviction - they are 'weak' cases. From the police's perspective that means 'why pursue it?' From the prosecutor's perspective it means 'no victim, no case'. For the judge it means one less case in an overcrowded court calendar. For the woman's advocate it represents a missed opportunity to use the power of the state to place controls on an abuser and protect the battered woman. Domestic assault cases often become 'shit' cases because battered women make bad victims: or rather because they make bad victims in *an incident-focused, adversarial criminal justice system.* Battered women make 'bad' victims because the crime of domestic assault needs to be understood in terms of ongoing patterns of behaviour rather than as a single criminal act or incident.

Thus the Duluth DAIP faces the continuing challenge of making an incident-focused, adversarial criminal justice system responsive to the kind of crime that must be understood in context. The point we want to make is that *institutional practices matter.* For example, changing how people in the legal system do their work can reduce homicide and felony assaults against women in their community. The task facing the DAIP was to identify, analyse and alter those processes and procedures used by different practitioners in the legal system (and in related human service agencies) which compromised victim safety. In addition, the Duluth DAIP wanted to organise a community response that would help women who wanted to leave their abusers do so safely, and to increase the protection available to women who stayed with violent partners.

Here are some of the practical changes introduced in Duluth:

- Dispatchers, patrol officers, jailers, prosecutors, probation officers and shelter workers are now all guided by inter-locking policies which coordinate their work.
- When police officers investigate an incident, their reports must now follow a format. The new format describes the incident but also records information from the victim about the overall pattern of abuse toward her and her children. If a woman reports a high level of ongoing violence, those reports

are forwarded to child protection workers and advocates for immediate follow up.

- Probation officers making sentencing recommendations to the court are provided with information from the police, women's advocates, jailers, civil court files and the DAIP. They are required to document the full pattern of violence used by the offender for the sentencing judge to consider.

- A sentencing matrix is used to ensure higher levels of sanctions and surveillance of repeat and dangerous offenders.

- In cases where victims of battering have used violence against their abusers, the prosecutor's office has developed a specialised prosecution policy for charging and prosecuting. This policy confronts victims' own use of violence while attempting to minimise the ability of batterers to use the criminal court as another weapon of control or intimidation.

Making women's safety central:
What do we mean by women's safety?

An inter-agency approach must decide what safety for a battered woman means. The Duluth project is based on the agreement that those who intervene, whether they be police officers, therapists, judges, or clergy, must intervene in ways that take the context of the violence and how it is experienced by the victim into account. For the victim's safety to be fully incorporated into case management routines, **each** part of the process must account for the following:

The pattern of abuse
A domestic assault-related crime, such as trespass, criminal damage to property, violation of a protection order, or kidnapping, is rarely an isolated incident. In order to design effective safety measures, the context in which violence occurred must be understood. Thus information which documents the patterns of coercion, intimidation or violence associated with a case, who is being harmed and to what extent, must be sought and recorded.

Power differentials
A battered woman and her abuser do not have equal power. The justice system acts as if they do. Gendered power relations in society generally, and the power gained from a sustained pattern of coercion, intimidation, and violence, give the perpetrator power

over the victim. They make the victim vulnerable to pressure, intimidation, and retaliation by the offender. The adversarial nature of the criminal court process rests on the false assumption that the individuals before the courts are separate, autonomous and have equal power. But that's not usually the case. The unequal economic and social relationship between an abuser and his victim, as well as the history of violence, shapes the meaning of every statement, affidavit, and action made by either party. For example, a man usually has economic, psychological or physical power over the woman he has beaten but when she is expected to act as the main witness against him, this is usually not recognised. Investigators and case processors must recognise and account for this fact or they may put victims at risk rather than providing safety.

The particulars of the case

The criminal justice system is structured in a way that classifies incidents as misdemeanour/minor or felony/serious assaults. This process often classifies extremely dangerous cases as minor assaults and in doing so can underestimate the actual danger posed to a victim. Interventions and safety measures should be based on the particulars of the case and not on predetermined legal or institutional categories of misdemeanour or felony or generalised categories.

The need to coordinate fragmented responses to domestic abuse

The DAIP gets practitioners to look at their own practices rather than focusing on the idiosyncratic characteristics of the offenders or victims. This means examining how those who work in as many as eleven different specialised agencies and five different levels of government can coordinate their work so as to protect victims' safety or discover why they fail to do so.

Victim perception of danger

There is no scale or measure that accurately predicts which offender will kill or seriously injure his partner. Yet evidence shows that victims of homicide or attempted homicide often try to tell others about the danger, but are ignored. We must examine how the victim's perception of danger is accounted for in the processing of a case. At what point is her knowledge screened out of the information gathering, and at what point is it given an authorised place in the construction of the case? A victim is often asked for data and information but rarely is she asked to *evaluate* that data. For example, she is asked if he has a weapon, if he was drinking, or if he has a history of mental illness, but rarely is she asked 'will he harm you?' or 'do you think he is dangerous?'

The differences among women's lives
There is no universal battered woman. Race and class shape the impact of interventions. For example, Lawrence Sherman's Milwaukee study of the relationship between arrest, police warnings and recidivism found that employed, married men were less likely to re-offend when arrested but not prosecuted. Unemployed, unmarried men of all ethnic backgrounds, however, were more likely to re-offend when arrested but not prosecuted (Sherman, 1992). Because so few men in either group were prosecuted, the effect of criminal justice intervention is unclear. We suspect that interventions that bring the legal system into violent relationships, but do not follow through on using the power of the state to control the offender, may make some women more vulnerable to abuse.

Assessing the risk
All women are not at equal risk. The criminal justice system cannot treat all acts of physical force, every shove, every push, every slap, as if these actions will escalate to homicide. Similarly, if a victim of ongoing abuse and violence or coercion herself responds with violence, her response cannot be treated as though it were the same as the violence used by her abuser to dominate her. Practitioners must develop working definitions of the significance of violence and the appropriate interventions that make safety a priority.

The eight essential activities of the Duluth Model

The key activities of the Duluth Model fall under one or more of eight objectives:

1. Creating a coherent philosophical approach which centralises victim safety
2. Developing 'best practice' policies and protocols for intervention agencies
3. Reducing fragmentation in the system's response
4. Building monitoring and tracking into the system

5. Ensuring a supportive community infrastructure
6. Intervening directly with abusers to deter violence
7. Undoing the harm violence to women does to children
8. Evaluating the system's response from the standpoint of the victim

1. Creating a coherent philosophical approach which centralises victim safety

Those involved in an intervention project must negotiate a shared practical philosophical framework around which they can organise. In Duluth, this core organising philosophy was the practice of referring all actions back to the priorities of victim *protection, accountability,* and *deterrence.*

A commitment to victim safety and to holding offenders accountable means, for example, that the pervasive victim-blaming that exists in most systems must be eliminated. People who work in the judicial system and other agencies must change how they understand domestic violence, how they understand the relationship of offender to the victim, and how they understand the potential for further violence. It also means that they must change whom they see as responsible for undoing the harm caused by the violence and what they see to be the respective roles of the offender, the victim, and the community in ending the violence.

A legal advocate describes what it is like to do this kind of work:

> *I think we spend a great deal of our time fighting against the notion that these assaults are logical extensions of relationship problems or dysfunction. We have picked up some allies in the mental health profession, but the mainstream is still a powerful force in the legal system and their way of seeing violence as an individual pathology has been hard to overcome. We also battle endlessly against the blatant and subtle ways that people in the system blame women for getting battered. But our biggest effort still comes down to getting systems people to develop a sense of urgency in these cases. In towns like ours, 80 to 90 percent of homicides are domestics, but the sheer volume of these cases lulls people into a passive intervention role.* (Women's Legal Advocate interviewed in Duluth, 1995)

The DAIP model means that practitioners, whether they work in the criminal justice system or in a community agency, must focus on concrete ways of defining victim safety. And then they must connect this to their work. The DAIP organisers stress that women's safety depends on having intervention practices which are rooted in *how women experience violence* and *not* simply in how the legal system abstractly defines violence.

2. 'Best Practice' policies and protocols

Victims will not be protected simply by having actors in a coordinated response system 'think' differently. They must *ACT* differently. And their actions must be both oriented towards victim safety and organised in ways that complement rather than undermine each other. With this goal in mind, practitioners' decisions and actions should be guided by sets of protocols and agency policies. These are sometimes referred to as 'best practice' standards.

But questions arise. When should the discretion of the individual practitioners be restricted by such protocols? When should police officers be required to arrest? Should prosecutors seek convictions when victims have asked to have cases dismissed? How can practitioners pay attention to the particulars of a case if they are constrained by generalising policies? These sorts of questions cannot be addressed from one site in the intervention project, but from several sites of change.

Protocols usually govern three things. First, they govern individual practitioners' responses to specific cases. For example, they specify under which conditions police will arrest, probation officers will recommend jail time, or jailers will release suspects. Second, protocols govern practitioners' interactions with other practitioners in the system, with victim advocates, and with other community-based agencies. Protocols should reduce system fragmentation. They help coordinate the often widely scattered parts of a legal response. Third, protocols address the issue of accountability by linking the agency with a monitoring system and a mechanism through which practitioners' actions can be recorded and, when necessary, questioned.

To make protocols responsive to victims, one must ask: Does this protocol enhance the victim's safety? Are case management considerations superseding victim safety? How does this policy or this procedure affect victims' self-determination and autonomy? And how does this policy deal with the power differential caused both by the violence and the differing social positions of the victim and offender?

DAIP staff coordinate the many levels of discussion needed to design, write and introduce new procedures and policies. They do this by organising thinking sessions, writing proposed drafts of policy or procedural guidelines, mediating conflict among participating agencies or practitioners, meeting with agency administrators and practitioners to explain the reasons behind and the direction of new procedures being proposed. They also work to lessen resistance to proposed changes.

3. Reducing fragmentation in the system's response

> *I can't tell you how many times I've seen a total breakdown in communication cause a case to be lost or dismissed. Every time somebody gets seriously hurt or killed, everybody scrambles to the files to make sure they didn't mess up. If they didn't there's a big sigh of relief, but there's always this awareness that on so many cases there's a screw-up.* (Court Clerk, Duluth)

Practitioners in the criminal justice system often develop a narrow definition of their tasks and of what being fair or protective means because their work is so specialised. Diane Winterstein's case (below) helps us make this point.

In Minnesota, as in most States, the seriousness of a crime depends on the bodily harm done or potential harm based on the use of a weapon. Bodily harm is categorised according to broken bones or permanent physical injury, so that a single slap to the side of the head that results in damage to the eardrum is a felony, whereas multiple blows to the body that result in deep bruising, cuts, and scrapes constitute a misdemeanour. This excerpt from a police report documents the arrest of a woman who, following a violent altercation with her husband, called the police for help.

> *I asked Diane Winterstein to tell me what occurred, she said her husband Philip had come home after drinking at the Y&R bar and was becoming very belligerent. She said he told her that people were 'reporting on her.' I asked what he might have meant by that and she said that he acts like everybody is his personal watch guard over her and that he makes up affairs she was supposed to have and then says his reporters saw her with someone. She went on to say that Philip started pushing furniture around. I noted that a chair was pushed over in the dining room. She then went into the kitchen and got out a steak knife and threatened to 'poke his eyes out' if he didn't leave the house immediately. I asked her if she was in fear of grave bodily harm*

*at this point and she said no, she thought he was going to leave.
Then according to Diane he started to call her names like 'whore'
and 'bitch' and 'cunt,' at which point she lunged at him and
'poked him in the right hand with the knife.' She said when he
saw the blood he started to cry and she called him a 'big baby,' at
which point she says, 'he grabbed me by my hair and began
pulling me toward the bathroom and kicking me.' She stated
that he kicked her three or four times in the legs and right hip
area. I asked her if there were any bruises. She showed me the
area of her right hip which was red and swollen and beginning to
bruise. I asked her if he did anything else to assault her and she
stated that he threw her up against the wall and told her that this
time she had gone too far. I asked her if she had been violent to
him in the past and she said that she often threatens him to get
him to leave her alone . . . . She said that he slapped her across the
face twice and then spit in her face. . . .I conferred briefly with
Officer Dickie and a decision was made to arrest both parties. I
informed Diane that I was placing her under arrest for 2nd
degree assault and took her into custody without incident. . . .
Officer Dickie placed Mr. Winterstein under arrest for 5th degree
assault (see Officer Dickie's report for more details). . . . Officer
O'Keeffe took pictures of both parties' injuries. Both refused
medical treatment. I placed a kitchen knife shown to me by Diane
Winterstein as the one she used to stab her husband into evidence.'*

Diane Winterstein was charged with second-degree assault
for 'stabbing her husband with a deadly weapon' and faced a
prison sentence of 10 years. As it was her first offence, she spent
only 11 days in jail and was ordered to classes for offenders.
Philip Winterstein plead guilty to a misdemeanour assault and
was sentenced to 1 year probation. He served 2 days in jail, and
was ordered to attend a men's educational group. The generalising
character of the law and the overly specialised work force
prevented practitioners from intervening in a way that would
have protected Diane from future assaults. She may well have
become more vulnerable to her abuser by this state intervention
than had the police never arrived at her door. Yet each
practitioner in this case did his/her job:

*I'm not so sure what you mean by how do I get involved in the
whole case. That's not really my job, to get involved in the whole
thing. I'm an investigator. That means I investigate. If I get to
having a need to own a case I'll go crazy with all the nutty things*

*that happen in this place. I do my job and I think I do a fairly
good job, but I don't want to be held responsible for how the whole
thing turns out. I've seen a lot of goofy things happen here and all
I can do is say, 'Did I do what I was supposed to do?'* (Police
Detective, Duluth)

Those who are aware that women's safety is compromised
often feel there is little they can do about it. The work of legal
practitioners, for example, is bureaucratically organised. They
have been trained in occupationally specific ways of handling the
specifics of individual cases so that they are institutionally
'actionable.' Thus they must fit battered women's experience of
the real world into the terms, categories, modes of organising,
accounting, and evaluating provided by their work. Individual
women's experiences of violence become translated into and
'absorbed' by bureaucratically sanctioned, objectifying accounts,
designed for 'case management' and the control of those people
who are part of 'the case'. The battered woman and her experience
of violence disappear. In her place, officially sanctioned
'knowledge' is expressed in terms of management-relevant
categories and becomes part of the way power works in the
reproduction of gender inequality.

*Resisting this kind of bureaucratic fragmentation of women's
experience*

A single case involves many actions by many different
practitioners. Established work routines, fragmentation of
responsibility and poor coordination among practitioners and
agencies compromise victims' safety. For example, before
incarcerating a suspect a jailor records all of his possessions. His
belt, shoe laces and other objects that he could use to harm
himself or others are removed, labelled and stored. During this
procedure the suspect may be muttering or shouting threats to
'get' his wife for 'doing this to him'. If you talk to jailers, they will
tell you they often hear such threats and they are often quite
specific and disturbing. Yet there is no institutionally organised
way for the jailer to routinely record and communicate those
threats to the victim, the pre-trial release personnel or the judge
who will set the conditions of the suspect's release.

There are very many occasions to either increase or
compromise victim safety during the months it takes to process a
case. The Duluth model holds that a detailed analysis or audit of
the system using *victim safety* as a criterion can generate an

inter-agency agenda for change. In Duluth, this inter-agency approach involves a fluid configuration of people whose composition is determined by the specific nature and area of change proposed. The Standing Interagency Committee of Agency Representatives is involved on only a general level. Such committees, sometimes called coordinating councils, are often fraught with inter-agency power differences and politics. This makes the kind of critical reflection and negotiation required for practical reforms in the day to day work practices of different agencies difficult. The DAIP reduces the consequences of bureaucratic fragmentation by promoting the coordination of the activities of the different agencies around the practical goal of victim safety. New procedures, such as the documentation of the history of abuse in all cases, promoting inter-agency consultations on cases, and helping different agencies change job descriptions become means to victim safety. The DAIP continually pushes the system to focus on the issue of justice and safety by linking each step in the legal process to the experience of the woman who has been beaten, asking, 'Does this community response protect women?'

4. Building monitoring and tracking into the system
Accountability is a crucial component of a community intervention program. Practitioners must be accountable for (a) maintaining the priorities of victim safety, (b) deterring individual batterers from further use of violence and (c) creating a general deterrence to the use of violence within intimate relationships. They must also be held accountable to each other.

> *We needed to keep pushing for accountability. We wanted the court to see itself as accountable to a community, to women who were being beaten, and to in turn hold the abuser to some standard of accountability.* (Legal Advocate interviewed in Duluth 1996)

To increase accountability and reduce fragmentation, the Duluth DAIP has an inter-agency tracking system to provide its participating agencies with information. The tracking system shares information, can follow a case from inception to closure, and can show trends in how cases are handled. A DAIP staff member collects information and disseminates it on a predetermined 'need-to-know' basis.

A tracking system allows one to review large numbers of cases in short periods of time. The DAIP issues a monthly report that alerts readers to patterns and problems not visible when cases are responded to individually. For example, a recent probation report from one Minnesota community revealed that there were 37 men on probation who had been reported by their rehabilitation program for failure to complete the program. All 37 of these defendants were thus in violation of the conditions of their probation. In 11 of these cases the probation officers had known about the violation for more than 14 days but had not issued a warrant or contacted the defendant; 9 of the cases belonged to the same probation officer.

The information in the monthly report has different implications for different people in the system. For example, information about men who drop out of their programs alerts the shelter worker system to contact individual women who may be at increased risk of harm: most men who re-offend in the Duluth project drop out of their groups just prior to using violence or shortly thereafter. It points out a potential personnel problem to the supervisor of the probation department. It warns the probation officer whose name appears on the list nine times to take action. It gives the legal advocacy project in the community a reason to meet with the probation supervisor.

A tracking system might also, for example, tell the reader that there are 60 outstanding warrants for batterers and that 35 of them are over 60 days old. Such a report can stimulate efforts to unclog the system. The data might show, for example, that 90 percent of all those cases in which a charge of assault was reduced to a disorderly conduct were handled by the same prosecutor. Perhaps it shows that one judge consistently denies petitions for protection orders, or that 20 men who have been assigned to batterers' groups have not yet made contact with the program. A tracking system allows a community to hold itself accountable to the policies and procedures it has adopted to protect victims.

5. *Ensuring a supportive community infrastructure of support*

> *Legal remedies are not enough. A community needs to provide some basic resources for women, like shelter, long-term housing, a decent income, and a place to talk with other women in the same situation.* (Shelter Advocate interviewed in Duluth, 1996)

In the USA the most effective legal reform programs such as the Duluth project tend to be located in communities with strong infrastructures of services for battered women. Coordinated community responses need to make some basic services available to women trying to negotiate a violence-free life for themselves and their children. These include emergency and long-term housing; legal advocacy; financial assistance, or access to employment, or both; a place to talk with other women, and help in understanding the social and personal forces in their lives; medical care; an opportunity to work in advocacy projects with other women; and community services that support women's roles as parents. In Duluth the Women's Coalition, a shelter and advocacy program for women, provides this kind of infrastructure.

6. Intervening directly with abusers to deter violence

For me the biggest shift was thinking about how to directly intervene with the man doing the violence. Do we try to fix him? When do we want to push for jailing batterers? Jails are not exactly places where men learn to respect women. I don't think we can claim to be standing with women if that means we say we're with you, except we won't ever deal directly with the person beating you up. On the other hand, trying to individually fix every man who beats his wife is futile. This is a tough one because as soon as you start to say, 'OK, let's do something with these men,' all sorts of screwballs show up to get in on it. (Legal Advocate interviewed in Duluth, 1996)

A coordinated community response to domestic violence must decide what the responsibilities of state and community agencies are regarding an abuser. Because we see that the violence reinforces unequal gender arrangements in society and is not simply a manifestation of individual pathology, the responsibility for addressing violence must be assumed by the relevant social and legal institutions and community organisations rather than left to individual women. The Duluth community therefore engages in direct intervention with the abuser, usually through three courses of action: (1) creating a safety plan for the woman, which may include such strategies as obtaining restraining or other court orders on the abuser; (2) imposing sanctions and deterrents, such as arrest, incarceration, and mandated community service, aimed at the individual abuser and at the broader community; and (3) providing abusers with an opportunity for rehabilitation. In our networking with activists from other communities this last component is hotly debated: after all, there is little evidence that batterers' rehabilitation groups are successful. Also, rehabilitation programs are usually run by mental health practitioners. Many women's advocates argue that rehabilitation programs typically de-politicise and de-criminalise the problem by psychologising male violence in ways that make neither individual men nor unequal gender arrangements in society responsible for the violence.

Right now, there is no agreement as to what position the battered women's movement in the US should take regarding rehabilitation programs for batterers. Most include monitoring such programs as part of their advocacy function. Some battered women's advocacy projects were drawn unwillingly into working with batterers; others have been more positive about their involvement. Our failure to offer alternatives to rehabilitation provided by the mental health field has been one of the big mistakes made by US activists. Despite early research which showed that highly structured education groups produce *lower* recidivism rates than groups using more clinical, psychological approaches with abusers, most batterers' groups are located in mental health centres rather than community-based education programs (Edleson & Syers, 1991).

Educational groups for batterers are a small but important part of the community's overall intervention strategy in Duluth. However, they neither define nor drive the community intervention plan. The DAIP's educational approach draws on Paulo Friere's literacy and popular education process because it emphasises the cultural aspects of working with an individual and links the individual to the social relations active in their lives (Pence & Paymar, 1993). Educational groups for batterers focus on participants' beliefs about the use of force in relationships, on the patterns of their controlling behaviour and on the ethics of their behaviour. They do not work on the abuser's relationship with his partner or wife, but confront him with his choice to use violence. Nor do the groups support the common illusion that the purpose of an abuser's participation is to get his partner to stay with him or to come back. Abusers who do not complete their required program will likely go to jail.

Abuser education programs must be designed so that they account for each of the factors described in the earlier working definition of safety for women. In the USA as elsewhere the commitment to fully integrating batterers' groups into an overall community response has been weak or even non existent. Early on in the Duluth experience a decision was made by the participating counselling agencies to hold off on starting groups for offenders until the courts and police had operationalised their policies for holding abusers accountable.

7. *Undoing the harm violence to women does to children*

Somehow the children are always labelled as the innocent victims of battering. I suppose that means their mothers aren't so innocent. The system needs to see that when a man beats a woman in front of her kids, there are two innocent victims. It's so artificial to separate out 'this is a child protection issue and this is a criminal court issue'. No matter what, mothers come with kids and kids come with mothers. (Visitation Centre Worker interviewed in Duluth, 1996)

The success of the DAIP in improving community and court interventions in domestic assault cases has not yet been matched by a similarly coherent approach to the visitation and custody issues which usually accompany the end of a relationship in which there has been violence (McMahon & Pence, 1995). Children who witness violence in their homes are also its victims. When an abused woman leaves a violent partner, therefore, issues raised about children are not simply those of custody, but of responding to the totality of harm that violence has done to the children. Advocates argue that the community, rather than individual women, has the responsibility to respond to this harm.

For women who have been battered, separation from an abuser often shifts the site of the conflict from the privatised setting of the home to the public arena of the judicial system. Custody and access workers report that abusive men are more likely than non-abusive men to fight for physical custody of their children (Taylor, 1993); evidence suggests that they are also more likely to receive favourable rulings from the courts (Saunders, 1992). Children and child custody issues are now a significant part of the politics of gender. Cain and Smart (1989) and Pollock and Sutton (1985) argue that a violent man's relationship with his children entails a power relationship with the children's mother, played out through the issues of custody and visitation.

Community intervention projects can play an important role in protecting children from violence, distress, and harm as their primary relationships are re-ordered. In 1990 the DAIP organised a visitation centre as a vehicle to work on court reforms in family court. The centre is a logical extension of criminal justice reform work and has become an integral part of the community's programming. One cannot think about children or the 'best interests of the child' as if children stand alone and are not integral to the power relations of which violence against women is part. To protect children and undo the harm done to them by domestic violence, the DAIP and shelter advocates argue that the mother's and child's interests must not be pitted against each other. The response of the system must be informed by an understanding of the role violence and power play in shaping the social relationships of families.

8. Evaluating the system from the victim's standpoint

It's important to agree on the standard that we will use to judge our work. If it's more arrests or more prosecutions or a speedier process, we may find a successful project that's failed to improve women's lives. We need to use what's happened to the women who are being beaten as the basis for judging ourselves. (Prosecutor, interviewed in Duluth, 1996)

Finally, a successful community response to domestic violence needs to have ways of evaluating State and community interventions from the standpoint of women seeking protection. This standpoint is quite different from a standpoint of effective case management which expresses bureaucratic or administrative priorities. It is also different from a socially conservative 'law-and-order' perspective that measures success in terms of arrests, conviction rates, and incarcerations. Sadly, most criminologists in the USA continue to be wedded to using quantitative research methods that are inadequate for addressing the problem of domestic abuse. Perhaps this is because their quantitative research allow them to speak with 'authority' to the voices of authority in the USA., rather than to speak from the marginal position of women's experiences. As a consequence much research offers activists little to deepen our understanding of the social relations that support violence against women; nor does it offer remedies that would be useful to women who struggle to stop the violence.

The DAIP approaches evaluation by examining how each part of the community response affects victim safety, autonomy and integrity. Each year, a different aspect of the responses is examined. These investigations then shape continued training, policy development, and case processing alterations. For example, working with the DAIP, the city of Duluth has recently completed an 'audit' of every aspect of case processing. This audit analysed the extent to which the work setting for dispatchers, jailers, pre-trial release agents, prosecutors, warrant servers and so forth were organised to centralise victim safety. The audit examined six aspects of each work setting: 1) the regulations that govern the worker; 2) the forms and procedures that are used; 3) the training provided the worker; 4) the resources and information available to the worker; 5) the technology of the work setting (e.g. proper computer access, use of dictaphones or video equipment); and 6) the communication links to other practitioners involved in the case. This audit provided a comprehensive list of practical changes needed in order to continue the community toward its goal of offering an institutional response that centralises the safety of women who turn to the legal system for help.

Conclusion

Sometimes it is easier to explain the Duluth model by pointing out what it is not. It is *not* a batterers' treatment program; nor is it simply a project which enhances the ability of the courts to convict batterers. The priority is neither social control nor therapy for violent men. The priority is women's safety. The model offers a way of doing legal advocacy that changes those institutionalised ways of doing things that put women at risk of domestic assault or fail to offer them protection from violence when it occurs.

Note

1. There are a few attempts in progress to duplicate the Duluth model in the UK (in Gloucester for example, and elsewhere). The most developed initiative is in Hammersmith & Fulham, named 'Standing Together'.
2. For more information on the Duluth Intervention Project, please write to Ellen Pence, The Duluth Domestic Abuse Intervention Project, 206 West Fourth St., Duluth, Minn. 55806.

References

Cain, M. & Smart, C. (1989). Series Editor's Preface in Smart, C. and Sevenhuijsen, S. (eds.). *Child Custody and the Politics of Gender.* New York: Routledge

Edleson, J. L. & Syers, M. (1991) 'The effects of group treatment for men who batter: An 18-month follow-up study', *Research in Social Work Practice* , 1, pp227-243

McMahon, M. & Pence, E. (1995). 'Doing more harm than good?' in Peled, E., Jaffe, P. G. and Edleson, J.L. (eds.). *Ending the Cycle of Violence.* Thousand Oaks, CA: Sage

National Clearinghouse for the Defense of Battered Women. (1995). *Statistics Packet,* (3rd Ed) Philadelphia: Author

Pence, E. & Paymar, M. (1993). *Education Groups for Men Who batter: The Duluth Model.* New York: Springer

Pollock, S. & Sutton, J. (1985). 'Father's rights, women's losses', *Women's Studies International Forum,* 8, pp593-599

Saunders, D. G. (1992). 'Women battering', in Ammerman, R. T. and Hersen, M. (eds) *Assessment of Family Violence: A clinical and legal sourcebook.* New York: Wiley

Sherman, L. W. (1992). *Policing Domestic Violence: Experiments and dilemmas.* New York: Free Press

Taylor, G. (1993). 'Child custody and access', *Vis-à-Vis: National Newsletter on Family Violence,* 10, 3. Canadian Council on Social Development

12
Is the glass half empty or half full? Action against domestic violence in Australia

Jennifer Gardiner

The title of this chapter conveys my ambivalence about action taken against domestic violence in Australia both Federally and by States/Territories. In reviewing the major initiatives with respect to taking action against domestic violence[1] over the last fifteen years, I *should* be feeling very positive. The process which began with the naming of the problem, the establishment of women's refuges in the mid 1970s and community education, has moved over the last ten years to encompass 'system' change. Laws have been passed enabling police to take a more pro-active role, considerable community debate has occurred about judicial attitudes and the treatment of women by the legal system, there have been State and Federal Task Forces[2] into domestic violence and gender bias in the law; State and Federal governments have endorsed a National Strategy on Violence Against Women which accepts a feminist socio-cultural analysis of 'power and control' as the underlying cause and advocates coordinated intervention citing the Duluth (USA) and Hamilton (NZ) community intervention projects (CIPs)[3].

However, if one talks to victim/survivors[4] of domestic violence it appears little has changed in the way responses are made to domestic violence. Thus, I finish this paper by highlighting the reasons for my negativity which include the conservative discourse about domestic violence now being given legitimacy through Government (Federal and State/Territory) approaches to domestic violence and the increasingly loud voices of men's rights supporters.[5]

I want to begin this paper with an overview of the peculiar nature of Australian constructions of masculinity to provide an understanding of the socio-cultural support for male violence against women in this country.

Australian constructions of masculinity

Violence against women in Australia is still supported by deep-seated cultural values of an aggressive masculinity and legitimisation of male dominance and female subordination in the private realm of the family. In the words of a popular song of the 1980s, in 'the land down under / Women glow and men plunder'.[6]

Miriam Dixon's 1976 publication The *Real Matilda* (Dixon, 1976) was one of the first to emphasise that masculine brutality towards women has been a pervasive theme in Australia since European invasion. Aboriginal women and female convicts were viewed as objects to fulfil the sexual needs of men and to provide physical care for them - convicts, soldiers, guards and free settlers alike.

The harshness of Australian early settlement conditions reinforced a rigid gender order with aggressive masculinity and male companionship ('mateship') an outcome of the physical privations and the lack of women. Aggressive masculine images and mateship still dominate. Heroes of contact sports and rugged pioneers past and present (such as the ANZACs[7] and Crocodile Dundee) are valorised as cultural icons (Evans 1992).

Very separate spheres developed in Australian gender relations with women relegated, in the main, to the private domain of home and children, with most men seeking sociability with their male 'mates' which excludes women.[8] A lack of female images – past and present - supports the low regard in which women have been held, despite the fact that Australian women were the first to get the vote.[9] It is claimed that, as a result of this segregation, Australian women have developed a strong sense of independence and self-sufficiency that is evidenced by the strength and vitality of Australian feminism (Evans 1992).

Notwithstanding the independence of Australian women, Easteal (1994) argues that Australian males generally still cling to traditional and outdated attitudes to women[10] even more than their peers in other western countries. Recent data show that Australia has one of the highest levels of sexual violence against women in the western world (Easteal 1992).

The women's and refuge movements

As in other countries, it was both the refuge and the broader women's movements in Australia which advanced the issue of domestic violence over the last 20 years. In comparing the women's movement in USA and Australia, Anne Summers (1994) argued that the Australian women's movement had been especially successful in advancing women's interests because of a strong involvement with and of the State, particularly through the Labor Party. Successive State and Federal Governments, since the Whitlam Labor Government of 1973-1975, have continued support for the notion of a 'special' women's department and units within mainstream departments to advance the interests of women.[11] The Federal Office of the Status of Women (OSW) has enjoyed a particularly influential location within the Department of Prime Minister and Cabinet.[12]

Much has been achieved since the first women's Refuge was established in 1975. Refuges have become institutionalised and provide the primary service for victims fleeing domestic violence. It has been the collaboration between the refuge movement and 'femocrats' that has enabled the refuge movement to make the political gains it has (Hopkins and McGregor 1991; McFerren 1990).

In the late 1970s, the Australian refuge movement took the position that volunteers would not be used because it was the responsibility of the patriarchal State to provide adequate funding for services for victims of male violence. This strategy was successful, given the 'progressive' political climate at the time, and Australia is the only country where refuges are fully funded by government under a shared Federal and State program for supported emergency accommodation[13] (McFerren 1990).

The national refuge organisation collapsed in the late 1980s due to internal political differences, despite (or perhaps because of) the success in obtaining government funding. This has meant there has been no combined powerful voice for the movement at national level. Refuge activism has generally become limited to negotiating funding and service delivery issues with government at State levels through the Supported Accommodation Assistance Program funding program. In 1996 a national women's organisation Women's Emergency Services Network (WESNET) was established for the women's supported accommodation sector which includes refuges as well as accommodation services for women who are homeless for reasons other than domestic violence, such as poverty, mental illness, etc.

Government funding and the policy of 'no volunteers' has also meant refuge work has become restricted to those in paid employment, many of whom do not identify as feminist and most of whom are not 'politically' active. There has been no means for survivors to translate their anger or energy into constructive action except through a limited number of paid positions as refuge workers. The only means for activist women to be involved in the issue of domestic violence has been through broader women's lobby or policy organisations such as the Women's Electoral Lobby. Those who argue for incorporating activists, survivors and volunteers in some capacity within domestic violence organisations point out that such involvement is a consciousness-raising and politicising experience and a numerically larger, diverse and more dynamic movement would result.

Advances by Federal and State Labor governments 1983-1993

The six States and two Territories of Australia have independent responsibility for considerable legislation and delivery of direct services (such as police, corrective services (probation), criminal and civil law, social welfare, health and education). However, policies adopted by the Federal government influence States, and initiatives by one State influence other States.[14] Thus, over time, a certain degree of uniformity develops.

In the mid-1980s, Federal and State governments agreed to a jointly funded Supported Accommodation Assistance Program (SAAP) which included refuges. Sexual abuse (rape/incest) support services were also incorporated into a Federal government health program (OSW, 1997).

In the 1980s virtually all State governments conducted Task Forces and Inquiries into the problem of domestic violence and what should be done about it (such as the Queensland Domestic Violence Task Force in 1988 and the Western Australian

Domestic Violence Task Force in 1986. Some States introduced specific Family Violence legislation, e.g. Victoria's Crimes (Family Violence) Act 1987, although the major emphasis of legislation dealt with protection or restraining orders, rather than changes to criminal codes.

For example, the Victorian legislation provides for police as well as victims of DV to seek an intervention order to provide immediate and on-going protection from violence within the home. A breach of the order constitutes a criminal offence and grounds for arrest of the offender. An adult is also able to seek an intervention order for the protection of a child. The proclamation of the Act was accompanied by the introduction of new police procedures. Officers are 'encouraged' to charge where it is evident that an offence has been committed (Seddon 1992). However, a review of the effects of the Victorian legislation (Wearing 1992) revealed that, overall, police are not utilising the powers that were granted to them under the Act.

The New South Wales Act of 1983 was amended in 1987 to become the Crimes (Personal and Family Violence) Amendment Act 1987. It introduced legal and procedural reforms that clarified and extended police powers to enter a dwelling where a DV offence is suspected to have occurred, including provision for police to obtain warrants by telephone to enter premises where entry was denied. Police Instructions were changed exhorting police to lay charges rather than requiring the woman to be the complainant and to take a tougher approach to decisions concerning bail. The compellability of spouses as witnesses in prosecutions for domestic violence offences was included. Finally, the Act created a procedure whereby a person who reasonably feared violence from their lawful or de facto spouse, even in cases where cohabitation has not ceased, could obtain an Apprehended Domestic Violence Order (where the onus of proof is on the civil standard of the balance of probabilities) with a maximum duration of 6 months. (Seddon 1992).

All States now have a system of protection or restraining orders and States recently agreed to the portability of protection orders across jurisdictions so that, where victims flee interstate to escape violence, protection orders obtained in one State will be valid in another. Some States have amended legislation to enable police to take a more pro-active role in arrest and/or in obtaining restraining orders. In addition, by the mid-1990s all States adopted stalking legislation, although not necessarily the most effective legislation. For example, Western Australia's stalking legislation (1995) required *intent*[15] by the stalker to cause fear or harm be proven rather than framing the legislation in terms of the *effect* of the stalking behaviour in causing fear or harm to the victim, which is the basis of sexual harassment legislation. This framing of the law led to the now famous comment by a Western Australian magistrate that a man who had stalked a woman for *seven* years was 'just like a puppy dog' and was not guilty of stalking because he did not intend to cause her fear or harm!

In response to various statements by judges and magistrates, considerable community debate has also occurred about judicial attitudes and the treatment of women by the legal system. In the mid-1990s Federal and some State governments held Task Forces into gender bias in the law (Chief Justice's Taskforce 1994).

More recently, the Federal and State governments have jointly developed model criminal codes on Sexual Assault and Domestic Violence (OSW 1997). The Federal Government reformed the Family Law Act in 1995 and now ' ... family violence and the need to ensure that family law matters do not jeopardise the safety of individuals are dealt with under the Act for the first time' (Attorney General's Dept, 1996). The Family Court must consider any violence order or incidence of violence and inconsistencies with existing orders must be avoided. The Family Court can order supervised contact as a safeguard and State magistrates' courts now have power to change an existing Family Court order for contact if it is determined to be in the child's best interests.

In the early 1990s, the Labor Federal government, through the Office of the Status of Women (OSW) convened a National Committee on Violence Against Women (NCVAW) with representatives from each State and Territory. The committee developed a position paper (NCVAW 1992) endorsing a feminist analysis of gender/power and identifying socio-cultural support as the underlying cause of male violence against women, and launched a National Strategy on Violence Against Women, in October, 1992. The aim of the National Strategy was to provide directions to State governments.

The Committee also developed a position paper on mediation that argued generally against mediation when there has been domestic violence (Astor 1991). An evaluation of the effectiveness of protection (restraining) orders in Australian jurisdictions (Egger and Stubbs 1993) and national guidelines for the training of service providers working in the area of violence against women (NCVAW 1993) were also commissioned by the Committee.

A number of media education campaigns have been run over the last 10 years by both Federal and State Governments, such as the Federally-funded 1993 'Real Men Don't Rape or Bash Women', Victoria's 1993 'Violence is Ugly' and Western Australia's 1994 'Abuse in Families'.

Community attitudes

In 1995 OSW commissioned a national study into Australian attitudes to violence against women, following-up similar research undertaken in 1987 under OSW's National Domestic Violence Education Program 1987-1990. The latest research was conducted to evaluate the effectiveness of the community education campaigns. It found that there is a much greater awareness and understanding of domestic violence. The report Stated: '... this level of understanding indicates the success of awareness raising and community education campaigns to date.' Domestic violence is now generally recognised as a problem and is now seen to include a range of abusive behaviours, with physical violence considered a crime. The major positive difference between the 1987 and 1995 studies is that the number of people who see provocation as an excuse has almost halved - 14% in 1987 to 8% in 1995.

While the changes in general attitudes are heartening, it is disturbing to note that those who perceive there are circumstances in which physical force by a man against a woman is acceptable has increased from 8% in 1987 to 18% in 1995 (OSW 1995). Furthermore, the study found that from the perspective of victim-survivors the situation is not much changed. The report Stated:

The community continues to be judgemental of victims with more than three-quarters (77%) not understanding why victims do not leave violent situations. The great majority (83%) also admits to not wanting to get involved. ... the greater community awareness and understanding of domestic violence has not yet been translated into improved personal responses.

The research also found that some groups are much better informed than others with the best informed being women who work, have post secondary education, and are less than 55 years of age. Women overall are better informed than men - blue-collar women are better informed than are white-collar men. Those born in non-English speaking countries are a generally less well-informed population group (Office of the Status of Women 1995).

In connection to the latter point, other reports (Easteal 1994; Bolger 1991; Elliott and Shanahan Research 1988) indicate that Aboriginal women and some overseas-born have much higher rates of incidence of domestic violence. Some of these women are particularly isolated and, thus, less likely to report and responses (including refuge) fail to meet their cultural needs.

Incidence of domestic violence in Australia

Until recently there has been no reliable data on the incidence of domestic violence in Australia. Domestic violence has rarely been an identified category in relevant data collection systems. A major difficulty in collecting valid data is obtaining agreement between various agencies and States on a common definition. Police around Australia are just beginning to discriminate between the types of incidences that are included under the category 'domestic' (i.e. any incident that occurs at a private residence). A number of State Police forces are now utilising a Family Violence Incident Form when the incident concerns abuse, threats to harm or violence.

Even if data collection becomes comprehensive and systematic we will still never obtain reliable data concerning the number of women and their families who experience abuse and violence through reports to service agencies because many victims or perpetrators do not seek outside assistance. The most reliable measure of the incidence of violence against women is a national survey. In 1995, OSW announced that it would commission the Australian Bureau of Statistics (ABS) to undertake the first national survey on the nature and extent of violence against women, similar to that undertaken in Canada (Statistics Canada 1993).

This survey (ABS 1996) asked about women's fear and experiences of violence in both public and in the home. It included questions about physical and sexual violence by strangers, previous and current partners and by other known men and women such as relatives, friends, acquaintances and professionals. The major findings were disturbing to say the least:

- In the 12 months prior to the survey 7.1% of women aged 18 and over experienced an incidence of violence.
- 38% of women had experienced at least once incident of violence since the age of 15.
- Younger women were more at risk than older women. 19% of women aged 18-24 had experienced an incidence of violence in the previous 12 months, as compared to 6.8% of women aged 25-44 and 1.2% of women aged over 55.
- 46% of women who said they had experienced violence by a previous partner said they had children who witnessed the violence. 38% of women experiencing violence from a *current* partner reported children being present.
- only 19% of women who were physically assaulted and 15% of women who were sexually assaulted in the last 12 months reported the incident to the police. Even fewer women used crisis and other services. The main action taken by victims was to talk to family and friends.

The results of this survey demonstrate that all the initiatives taken to date are like a drop in the ocean. These results are part of the reason that I see the glass as half empty rather than half full.

Non-government initiatives to prevent domestic violence

Until recently few services beyond refuge had been developed for either victims or perpetrators.[16] The notable exceptions were the Canberra Domestic Violence Crisis Support Service, the Domestic Violence Court Support Scheme in the inner Sydney area of Redfern, and the Domestic Violence Resource Centre in Brisbane. Recently, however, a range of initiatives has been developed in various States and Territories.

Court support schemes
Despite criticisms[17] that restraining orders or orders for protection are 'not worth the paper they are written on', Domestic Violence Court Support schemes are currently being developed in selected locations in all States in recognition that restraining orders provide an important means of assisting the safety of many victims. The experience of the Redfern Court Support Service has been that they are effective in preventing further violence if

the victim is provided legal advice, advocacy and support and agreement is obtained from the abuser to the conditions (Blazejowska 1994).

One model has been to hold 'special' protection order courts at certain times of the day and/or on certain days of the week utilising a lawyer from the local community law centre to provide legal advice, to draw up the relevant conditions and negotiate with the abuser. Redfern also utilises workers from various social service agencies to provide victims with support and advocacy with social services (Blazejowska 1994).

There is some debate about whether it is necessary to have lawyers undertake this work or whether trained para-legal workers (who are cheaper) can be effective. In support of lawyers, it is argued that magistrates will only allow lawyers to represent victims. However, the experience with para-legal workers in both Hamilton, New Zealand, and in Western Australia is that, as magistrates come to know and respect the value of victim advocates they allow them to 'represent' applicants for *ex-parte* restraining orders. At the same time, experience also in Western Australia indicates that where a magistrate is 'unsympathetic' to victims, they are better served by being represented by lawyers until the magistrate has been 'educated' and is supportive of victims and para-legal workers. A lawyer is then only required if there is a defended hearing.

Certainly, when a charge comes before criminal court, para-legal advocates are able to provide victims with support and information should they be required to give evidence as a witness.

Domestic violence outreach services

In 1995, the Federal SAAP program made a limited amount of funding available that had to be matched by each State, for the development of domestic violence outreach services. These outreach services were to provide support, advocacy and assistance to women in the community and help with the decision as to whether to seek refuge.

At the time Western Australia did not take up the offer, although Victoria chose to and established a number of outreach services in Melbourne and some rural towns. In Western Australia, with the adoption of the family and domestic violence action plan incorporating a 'whole of government' response and regional committees, the Department of Family and Children's Services has provided funding for eight Domestic Violence Victim Advocacy Services in both Perth and some rural towns.

Education and counselling for victim-survivors

Until recently, the larger mainstream non-government 'counselling' services such as Relationships Australia[18] and church-based agencies such as Centrecare[19] and Anglicare[20] provided individual and group counselling for women. Many refuges had also offered groups although, on the whole, the groups offered by refuges were not as well supported as those run by the counselling agencies; refuges did not usually receive funding to run groups.

More recently, with a greater awareness of domestic violence and an increase in available funding, a more varied range of services are offering individual and group counselling for victim/survivors, such as women's health centres, refuges, sexual assault centres.[21]

Programs for children who experience domestic violence

The effect on children of experiencing domestic violence has recently become an important issue for the government and the field. Funding is now becoming more available for services for children both within refuges and in the community. SAAP have also recently established guidelines for children who are in refuges (SAAP 1997)

Coordinated inter-agency responses

In most States in Australia there are now local Domestic Violence Action Groups or Committees comprised of interested government and non-government service providers from a range of agencies in a community. These groups have adopted mandates that are variations on a theme. Almost all undertake inter-agency networking and education of service providers. Most engage in some community education.

There is interest in all States and Territories in establishing coordinated inter-agency community interventions, sparked by awareness of such projects in USA, particularly Duluth, and the New Zealand project in Hamilton (Robertson and Busch 1993), modeled on the Duluth project. Some local groups are attempting to initiate a full-fledged 'Duluth' model Community Intervention Project (CIP)—Duluth has become a 'benchmark' internationally for an effective response to domestic violence. It features a coordinated inter-agency criminal justice focused response to domestic violence with a range of victim support services (e.g. crisis, court support and advocacy) and a rehabilitation program for offenders based on challenging men's power and control of women. The key to inter-agency coordination is the development of inter- and intra-agency policies and protocols and the monitoring of practices to ensure compliance (Pence 1985).

The first Australian attempt to establish a Duluth-style coordinated inter-agency CIP was in Western Australia in 1993, in the outer-Perth district of Armadale (Gardiner 1996). Just as in Duluth and Hamilton, New Zealand, it was a small group of 'activists' who initiated the project, including domestic violence counsellors, refuge workers and others who were convinced that the Duluth project provided the best model of intervening in male violence against female partners. The challenge for us, and for all 'community' initiated projects, was to convince succeeding layers of government service providers and policy makers to make changes to legislation, policy, protocols and practices with respect to domestic violence. In the early stages of establishing the Armadale project, support was not forthcoming from the Western Australian State Government and senior departmental managers. What soon became obvious was that the particular minister with responsibility for domestic violence held an extremely conservative notion of the family and gender roles. He let it be known that he did not support a criminal justice response to domestic violence and that he considered intervention to be interference in the family (Nicholls 1993).

However, after little over a year the minister was removed after generally upsetting the 'welfare' sector and sending it into chaos. The new minister, a woman who had been the Attorney General, established a Task Force into Family and Domestic Violence, which released an Action Plan in November 1995 (Family and Domestic Violence Task Force 1995). This Action Plan supported a 'whole of government' approach to addressing domestic violence and the establishment of Regional Domestic Violence Committees. As a result of this Action Plan, funding has recently been forthcoming for a number of victim counselling and court support and advocacy services and for perpetrator group programs, principally in rural areas that previously had few, if any, services.

Programs for abusive men

Within a coordinated, inter-agency response that is attempting to change the way domestic violence is responded to by the criminal justice system, rehabilitation group programs for domestic violence perpetrators are considered necessary to obtain system change. Police, judiciary, corrective services as well as the community and often the victim-survivors, share the desire for 'something' to deter and rehabilitate abusers and/or to 'preserve families'. As is often said, 'something most be done about the men, they are the problem'.

However, the establishment of 'perpetrator group programs' has not had an easy road in Australia. Many in the refuge and women's movements have been very wary of programs for abusers for three main reasons. First, resources and energy may be taken from needed victim services. Second, rather than becoming non-violent, abusers may learn new methods of abuse through exploring the range of abusive behaviours. Third, women may stay in unsafe relationships because the man is attending a program which the woman hopes will change him.

In NSW the refuge and women's movements were successful in convincing the government that no funding should be made available for abuser programs (Stewart 1991). A few abuser programs for 'voluntary' men have been established by non-government counselling agencies without government funding or support.

However, a very different situation exists in Victoria where a network of some 25 abuser programs around the State has been established, targeting 'voluntary', rather than court mandated, abusers. This network draws its members principally from the counselling professions and the 'men's (health) movement'. They argue that men are choosing voluntarily to do something about their violence as a result of government community education campaigns in the media. The network has a policy of no more than 20% mandated abusers in any one group. The network has successfully lobbied the Victorian Department of Health and Community Services to provide 20% of its family violence budget to abuser programs (V-Net 1995).

In Australia generally, abuser programs have not been employed as a stimulus for change in the criminal justice system responses and compliance from the police, contrary to developments in Great Britain and USA. In Victoria and New South Wales much effort has been put into changing police practices through legislation and policy although research has revealed that this is not particularly effective (Wearing 1992). South Australia has developed a 'diversionary' abuser program model where abusers undertake a program before being sentenced (Kunst 1997), rather than as an option for sentencing or probation once there has been a finding of guilt. However, in Western Australia, as in Great Britain, corrective services have generally welcomed abuser programs as a means of providing a rehabilitation option for convicted abusers.

Aboriginal 'family' violence

Recent research indicates the incidence of violence against women is higher for some segments of society where class, gender and race/ethnicity intersect (Ferrante, Morgan et al. 1995). A study of murders by adult sexual intimates (Easteal 1993) found that overseas born and Aboriginal women were disproportionately represented. Reports to authorities indicate that Aboriginal women are at 45 times the risk of being assaulted than are non-Aboriginal women (Ferrante, Morgan et al. 1995).

At the same time, interventions to prevent domestic violence for Aboriginal and minority women are problematic, confounded by both the cultural meanings of the Aboriginal communities and the racism and discrimination prevalent in the discursive practices of the State. Paradoxically, the analysis and solutions to the problem of male violence against women offered by non-Aboriginal feminists and others in the broader community are often contrary to the analysis and solutions offered by the Aboriginal community and Aboriginal women.

Aboriginal people have made strong claims that even the term domestic violence is not appropriate to their experience, preferring the term 'family violence' which many feminists find problematic. Aboriginal argument is that under the practice of 'pay-back' the violence extends from husband to wife to the extended families of the victim and perpetrator who become involved in what is known as 'family fighting'.

There are three major concerns for Aboriginal communities about intervention to prevent violence against women and children.

The first concern is to preserve the family. There is fear that the family unit will be destroyed. This fear stems from the fact that, traditionally, the family is the principal unit of support, socialisation, social control, etc. Furthermore, the survival of Aboriginal people in the face of virtual genocide has been credited to the strength of the family. For almost 100 years, the destruction of Aboriginal families by taking 'part-Aboriginal' children and raising them in institutions and foster-families administered by

Anglo-Australians was official policy and practice in the name of assimilation. Thus, Aboriginal people are anxious that nothing further be done that might threaten to destroy their families.

The second concern of many Aboriginal people is that the cause of violence is understood to result from conquest/ colonisation and/or alcohol. Many want something done about the 'grog', believing that then the violence will stop.

Finally, Aboriginal women and men have been vocal in rejecting an enhanced criminal justice response to domestic violence. This is understandable in light of the discrimination experienced by Aboriginal people, principally men, caught up in the criminal justice system and the high rate of 'black deaths in custody'. Unfortunately, often what is ignored is that many more Aboriginal women are dying at the hands of Aboriginal men than Aboriginal men are dying in custody!

Nonetheless, Aboriginal women are beginning to speak out against the violence they experience. They are condemning many men's excuses that violence against women is 'traditional' as 'rubbish tradition' (Bolger 1991) .

At this point, Aboriginal people are relatively united in knowing what they do not want. There is also the beginning of a vision of what can be done to prevent violence, articulated as 'whole healing' similar to that being promoted in Native American and Native Canadian communities. Many Aboriginal people are arguing that the whole community has to be 'healed' from the trauma that has been experienced as a result of invasion, genocide and cultural annihilation (Atkinson 1996).

In the meantime, to the extent that the police and judiciary are taking a more pro-active approach to domestic violence, Aboriginal men will become caught up in the criminal justice system in increasing numbers, particularly in urban areas. Where Aboriginal people live in communities with functioning forms of social control that respect and include women, as was traditional practice, it is possible that customary law can be revived to prevent violence against women and children. However, many Aboriginal women do not have recourse to customary law. Culturally appropriate support and advocacy services for victims and perpetrator programs are urgently needed along with changes in the ways the criminal justice system responds to Aboriginal people. One of the recommendations to have come out of the Deaths in Custody Royal Commission currently being considered in Western Australia is much greater use of suspended sentences (Aboriginal Affairs Department 1995).

Why it feels we are going backwards

Perhaps I am negative by nature but despite all the initiatives I have documented (and many more) little seems to have changed for women and children who are subjected to domestic violence.

The resistance of helping professionals (e.g. social workers, psychologists, doctors, clergy, police, judiciary, corrections officers) to intervening and assisting in ensuring the safety and protection of women and their families derives from the dominant discourse of women's subordination that includes blaming the victim. Research into responses to domestic violence by General Practice doctors has led Easteal (1990) to conclude that:

> ... *the great majority of doctors are not adequately trained to recognise the signs of violence against women, or to perceive their role as interventionist, or to understand the dynamics of family violence such as its consequences for victims' self-esteem and their inability to act.*

If victim-survivors are to experience a difference in response when they seek assistance the prevailing 'psychology of denial' must be changed to a 'psychology of care and concern'. The National Strategy has recognised that training of helping professionals to identify and intervene supportively is essential. However, training has not been delivered in any consistent manner. Nowhere in Australia, is there a project like the Leeds Inter-Agency Project in England, which has trained over 500 front-line workers. To the extent that training has been provided it has been sporadic and short e.g. one day. To bring about effective change in knowledge, attitudes and practice, training needs to be cumulative over time, consistent within a professional group or agency, and supported by effective policy and protocols with monitoring of actions of individual service providers for compliance.

Research in Australia has demonstrated that, like other countries, the criminal justice system, is generally less than helpful, even following changes to the law designed to make it clearer for police to know how to act appropriately to provide victims with needed safety and protection. Furthermore, some magistrates and judges are not enforcing laws concerning criminal assault in cases of violence against wives (Wearing 1992). According to (Easteal 1994):

The body of evidence indicates that although the laws may be in place and lip service is paid, a general attitude of minimizing or trivializing domestic violence exists that translates into limited legal intervention..

Although in all States laws exist that declare sexual assault in marriage a crime and although it is well known, certainly by those providing victim support, that sexual assault is a common pattern in much domestic violence, very few reports of sexual assault by a partner are made to police. The incidence of partner sexual assault of adult women is thought by domestic violence and sexual assault workers to far exceed that of stranger sexual assault. Yet only 1% of sexual assault reports to West Australian police named the spouse as the offender (Broadhurst, Ferrante et al. 1992).

Despite the supposed changes in community attitudes, the Women's Safety Australia Survey discovered that 40% of women had experienced at least one incidence of violence since the age of 15 while 19% of women aged 18-24 had experienced an incidence of violence in the previous 12 months (compared to 6.8% of women aged 25-44). These figures heighten my concern for all young women and men both as victims and perpetrators. Until now we have had no idea if violence in our society (particularly against women) is increasing or diminishing although we did know reporting rates have increased. Now we will be able to regularly replicate the Women's Safety Survey to determine if the level of violence experienced by women is decreasing with all our efforts.

In developing legislation, policies and practices to address domestic violence, most State governments want to at least appear to address Aboriginal concerns. However, the fear held by some in the pro-feminist movement against domestic violence is that a 'pro-victim' or feminist perspective, particularly in relation to the individual rights of women to leave violent 'families', will be jeopardised by governments' implementing policy and services for all the population based on conveniently appropriated Aboriginal concerns. This has already started in Western Australia. The challenge is to dialogue across the two very different understandings of violence against women held by those with a gender/power analysis and Aboriginal people.

Initiatives by conservative Federal and State governments 1993-1998

From 1983 to 1996 Australia had a Federal Labor government. During this time the majority of the States also had Labor governments. However, around 1993 this began to change with the election of Liberal governments in most States and in 1996 a Liberal Government was elected Federally.[22] Many of us active in the movement against violence against women were concerned that the Liberal Governments would dismantle all the gains made under Labor, and in some respects this has occurred in general areas relating to women as well as other areas of social policy. But paradoxically, this has not occurred in the area of domestic violence. In fact, it has transpired that considerably more funding and policy development has resulted than under the last terms of Labor Governments generally.

Western Australia conservative government - 1993 onwards

In Western Australia, the domestic violence field experienced demoralising two years under the first minister appointed by the Liberal Government elected in February 1993. However, with a change in ministers to the woman who had initially served as Attorney General, the issue of domestic violence was taken up seriously, with a Task Force into Family and Domestic Violence being convened in early 1995, as previously noted. Some of us who have been active in the field for a number of years would like to think that the change of direction was because, through our lobbying and activities, we had convinced the government that something serious needed to be done about domestic violence.

The outcome of the Task Force was the Government's Action Plan on Family and Domestic Violence (Family and Domestic Violence Task Force 1995). The Action Plan adopted a considerable part of what we had been lobbying for under calls for 'a coordinated inter-agency community approach'. It mandated the establishment of Regional Domestic Violence Committees in all 16 Police Regions in the State with representatives from the government departments of Family & Children's Services, Health, Education, Police and Justice (including both Court and Corrections officers). The Regional Committees were to also include relevant non-government services such as refuges, women's health services, counselling agencies, etc.

The government established the principle of 'responsiveness to grass roots needs' through the development of regional plans and took up issues of collaboration and coordination, improved responses to assist victim safety, provision of appropriate services for victims and perpetrators and a community education program. It also endorsed education and training for workers in fields related to family and domestic violence.

However, the Action Plan did not explicate a clear gender/ power analysis and a criminal justice focus as the framework, nor did it endorse a particular model or structure (such as Duluth)[23] to guide the coordination of responses and services. In fact, the government and the unit it established to implement the plan have consistently said that they 'do not want to be prescriptive' but want to allow regions to develop their own structures and responses according to their needs. Thus the committees were dominated by public servants with few, if any, members who had a critical awareness of the complexities that confront and confound interventions in domestic violence. A few of the refuges were committed to the process but most found their representative had little influence in the committees dominated by representatives from government departments with little understanding of the issues.

The problem is that without critical awareness of the complexities that confront and confound interventions in domestic violence this laissez faire strategy, in fact, allows for the development of 'worst' practices rather than encouraging 'best practice'. An example of this arose in the last year. In response to an announcement of available funding, a regional Crime Prevention Committee (chaired by the local community policing senior officer) thought it would be a good idea to have a 'refuge' for men. It was envisaged as somewhere police could take men to 'cool off' following their violence to their female partner and a safe place for men who were victims of domestic violence committed by their wives. The committee was successful in obtaining the funds and established the service to accommodate both male perpetrators and male victims of domestic violence. There is no prize for guessing the outcome of this initiative in response to need as 'perceived' by the local Crime Prevention Committee. It closed down because of lack of use. Not having a critical knowledge of the complexities of intervening in domestic violence these well-meaning but naive people obviously did not consider whether abusive men would actually leave the family home voluntarily on the suggestion of the police and stay at the 'refuge'. Nor were they sufficiently aware to query whether there are sufficient male victims who are abused by their female partner who would identify themselves and seek 'refuge'.

Those of us involved in preventing domestic violence are caught in a dilemma. If victims and perpetrators are to be responded to appropriately and effective services provided we must involve a broad range of service providers, from both government and non-government sectors. However, because most of these services providers participate in the dominant discourse which supports women's subordination and victim blaming, the challenge is to develop critical knowledge of the complexities that confront and confound attempts to intervene in domestic violence amongst a considerable number and variety of service providers.

From my perspective, the most effective method of changing current responses to domestic violence is for every community to establish a coordinated inter-agency criminal justice-focused intervention project with leadership from those who have a critical pro-victim understanding of the complexities of domestic violence. Such a project involves education and close monitoring of service providers.

Federal conservative government 1996 onwards

Social programs have been drastically cut since the Liberal Government took office in March 1996 and the government is fast retreating on women's and other social justice issues. The Federal 'Office of the Status of Women' (which is located within the Department of Prime Minister and Cabinet) has experienced the same drastic cuts as have almost all areas of Federal government. The magnitude of the funding cuts will have serious ramifications for women generally and particularly for those escaping domestic violence.

Funding to the States for Legal Aid is being cut drastically with the Federal Attorney General stating that legal assistance will only be funded by the Federal Government for Federal issues, such as family law matters. Civil and criminal laws relevant to domestic violence are State matters and funding will now have to be provided by the States. However, the States do not have the tax base to raise money like the Federal Government.

Paradoxically, the government has just announced that

$25million will be spent on domestic violence over the next four years 1998-2001 under the title 'Partnerships Against Domestic Violence'. This money is divided between national and State/Territory initiatives - $12 million and new Federal portfolio initiatives to be developed in consultation with the States/Territories - $13.3 million (Office of the Status of Women 1997).

In September 1997 the government held a National Domestic Violence Forum with approximately 150 invited 'experts' from government and non-government sectors including police, service providers, researchers, judiciary, medical practitioners and representatives of national peak welfare bodies. The recommendations made by this forum became the foundation for the 'Partnerships' initiative and the principles espoused at the Domestic Violence Summit of Federal and State Heads of Government. The agreed Principles announced at the Summit (Office of the Status of Women 1997) were:

We believe that:
- *all individuals have the right to be free from violence;* and
- *all forms of domestic violence are unacceptable*

We are committed to:
- *the safety of those subjected to domestic violence as a first priority;*
- *Making those who commit domestic violence accountable for their actions;* and
- *Encouraging offenders to take responsibility for changing their behaviour.*

These are fine principles and ones most of us active in the field endorse. The challenge is in how they will be actioned: whether discursive practices will change to reflect these fine principles.

Men's rights supporters

A further impediment to appropriately preventing male violence against their female partners particularly evident in the last few years are the 'men's rights supporters'.[24] This 'group' has various forms, most of which include strong elements of 'backlash'. It is generally characterised by attempts to highlight:

- the supposed current bias in favour of women by various State instrumentalities such as the Police, Family Court, Social Security, etc;
- that women are just as violent, if not more violent than men. In support of their case they draw on research using the Conflict Tactics Scale (Straus and Gelles 1990) the limitations of which have been clearly demonstrated. They also include cases of neglect of children, which usually relates to poverty. Further, no acknowledgement is made for the fact that women spend considerably more time caring for children than do men. Women, not men, are also held responsible for 'providing care and protection' for children even in situations where a male partner is abusing a child (and often also abusing the mother).
- that men's violence is the result of men's individual psychology (which is the fault of others, such as, of a distant father, an over-involved mother, fear of failure, childhood experiences of witnessing or experiencing violence and abuse, etc), rather than socio-cultural factors.

Conveniently ignored in this discourse are the links between culture, social institutions and discursive practices. Also ignored are the official reporting statistics that show that in the vast majority of cases it is men who are violent to women and children. Similarly, the different contexts of women's and men's behaviours[25] are totally ignored, making comparison as relevant as comparing apples with oranges.

Even the Federal Minister for the Status of Women was recently moved to say (Moylan 1997)

> ... *let me say loud and clear to those who doubt the data:* men must stop bashing women and their children. *The statistics clearly indicate women are the main victims of domestic violence. There is absolutely no point in men arguing – as I see from time to time in media reports – they are the victims, or the even more ludicrous assertion, that women are the majority initiators of domestic violence.*

Conclusion

Despite legislative and policy changes, the National Strategy, media campaigns and changes in attitudes, little change has resulted for victim-survivors of domestic violence once they seek assistance.

As Patricia Easteal (Easteal 1994) has argued:

> *Although there have been many positive structures and policies implemented during the last 20 or so years, it is important not to be overly optimistic and hence not to be complacent. There continue to be many who are still denied the right to a secure and supportive home. It is therefore important to continue working to stop violence against women and initiating changes on their behalf until safe families are the reality for all women and children.*

While those of us working against violence against women[26] have been calling for increased action the dilemma is now that very few people have a sufficiently comprehensive understanding of this complex field to develop policies and deliver services. It is naïve in the extreme to expect politicians, policy makers and service providers, who have limited understanding of the complexity of domestic violence and who share general community discourses regarding family, masculinity, violence and women, to develop and implement appropriate initiatives.

Now is not the time for those of us who have worked against violence against women to remove ourselves from the struggle - either congratulating ourselves for the initiatives taken or because of the frustration at what still needs to be done. We must continue to be engaged in the dialogue and debate as affirmative post-modernists (Rosenau, 1992), convincing others to join us. Discursive practices and organisational culture within government departments have to be changed. We must be there to work through the dilemma raised by increased action to domestic violence being undertaken by those who do not have comprehensive knowledge of the issues. We must be politically astute, particularly in lobbying government for appropriate legislation and policies, which challenge dominant discourses. We must continue to undertake community education, write letters to the editors of newspapers and get on talk-back radio and television. We must sit on government committees and relevant boards wherever we can, we must establish lobby organisations, develop and demonstrate appropriate pro-victim/ survivor services, undertake research and most importantly educate those who have a responsibility to 'do something' about domestic violence. Needless to say this is risky work in terms of our reputations – we will continue to be challenged and labeled. If we look back over the last fifteen years, without a doubt a tremendous amount was achieved, but now is certainly not a time to be complacent.

References

Aboriginal Affairs Department (1995) *Royal Commission into Aboriginal Deaths in Custody*. Perth: Government of Western Australia

ABS (1996) W*omen's Safety Australia*. Canberra: Australian Bureau of Statistics, Office of the Status of Women, Department of Prime Minister and Cabinet

Astor, H. (1991) *Mediation and Violence against Women*. Canberra: National Committee on Violence Against Women, Office of the Status of Women, Department of the Prime Minister and Cabinet

Atkinson, J. (1996) A *Pebble in the Pond and a Hole in the Blanket. Moving On: Traditional wisdom in contemporary practice*. Brisbane: unpublished

Attorney General's Department. (1996) *Family Law Reform Act 1995: Overview*. Canberra: Family and Administrative Law Branch, Commonwealth Attorney-General's Department

Blazejowska, L. (1994) *Court Support Schemes - Improving Women's Access to the Legal System. Challenging the Legal System's Response to Domestic Violence*. Brisbane

Bolger, A. (1991) *Aboriginal Women and Violence*. Darwin: Australian National University North Australia Research Unit

Broadhurst, R.G., Ferrante, A.M. et al. (1992) *Crime and Justice Statistics for Western Australia: 1992*. Perth: Crime Research Centre, University of Western Australia

Chief Justice's Taskforce (1994) *Report on Gender Bias and the Law*. The Hon Mr. Justice D.K. Malcolm AC: Chief Justice of Western Australia

Dixon, M. (1976) Th*e Real Matilda*. Melbourne: Penguin Books

Domestic Violence Task Force (1986) *Break the Silence*. Perth: Women's Interests Division, Department of the Premier and Cabinet, WA

Easteal, P. (1990) *Doctors and Spouse Assault Victims: Prevention or perpetuation of the cycle of violence*. Canberra: Criminology Research Council, Institute of Criminology

Easteal, P. (1992) *Rape. Violence Prevention Today*. Canberra: D. Chappell/ Australian Institute of Criminology

Easteal, P. (1993) *Killing the Beloved: Homicide between adult sexual intimates*. Canberra: Australian Institute of Criminology

Easteal, P. (1994) 'Homicide between adult sexual intimates in Australia: Implications for prevention', *Studies on Crime and Crime Prevention: Annual Review* , 3

Easteal, P. (1994) 'Violence against women in the home: How far have we come? How far to go?', *Family Matters* , 37, pp86-93

Egger, S. and J. Stubbs (1993) *Effectiveness of Protection Orders in Australian Jurisdictions*. Canberra: National Committee on Violence Against Women

Elliott and Shanahan Research (1988) *Summary of Background Research for the Development of a Campaign Against Domestic Violence*

Evans, R. (1992) 'A gun in the oven: Masculism and gendered violence' in Saunders, K. and Evans, R. (eds) *Gender relations in Australia: Domination and negotiation*. Sydney: Harcourt Brace

Family and Domestic Violence Task Force (1995) *It's Not Just a Domestic: An action plan on family and domestic violence*. Perth: Western Australian Government

Ferrante, A., F. Morgan, et al. (1995) *Measuring the Extent of Domestic Violence*. Melbourne: Federation Press

Gardiner, J. (1996) *From Private to Public: Creating a coordinated approach to preventing wife abuse: The Armadale Domestic Violence Intervention Project*. Perth: Criminology Research Council, Australian Institute of Criminology

Hopkins, A. and McGregor, H. (1991) *Working for Change: The movement against domestic violence*. North Sydney: Allen & Unwin

Kunst, L. (1997) Personal communication

McFerren, L. (1990) 'Interpretation of a Frontline State. Australian Women's Refuges and the State', in Watson, S. (ed) *Playing the State: Australian Feminist Interventions.*. Sydney: Allen and Unwin

Moylan, H. J. M., Minister for the Status of Women (1997) *National Directions: how to move our decisions forward*. Randwick: WESNET National Conference, University of NSW

NCVAW (1992) *National Strategy on Violence against Women*. Canberra: National Committee on Violence against Women, Office of the Status of Women, Department of the Prime Minister and Cabinet

NCVAW (1993) *Training in the area of violence against women: incorporating National training guidelines; Training of key occupational groups; and Train the trainer programs*. Canberra: National Committee on Violence against Women, Office of the Status of Women, Department of the Prime Minister and Cabinet

Nicholls, R. (1993) *Address to Domestic Violence Action Groups of Western Australia*. Annual General Meeting of Domestic Violence Action Groups of Western Australia, Inc., Perth

Office of the Status of Women (1995) *Community Attitudes to Violence against Women: Detailed report.* Canberra: Department of the Prime Minister and Cabinet

Office of the Status of Women (1997) *Partnerships against Domestic Violence.* Canberra: Department of Prime Minister and Cabinet

Pence, E. (1985) *The Justice System's Response to Domestic Assault Cases: A guide for policy development.* Minneapolis: Minnesota Program Development

Queensland Domestic Violence Task Force (1988) *Beyond These Walls,* Queensland: Department of Family Services and Welfare Housing

Ralph, A. (1992) *The Effectiveness of Restraining Orders for Protecting Women from Violence.* Perth: Western Australian Office of the Family

Robertson, N. and R. Busch (1993) *Two Year Review,* Hamilton NZ: Hamilton Abuse Intervention Pilot Project

Rosenau, P. (1992) *Post-Modernism and the Social Sciences: Insights, inroads and intrusions.* Princeton NJ: Princeton University Press

SAAP (1997) *Case Management with Children in SAAP Services: A family oriented approach.* Canberra: Supported Accommodation Assistance Program, Commonwealth Department of Health and Family Services

Seddon, N. (1992) *Domestic Violence in Australia: the Legal response.* Sydney: The Federation Press

Statistics Canada (1993) *The Violence against Women Survey.* Ottawa: Statistics Canada.

Stewart, J. (1991) Personal communication

Straus, M. and Gelles, R. (eds) (1990) *Physical Violence in American Families: Risk factors and adaptations to violence in 8,145 families.* New Brunswick, NJ: Transaction Publishers

Summers, A. (1994) 'Feminism on two continents: The women's movements in Australia and the United States' in Grieve, N. and Burns, A. *Australian Women: Contemporary femininst thought.* Melbourne: Oxford University Press

V-Net (1995) *Stopping Men's Violence in the Family: A manual for running men's groups.* Melbourne: Victorian Network for the Prevention of Male Family Violence

Wearing, R. (1992) 'Family Violence: Has anything changed in 4 years?' *The National Centre for Socio Legal Studies,* pp4-5

Wearing, R. (1992) *Monitoring the impact of the Crimes (Family Violence) Act 1987.* Melbourne: La Trobe University

Notes

1. I use the term 'domestic violence' generically to encompass violence (usually by men) against an intimate partner (usually female). At one level I support the argument that because language shapes reality we should use terms that describe who is doing what to whom and the type of relationship eg 'violence against women and children by known men', 'male violence and abuse of their female partners and children'. 'male violence of females with whom they have an intimate relationship', 'violence by a lesbian/gay man against her/his partner'. However such terms are quite cumbersome and readability is also important.

2. For the sake of readers not familiar with Australian political structures, which have a bearing on preventing domestic violence, I provide the following description. The Federal (national) Government has responsibility for matters of national significance and external affairs. Thus, taxation is a Federal matter with the Federal government funding State expenditure on State responsibilities. The Federal government is responsible for income support. States are responsible for civil and criminal law but family law is a Federal responsibility. States are also responsible for the provision of direct services in Health, Education and Human Services.

3. My knowledge of domestic violence policy is most developed for my own State of Western Australia, where I am located in Perth. I therefore do not attempt to provide a complete summary of Federal and State initiatives, including legislation, policy development, funding programmes and practices. I hope, though, to provide readers with a sense of the landscape of the domestic violence field in Australia over the 15 years from 1983 to 1997.

4. I use this form to represent women's experience of being a victim of violence and abuse and at the same time, to represent the movement from being a victim to being a survivor.

5. Some people are referring to the current articulation issues concerning men as the 'men's movement'. While the primary focus remains on the maintaining of men's advantages and not on the recognition of women's disadvantages, I would not consider this a 'movement'.

6. The phrase is from the song 'Down Under' by the Australian

rock group Men at Work.

7.   ANZAC refers to the Australian and New Zealand Army Corps, many of whose members fought futilely under the British flag at Gallipoli in Turkey in the First World War.

8.   Even today at an Australian heterosexual party, women are usually in one space/room and men in another, such as around a keg of beer, barbecue, fridge or other symbolic male space.

9.   In 1893, South Australia became the first government in the world to enfranchise women. Women have had the right to vote in Federal elections since 1901.

10. Such as the comment by a South Australian judge that 'rougher than usual handling' was to be expected by a man when his wife was unwilling to have sex.

11. The women working in women's departments/units generally identified with feminism and have become known as 'femocrats' (ie feminist bureaucrats). There has been much debate about the tension between commitment to a cause and being a bureaucrat/public servant.

12. The Office of the Status of Women (OSW) was established by a Labor government in the 1980s, and located within the Department of Prime Minister and Cabinet.

13. Now the 'Supported Accommodation Assistance Program' (SAAP).

14. However, the Federal government has no power to require States to adopt any policy initiatives it may develop except through funding agreements.

15. My emphasis.

16. One of the difficulties in establishing non-governmental services in Australia is that they rely on Government funding. Australia has a tradition of a welfare State (although this in now undergoing rapid change) and so, unlike the USA or the UK, does not yet have a system of philanthropy, corporate sponsorship or volunteerism.

17. Many abusers ignore restraining orders as they believe they will not be acted upon. Police often fail to give a high priority to serving them and in most cases do not act on breaches of their conditions. Furthermore, the offences which brought about the need to obtain a restraining order are in effect decriminalised as they are invariably ignored by police and/or the judiciary (Ralph, 1992).

18. Formerly, Marriage Guidance Council.

19. The social services agency of the Catholic Church.

20. The social services agency of the Anglican Church.
21. In the past, Marriage Guidance also provided 'couple' counselling. However, Relationships Australia now offers specialised programmes for clients experiencing domestic violence.
22. After the Second World War, the Australian conservatives called their new organisation the 'Liberal' Party!
23. We had been forced to drop the name Duluth as a descriptor of the approach for which we were lobbying as the first minister under this government has given clear indications that he did not support the Duluth model.
24. I believe we give too much credence to the activity of a few men to identify it as a social movement. Some of this activity emanates from men who accept a feminist analysis that masculinity is a social construction, which has many negative implications for men (and women and their children). However, within this group there are many variants of critique and solutions from Robert Bly's valorous Wild Man to pro-feminist men who are supportive of women's struggles and envisage androgynous sharing of power and choices. Other activity is just plain old-fashioned back-lash.
25. Girls witness and/or experience more violence and abuse in the family than boys but most do not become violent or abusive.
26. Including myself, as an activist academic.

13
Housing agencies, domestic violence and multi-agency work

Ellen Malos

Local authority housing departments in Britain have had a crucial role in providing accommodation for women escaping from violent relationships, especially over the last twenty years. In world terms Britain has had a unique public housing system combining a high degree of local autonomy with a framework of extensive statutory duties devolved from central government, both for people homeless in an emergency (among whom women escaping domestic violence have been included since 1977) and for the provision of permanent accommodation in the form of publicly owned rented housing which formed a high proportion of the total housing stock.

This role has been eroded in recent years, first by the expansion of the provision of 'arms length' socially rented accommodation by housing associations and later by the reduction in the public rented sector through massively expanded sale of council housing under 'right to buy' legislation and stringent controls on building programmes. Despite the protestations of the Conservative government of the time, this loss was not offset by the expansion of provision of social rented accommodation by housing associations (OPCS, 1997). Nevertheless housing departments still have a key role to play, despite these changes and despite the removal by the 1996 Housing Act of the mandatory duty to provide permanent follow on accommodation to homeless people (discussed further below).

Indeed, it could be argued that the curtailment of the provider role of housing departments and the expansion of their role as 'enablers', advisers and facilitators should make their participation in multi-agency initiatives even more vital if they are to help to provide an adequate service for women experiencing domestic violence who seek their assistance either for themselves or for themselves and their children.

Housing and domestic violence

A two year research study into local authority responses to domestic violence by a team in the Domestic Violence Research Group at the University of Bristol documented the continuing need of women experiencing domestic violence for safe permanent housing as well as safe emergency accommodation. It also demonstrated the continuing importance of access to local authority and social rented housing (Malos and Hague, 1993). Similarly a study commissioned by the Department of the Environment demonstrated the significant part played by local authority housing entitlement for women experiencing violent relationship breakdown (Bull, 1993).

Women's lesser access to better paid work and to financial resources generally, especially when they have children, has been firmly established. This means that they are less able to afford acceptable housing in the private housing market, either as owners or as tenants (Watson, 1984; Watson and Austerberry, 1986, 1983a, 1983b; Logan, 1986; Ross, 1990; Muir and Ross, 1993). It is, therefore, all the more important for women seeking safety from violent partners that there should be safe emergency or temporary accommodation of a reasonable standard in the short term. If a safe return to their previous home would not be possible, they also need access to an adequate, secure and affordable permanent home in which they and their children can live. Our research demonstrated that, despite the increasing problems it faces, the public housing sector has remained an important, if diminishing, resource for women and children in this situation. In the last twenty years this has often been possible only through the special provisions made for homelessness, with local authority nominations to housing associations as an valuable supplement. However, the 1996 housing law, which permits and encourages local authorities to discharge their duties to homeless people by referring them to the private rented sector, after emergency rehousing, weakens this safety net and creates dangers that it may be withdrawn altogether in some areas of the country. This danger remains despite the fact that the impact of the law has been softened by changes brought about through regulation .

Under The Homelessness (Suitability of Accommodation) (Amendment) Order 1996, in force since the 1st September 1997, the previous government accepted the force of some of the criticisms made of the possible effects of an uncritical recourse to assured shorthold tenancies. Therefore, accommodation is not to be regarded as suitable unless the local authority are satisfied that it will be available for occupation by the applicant for 'at least two years beginning with the date on which he secures it'. Subsequently, the Labour Government elected in May 1997, although not as yet fulfilling its pre-election promises to repeal the sections of the 1996 Act referring to homelessness, has taken action by way of regulation and guidance which mitigates some of the worst effects of the new law, for example by making it clear that homelessness is a factor which should be given due weight in the allocation of points on the waiting list and the provision of permanent accommodation. But this change is not mandatory and does not restore the situation under the previous law. Each authority will have the power to decide what weight to give and of course many authorities have now divested themselves of all housing stock.

However the Act itself does appear to be potentially beneficial to some women already in local authority tenancies (still a significant proportion of women applying as homeless in our research on homelessness and domestic violence (Malos and Hague, 1993). Within the new grounds the Act introduces for repossession for nuisance and anti-social behaviour domestic violence becomes a ground for eviction from secure tenancies and assured tenancies with social landlords (Cowan, 1996, Arden and Hunter, 1997). But this ground for possession only comes into play where the couple are married or living together as husband and wife and the partner leaving is unlikely to return. It therefore does not cover 'McGrady' cases (a procedure, based on case law, used by some councils to allow the woman to return to the tenancy after a notice to quit had been served to joint tenants). It remains to be seen therefore whether the new eviction provision is able to be used creatively to allow women and their children to be transferred to a new tenancy without falling foul of the new homelessness provisions.

Past research indicates that the nature of the response to the new law and regulation and therefore its impact on women and children escaping domestic violence will vary enormously, with sympathetic authorities doing their best to develop good policy and practice (though these may not always be applied consistently) while others make little attempt to provide a supportive housing service.

Varying responses of local housing authorities

Our research into local authority responses under the previous law, looked at policy and practice in seven local authorities. In four of these it centred on in-depth interviews with women who had experienced domestic violence and were seeking rehousing in each of four local authorities (20 in each authority) with a follow-up approximately six months later.

Although the majority of the women were or had been in Women's Aid refuges, the study included women from bed-and-breakfast, local authority homeless hostels, and temporary private accommodation. These four authorities were one rural and one London borough and two urban district authorities. We interviewed workers from a large number of local voluntary agencies in all seven study areas, as well as from women's refuges, housing associations and the local authority housing departments.

The majority of the women interviewed had dependent children and were therefore a priority under the law, and the Code of Guidance current at the time advised local authorities to give special consideration to women without dependent children because they had been made homeless through violence. A sizeable proportion of women in the study came from minority ethnic communities.

Contrary to recent suggestions, our research showed no evidence that these groups received unfair precedence over other homeless applicants for local authority housing or were given 'fast track' access to permanent tenancies on more favourable terms than others.

The authorities varied in the sympathy of their response but none went significantly beyond the law and the advice of the government's Code of Guidance as to which groups of applicants they accepted for rehousing. Some did show more consideration for the problems faced by women escaping violence in their approach to interviewing women, in the facilities they provided to help ensure a safe and sympathetic interviewing environment, or in allowing them to specify areas in the authority in which they would not wish to be rehoused. Such authorities were often developing written guidelines on policy and practice in relation to domestic violence and were carrying out training programmes for all staff.

On the other hand some authorities interpreted their duties very narrowly: for example by adopting a stance of 'minimum compliance' with the law and attempting to deter women from pursuing their applications: pointing them in the direction of legal remedies, which are often ineffective; or demanding a high degree of 'proof' and conducting stringent and detailed investigations into the violence they had experienced (which can often be very distressing for women in these situations because of the very private and intimate nature of the abuse experienced). Some authorities would not consider for rehousing women escaping violence who did not have dependent children with them, or interpreted the 'local connection' clause of the homelessness law more narrowly than the law prescribes in situations involving domestic violence. This might involve the authority attempting to refer women on to another authority even if they might be in danger there, or keeping them in uncertainty about whether they would be accepted for rehousing for very long periods of time.

Overall, our impressions from the research were that the queues of women waiting for rehousing were lengthening as an effect of the cut-back in public housing and the recession, especially in London and the rural authority. There was little evidence that housing associations were making up for the shortfall although they did make a valuable contribution, especially in rehousing single women and women from minority ethnic communities who might otherwise have had special difficulty in some areas.

A significant proportion of women, especially in London and the rural borough, had difficulty in establishing their claim to be accepted for rehousing. The great majority of the women and children spent periods varying from four months to several years in temporary accommodation and in the rural and the London borough most had still not been rehoused at the end of the study.

Our research confirmed the existing evidence that local authority responses vary widely from one area to another, in terms of the use of their discretion under the homelessness legislation to accept or attempt to limit their acceptance of homeless people (Thomas & Niner, 1989, Evans and Duncan, 1988, Evans, 1991). We found that women who become homeless because of domestic violence are no exception to this pattern. This response is not always explicable in terms of the amount of housing stock the authority controls although, not surprisingly, the length of time that women had to wait for housing once they had been accepted *was* affected by the availability of housing in the area.

In the new situation created by the catastrophic decline of the public rented sector as a result of the policies of the previous Conservative government and the inability of the housing associations to fill the gap (especially in view of government pressures to force them to borrow in the commercial market) it has become even more important than before for local authorities to seek sympathetic and creative use of the human and material resources they do have at their disposal. At the time of our research into local authority responses, as we have seen above, housing departments in some areas had begun to examine their practices and policies towards homeless people in general and women escaping domestic violence in particular, developing codes of practice, providing training for staff and developing better facilities in relation both to the allocation of the available accommodation and to the process applicants must go through in applying to the homelessness section for accommodation. In existing accommodation, for example, the provision of alarms and door phones to control access and policies in relation to easing transfers to other accommodation could lessen the need for women and their children to become homeless in the first place. Changes in their homeless section could also be important: taking a sympathetic, informed and 'believing' approach, allowing for more privacy in interviews, providing information and interpretation in a variety of languages, giving clear information of the progress of their application were some of these. In some cases these changes took place in conjunction with the development of multi-agency initiatives on domestic violence. Also, in many urban areas, the local authority was providing a significant proportion of the funding for Women's Aid refuges which provided emergency and temporary accommodation, support and advocacy for women experiencing such violence.

The current situation of housing agencies in multi-agency work

As described in chapter 2 research by the Bristol Domestic Violence Research Group into multi-agency initiatives in domestic violence (Hague, Malos and Dear, 1995 and 1996; Hague and Malos 1996) combined a survey of all local authority areas in the country with more detailed studies of eight differing and geographically dispersed areas in which multi-agency initiatives existed. Our previous research on housing had led us to expect a relatively high degree of participation by local authority housing departments and indeed this was true in six out of our eight study areas (Hague, Malos and Dear, 1996, p.25). However the picture is rather different nationally, as shown by a sample of 50 randomly chosen domestic violence forums from the national survey where housing department representative were active in only 27 (this compared with 28 for social services departments which, at the time being a county based service, were fewer in number overall, 26 for probation services and 43 for police) (Hague, Malos and Dear 1996, p.53).

However this is not to say that housing departments did not play a significant role in many instances. In some areas, local authority agencies are important in stimulating and supporting the development of multi-agency initiatives and in a number of instances housing departments have either taken the lead as in Bristol in 1992/93, where the Housing Department initiated a city wide forum in parallel with their development of a new domestic violence and housing policy, or in Greenwich where a multi-agency forum was initiated jointly by the London Borough of Greenwich Equalities Unit, the police, and a parallel multi-agency group, the Greenwich Fightback group (now wound up), with representation from refuges; while the local housing authority took on the development of housing policy and training modules for housing officers (Hague, Malos and Dear, 1996, pp. 16/17, p.56).

Housing departments are most often represented on multi-agency forums through their homelessness section or homeless persons unit. It is to this part of the housing service that women and children who are escaping from domestic violence most frequently turn since one of their greatest needs is for safe permanent accommodation. However, in some areas the need for a policy that embraces all sections of the housing service as one part of an overall corporate policy on domestic violence for the council as a whole has long been recognised (as in the London Borough of Hammersmith and Fulham).

In future as the new Housing Act comes in to effect it will be even more important to broaden the concept of multi-agency work as it effects housing and domestic violence. It is not sufficient to leave representation to basic grade workers. Instead, as is already the case in some areas, there is a need for back-up at managerial level and for greater cooperation, within the Housing Department and between departments.

In some areas, as in Islington, housing departments may make use of either multi-agency or corporate practice guidelines to improve policy and practice. For example there is the possibility of action by local housing area offices to implement the new clauses on anti-social tenants in the 1996 Housing Act as applied to domestic violence, and to develop policies on transfers which can remove the necessity for women to declare themselves homeless and thus possibly lose the right to a permanent tenancy.

Homelessness sections can develop cooperation with community safety units, where they exist, and with the police, to improve the safety of women in their homes. Particularly where a local authority's own stock is severely diminished or its management has been handed over to other agencies there will be a need to build up liaison and policy and practice guidelines between the local authority and housing associations; and in some cases with private landlords or property companies where these play a significant part in the provision of housing to women who may formerly have been directly housed by housing authorities.

In such new developments it is particularly crucial that Women's Aid groups and the Women's Aid Federations are involved in multi-agency consultation and multi-agency initiatives and that housing authorities and housing associations continue to work with them to attempt to ensure that the new legislative framework does not result in women and their children remaining trapped in violent relationships or forced to return to them after a period in a refuge or other temporary accommodation because the route to safe permanent housing is blocked.

One way in which multi-agency initiatives can have an impact on housing issues is by the formation of housing sub-groups to work on policy, to develop training packages and to highlight good practice.

Another important area in which multi-agency initiatives can be of assistance to housing departments in relation to domestic violence is the development of good practice on race and equality issues. In our housing research some authorities had already begun to develop culturally sensitive approaches which included the provision of interpreters and the option of being interviewed by women officers if desired. Others had not even begun to consider such matters. Multi-agency initiatives often develop sub-groups or working groups to consider equalities issues in detail and to incorporate the insights of women from minority ethnic communities in depth. The consideration of these matters across the whole field of domestic violence for the community as a whole can overcome the patchiness of a fragmented approach within single agencies.

It will also be of importance, as noted earlier, for participation in such initiatives to be seen as a serious responsibility of the housing department rather than an optional task to be undertaken by basic grade staff as an extra or 'spare time' responsibility. Especially where local authorities have little remaining housing stock or where they have divested themselves of direct responsibility by devolving its management to other bodies it will also be critically important for such organisations, whether housing associations or property companies, to be kept aware, within a multi-agency setting, of their responsibilities to women experiencing domestic violence. Such developments have already taken place in a number of areas and some housing departments are very active in multi-agency forums. As noted above, this was the case in a number of our study areas. Some housing officers not only took a very active part in the work of the forum itself but were also very helpful in assisting with the research, locating potential interviewees as well as giving their own time very generously in the survey and the in-depth interviews

The current housing situation

Homelessness of all kinds remains a significant social problem and the current shortage of social rented housing will continue to create enormous difficulties for a woman seeking to escape from a violent relationship and to make a new home for herself whether or not she has children. Although the new Labour government has promised to release the proceeds of the sale of council housing for the building of public housing, the scale of the shortfall of public and housing association properties and the continued restrictions on public spending in general make it very unlikely that the shortfall can be made good. Greve (1991) and others have estimated that there is a need for somewhere in the region of 100,000 new homes in a ten year period. This is far in excess of what is likely from the easing of restrictions on the use of the proceeds of sales alone, especially since the bulk of marketable properties have already been sold.

Similarly, at the time of writing, we are waiting to hear the government's plans for further reform of the homelessness provisions of the 1996 Housing Act, which they promised to repeal in the lead up to the May 1997 general election. So far the most significant change has been to allow councils to restore a degree of priority for homelessness for applicants on the waiting list for permanent re-housing, a step which a number of housing authorities had already taken in effect through their new points system, some of them as a direct result of discussions within multi-agency forums.

It also remains to be seen what the impact will be of the strengthening and widening of the scope of civil protection orders for women and children experiencing violence in the home under the Family Law Act 1996. Past experience suggests that it will take time for the new provisions to settle in and that judicial practice may not match up with the hopes that the possibilities of the new legislation, including the provision for greater use of powers of arrest, may give rise to. It is thus vital that housing authorities, in considering whether it is safe for women and their children to remain in or return to their own homes, should have the kind of access to up to date information that participation in a multi-agency initiative with front line services for women experiencing domestic violence can bring. It will also be important, for reasons of housing security, as well as for other reasons, that some way is found to remedy the present rarity of participation by the judiciary, the magistracy and of other court staff, in multi-agency initiatives. In this respect specific guidance from the Department of the Environment, Transport and the Regions, the Home Office and the Lord Chancellor's Department will be of vital importance in encouraging participation at local level of personnel from the relevant agencies, including local authority housing departments.

There will also be a need, almost 25 years after the formation of the Women's Aid movement, finally to address seriously the question of adequate funding to ensure sufficient refuge provision as part of an overall national strategy in conjunction with the national Women's Aid federations of England, Scotland, Wales and Northern Ireland. There has been a disturbing trend in the opposite direction recently with some local authorities cutting back on funding to Women's Aid groups and of housing associations taking refuges previously run through the agency of Women's Aid groups into direct management.

It will only be in this way that the commitment expressed in the government Inter-agency Circular (Home Office, 1995) to ensuring 'the provision of safe accommodation and support services both emergency and long term for women and their children who feel compelled to leave the family home' can begin to become more than a pious hope.

Note

The two research projects on which this chapter is based were supported by the Joseph Rowntree Foundation. The facts presented and the views expressed, however are those of the author and not necessarily those of the Foundation.

References

Arden, A. and Hunter, C. (1997) *Women and Allocation.* London: Legal Action Group

Barron, J. (1990) *Not Worth the Paper? The effectiveness of legal protection for women and children experiencing domestic violence.* Bristol: Women's Aid Federation of England

Bradburn, H. (1994) *Home Truths: Access to local authority and housing association tenancies. Responses to the Consultation Paper.* London: Shelter

Bull, J. (1993), *Housing Consequences of Relationship Breakdown.* London: HMSO

Charles, N. (1993), *The Housing Needs of Women and Children Escaping Domestic Violence,* Cardiff: Tai Cymru (Housing for Wales)

Cowan, D. (1996) *Housing Act 1996: A practical guide.* Bristol: Jordans

Department of the Environment (1994) Consultation Paper, *Access to Local Authority and Housing Association Tenancies.* London: HMSO

Department of the Environment (1993) *Report and Recommendations of the Working Party on Relationship Breakdown.* London: HMSO

DOE 0919 (1996) *Housing England and Wales: The Homelessness (Suitability of Accommodation) Order 1996*. London: The Stationery Office

DOE 1086 (1997) *Housing, England and Wales: The Allocation of Housing (Reasonable and Additional Preference) Regulations*. London: The Stationery Office.

Evans, A. (1991) *Alternatives to Bed and Breakfast, Temporary housing solutions for homeless people*. London: National Housing and Town Planning council

Evans, A. and Duncan, S. (1988) *Responding to Homelessness: Local authority policy and practice*. London: HMSO

Family Law Act 1996. London: HMSO

Gilroy, R. and Woods, R. (1994) *Housing Women*. London: Routledge

Greve, J. (1991) *Homelessness in Britain*. York: Joseph Rowntree Foundation

Hague, G. and Malos, E. (1994) 'Domestic violence, social policy and housing' *Critical Social Policy*, 42

Hague, G. and Malos, E. (1996) *Tackling Domestic Violence*. Bristol: Policy Press

Hague, G. and Malos, E, (1998) *Domestic Violence; Action for change*. (2nd Ed) Cheltenham: New Clarion Press

Hague, G., Malos, E., Dear, W. (1995) *Against Domestic Violence: Inter-agency initiatives*, Bristol. University of Bristol: SAUS Publications

Hague, G, Malos, E., Dear, W. (1996) *Multi-Agency Work and Domestic Violence: A national study of inter-agency initiatives*. Bristol: Joseph Rowntree Foundation and Policy Press.

Home Office (1994) *Consultation Document on Inter-agency Responses to Domestic Violence*. London: Home Office,

Home Office (1995) *Inter Agency Circular: Inter-agency Co-ordination to tackle Domestic Violence*. London: Home Office and Welsh Office

Homer, M.., Leonard, L., and Taylor, P. (1984) *Public Violence, Private Shame*. Bristol: Women's Aid Federation (England)

House of Commons Home Affairs Committee (1993) *Inquiry into Domestic Violence*. London: HMSO

Housing Act 1996. HMSO: London

Law Commission (1992) *Family Law, Domestic Violence and the Occupation of the Family Home*. London: HMSO

Logan, F. (1986) *Homelessness and Relationship Breakdown: How the law and housing policy affects women*. London: One Parent Families

Malos, E. (1993) *'You've got No Life' : Homelessness and the use of bed and breakfast hotels*. Bristol: University of Bristol, School of Applied Social Studies

Malos, E. and Hague, G. (1993) *Domestic Violence and Housing.* Bristol: Women's Aid Federation (England) and University of Bristol, School of Applied Social Studies

Mama, A. (1996) *The Hidden Struggle*, (2nd Ed). London: Whiting and Birch

Muir, J. and Ross, M. (1993) *Housing The Poorer Sex.* London: London Housing Unit

Office of Population Census and Statistics (1997) *Social Trends*, 27. London, HMSO

Pascall, G. and Morley, R. (1996) 'Women and Homelessness, 1: Proposals from the Department of the Environment: Lone mothers, *Journal of Social Welfare and Family Law*, 18(2)

Pascall, G. and Morley, R. (1996) "Women and Homelessness, 2: Proposals from the Department of Environment: Domestic violence', *Journal of Social Welfare and Family Law* , 18 (3)

Ross, M. (1990) *A Summary of Research into Women and Homelessness.* London: London Housing Unit

Sexty, C. (1990) *Women Losing Out: Access to housing in Britain today.* London, Shelter

Taylor, M. (1994) *Housing and Domestic Violence in Scotland.* Scotland: Scottish Women's Aid

Thomas, A. and Niner, P. (1989) *Living in Temporary Accommodation: A survey of homeless people.* London: HMSO

Watson, S. (1984) 'Definitions of homelessness: a feminist perspective', *Critical Social Policy*, 11

Watson, S. and Austerbury, H. (1983a) *Women and Housing Research: Future directions for the next decade.* London: SSRC

Watson, S. and Austerberry, H. (1983b) *Women on the Margins: A study of single women's housing problems.* London: The City University

Watson, S. and Austerberry, H. (1986) *Housing and Homelessness: A feminist perspective.* London: RKP

14
Policing domestic violence and inter-agency working

Sharon Grace

Introduction

The importance of effective inter-agency work in the field of domestic violence has been widely acknowledged (see, for example, National Inter-Agency Working Party, 1992 and Hague and Malos, 1993). The value of involving the police in such work has also been recognised. As Hague and Malos point out:

> *The police role in combating domestic violence is one of the most essential, and their handling of violence cases is of key significance to women because of the traumatic and crucial point at which they are asked to intervene on women's behalf. In addition, the police have not been previously noted for pro-women sympathies, so the new police policies are demanding changes in long-established police practices and attitudes. For all these reasons, domestic violence training and inter-agency cooperation can be even more vital for the police than for other agencies.* (1993)

One of those police policies, the Home Office circular (60/1990) on domestic violence, recommended:

- that the police take a more interventionist approach in domestic violence cases - with a presumption in favour of

    arrest;
- that domestic violence crimes are recorded and investigated
  in the same way as other violent crimes; and
- that the police adopt a more sympathetic and understanding
  attitude towards victims of domestic violence.

Forces were also encouraged to set up dedicated units or
appoint officers to deal specifically with domestic violence cases
and to liaise with other agencies working in the field.

A research study was carried out by the Home Office Research
and Planning Unit between 1992 and 1994[1] to discover how far
such recommendations were reflected in current police policies
and practice. Five forces were selected to be studied in detail -
Northamptonshire, Nottinghamshire, South Yorkshire, Thames
Valley and West Midlands.

This chapter focuses on the part of the research study which
examined the role of the police in inter-agency work. It reports on
discussions held with agencies involved in dealing with domestic
violence victims and with the police, in each of the study areas,
namely: the Crown Prosecution Service[2]; women's refuges; local
authority housing; and Victim Support Schemes[3]. As well as
these core agencies, interviews were also conducted with agencies
who had developed some role in domestic violence issues in the
various force areas. The discussions focused on how the particular
agency saw their own role in respect of domestic violence; how
they saw the role of the police; and their views on the police
response to domestic violence in their area. The chapter also
describes what domestic violence officers (DVOs) and senior
police officers thought about inter-agency working.

Crown Prosecution Service

Views on the police
The Crown Prosecution Service (CPS) were generally supportive
of the police response to domestic violence. They saw themselves
and the police in complementary roles - working towards the
arrest and prosecution of domestic violence offenders - and
because of this thought it important that they all worked well
together.

However, some prosecutors voiced concerns about the police
response. They thought older police officers were set in their
ways and had not incorporated the new guidelines into their

practice. Younger officers were thought to have a better attitude, but also to be at risk of becoming quickly disillusioned when victims withdrew their complaints or when they came under the influence of older officers. Prosecutors understood that the police were, in general, keen to prosecute domestic violence cases as they saw this as the best way to teach the abuser a lesson. Because of this, the CPS were aware that the police became very frustrated if a case did not proceed to court. In order to avoid this, prosecutors thought it was vital to emphasise to the police that the evidence in domestic violence cases needed to be of very high quality to ensure the greatest chance of securing a conviction.

Contact with Domestic Violence Officers

Most prosecutors supported the idea of DVOs and had established good working relationships with them. This made liaison and information exchange with the police much easier and prosecutors found the DVOs' detailed knowledge of individual cases very useful. The DVOs often acted as a contact point for the CPS and respondents felt that this ensured a consistency of approach. Most respondents also thought that DVOs showed more understanding to victims and that, by supporting victims throughout the criminal justice process, aided successful prosecutions. However, one prosecutor expressed reservations about the role of DVOs and said that he preferred to deal with arresting officers rather than DVOs because they knew more about the initial incident.

Retraction of complaints

All CPS respondents said that they insisted on a formal retraction statement if a victim decided to withdraw her complaint, and would not terminate a case without such a statement. Several admitted that this was a relatively new system and the practice had been rather haphazard in the past. Most also said that they would ask the police to find out the reasons why a victim was withdrawing, to check that she had not been intimidated. Again, DVOs were considered to be best placed to know whether the withdrawal was voluntary. One prosecutor said that she was keen for victims to come to court to withdraw a complaint, as this served to emphasise the seriousness to the victim of making a complaint. However, she had taken account of her local DVO's reservations about this practice and did not insist that it happened.

Most prosecutors said that the best option for victims was to take their violent partners to court and that victims could help to make the system work by not withdrawing their complaints. Prosecutors said that unless the victim cooperated with the prosecution process there was very little they could do to help her. However, some prosecutors did say that they felt the CPS could do much more to support victims when they came to court and by doing so they might help to reduce the number of withdrawals.

All the prosecutors said that they would be willing to pursue a case without a victim's support but only if there was independent evidence of an assault (usually a witness) and/or the case was serious enough to warrant going ahead. Most thought that compelling witnesses should be reserved for the most serious cases where the defendant posed a considerable danger to the victim.

Several respondents mentioned that Section 23 of the Criminal Justice Act 1988 allowed written evidence to be offered in court if a witness felt intimidated and did not want to give evidence in person. Some thought that this might be useful in domestic violence cases - but most were in agreement that judges preferred to see the victim in person and that consequently Section 23 was rarely used[4].

Charge reduction and bind overs

All prosecutors said that they were prepared to use the full range of possible offences from, for example, common assault to wounding, in domestic violence cases. However, they explained that while the first charge laid would probably be the most serious possible for the given facts, this might be reduced if a lesser charge 'offered appropriate penalties for the injury sustained'. In addition, several said that they were very keen to use summary-only offences because it was better to prosecute cases in the magistrates' court where they would be dealt with more speedily and where, one prosecutor said, a conviction was more likely. The same prosecutor described this decision-making process as a balancing act between ensuring a serious enough charge was brought and making sure the case was dealt with swiftly and efficiently - 'for the victim's sake'.

Most prosecutors thought that 'bind-overs' (binding an offender over to keep the peace) could be useful in less serious cases and only one respondent thought that this practice 'devalued' the offence. It was generally thought that bind-overs should be considered where the victim was reluctant to give evidence or the evidence was rather weak. However, most prosecutors admitted that a bind-over offered little protection to the victim and would not have any deterrent effect on persistent abusers.

Women's refuges

Background

Women's refuges are the front line agencies for domestic violence and 'stand at the heart of the battered-woman movement' (Dobash and Dobash, 1992). A variety of refuges were visited. Some refuges were affiliated to Women's Aid; other refuges were 'independent' organisations. The services the refuges offered varied. All provided emergency accommodation for women fleeing violence. How long the women could then stay at the refuge depended on their individual policy. Some of the independent refuges restricted the number of women they took so that residents could stay as long as up to a year. Others provided 'half-way' houses for women to stay in while awaiting permanent accommodation.

As well as accommodation, most of the refuges provided advice and support to victims of domestic violence and referred them on to other agencies. Some had drop-in advice centres and/or ran telephone help lines.

Views on the police

Refuge workers within the study were generally very critical of the police response to domestic violence. From their responses it was obvious that there was frequently a degree of mistrust and misunderstanding between the two agencies. Overall, there was little direct contact between the police and the refuges.

Respondents said that referrals to refuges were rarely received directly from the police, and many felt that the police did not tell women about the services which they could provide and, moreover, did not have any respect for the work refuges did. Some workers thought that the police only used the refuges in an emergency and did not consider that they could offer anything other than temporary shelter. However, some respondents also said that because they could not allow the police to just 'pop round' to the refuge it was difficult to develop good informal relations with the police.

While the refuge workers welcomed the Circular, many felt that the police had only paid lip service to its guidelines and that it had not affected the way in which domestic violence was policed at ground level. They felt that the police displayed a lack of understanding of domestic violence issues and were largely ignorant of the law - in particular the civil law. The majority of refuge workers interviewed felt that the police had not had sufficient training on domestic violence and on the recommendations of the Circular. Many said that they were involved in trying to rectify this situation through offering to train police officers.

Several workers made the point that most women with whom they came into contact had never called the police - because they did not believe it would help. Most of the respondents complained that the police were slow to respond to domestic violence calls and cited examples of women waiting up to three hours for the police to arrive. The workers said that, when they did arrive, the police would do nothing without definite evidence of an assault; would not arrest unless there were severe injuries; and were generally not interested unless there was a strong chance of a conviction.

One of the main services the police provided was to act as an escort for refuge clients so that they could collect their belongings (and sometimes their children) from home. While some respondents said that the police carried out this function very well and were quick to respond to such requests, others said that they were reluctant to do it, and often sided with the violent partner when they took the woman to her house. Several respondents thought that the police were keener to help if there were children involved and said that women with children were generally more satisfied with the response they had from the police.

Several respondents said that the police were good at offering advice to both individual women and the refuges about security and at dealing with cases where the injuries were severe and prosecution was very likely. However, they said that because domestic violence was not like other crimes (which tend to be one-off events from a victim's perspective) the police found them difficult to deal with.

One respondent made an observation about the usual kinds of cases in which the police were involved which she felt might help to explain why they find dealing with such cases so difficult. She said that the women the police refer to the refuge are often in a state of immediate crisis - leaving home without preparation or forethought. Women in this position, the worker considered, are the most likely to return to their partners, unlike those who come directly to the refuge having planned their escape over a period of time. The respondent felt that because the police come into contact most frequently with women in crisis they see a lot of women returning home and they therefore become cynical about what can be done to help them and are then less keen to get involved in other cases.

Contact with DVOs

The refuge workers rated their contact with DVOs more positively than their contact with general officers and many had developed good working relationships with a DVO. Because of this, they had become less reluctant to work with the police in general. Most of the referrals which came from the police came via DVOs. However, several workers observed that DVOs were often marginalised, unsupported and isolated from the rest of the police and therefore had little impact on the general police response.

Asian women's refuges

In the main, the problems described by workers in refuges for Asian women were similar to those for general refuges but were further exacerbated by the particular sensitivities associated with domestic violence in Asian communities. Workers said that the police failed to appreciate sensitivities about violence in Asian families. Ironically, this sometimes meant that the police were sometimes more helpful to women trying to leave such families, as they thought this was their best option. On the other hand respondents said that the police were typically very reluctant to get involved, knowing that any action they took could have repercussions for their dealings with the Asian community as a whole.

One worker said that it was very important for the address of the refuge to be kept secret because if it became known in the general Asian community it would soon become known to the violent partner. She said that the police had often given the address to inappropriate people. In particular, she suggested that officers in a community liaison role can have divided loyalties and might cooperate with community leaders, risking the safety of the refuge clients.

Local authority housing departments

Background

(Note: This research was conducted before the Housing Act 1996.)
Most housing departments deal with domestic violence victims
through their homelessness units. Women fleeing violence are no
longer regarded as 'intentionally homeless' (which used to be a
general housing policy) and thus receive the same priority as other
homeless people. Most of the authorities were able to offer
temporary accommodation - often in their local refuge - while
women were waiting to be permanently re-housed. Many workers
expressed sympathy with victims who had to move because of their
partner's violence and some workers said that they tried to evict
the abuser and allow the woman to stay in her home if this did not
jeopardise her safety. While some respondents said that their
priority was to house women with children, others said being a
mother had no influence on how quickly a client was found a new
home. Some workers said that they offered women the choice to see
a female housing officer if they preferred. A policy of making only
one offer of re-housing was in force in some departments.

Most housing officials said that they sought confirmation of
the women's stories of violence from various sources - often the
police or a solicitor with whom the woman had had contact. The
level of proof required varied from worker to worker, but most
said that, even if the woman could not prove her story or had
been subject to mental rather than physical abuse, they were
usually willing to give her the benefit of the doubt. All but one of
the workers said that in their experience the vast majority of
cases were genuine and that they often saw the same woman
several times - still trying to escape from her partner. The
exception was a worker who seemed to have a one-person
campaign against women making fraudulent claims of violence
as a means of getting to the front of the housing waiting list. This
worker thought that at least 50 per cent of the applications she
received were bogus. However, her views were not shared by any
of the other housing officials interviewed.

Views on the police

Most housing workers said that very few of the domestic violence
victims they saw spoke highly of the police and that victims'
perceptions that the police will do little to help was still very
prevalent. However, most also said that they thought the police

response was improving but that policy changes had been slow to reach the lower ranks of the police and that a cultural and attitudinal shift was still required among these officers. The number of referrals they received from the police had increased, particularly in areas with DVOs, with whom several officers were in regular contact. The police also seemed more prepared to escort victims to their homes.

Respondents said that DVOs were particularly helpful in verifying victims' stories and had speeded up and simplified this procedure greatly. Respondents said that they often referred their clients to DVOs for further advice and also received clients via the DVOs. Several workers mentioned having liaised with DVOs about fitting panic alarms in victims' houses.

Victim support schemes

Background

All of the Victim Support workers interviewed described being at the very early stages of developing a response to domestic violence victims. Some schemes were still not involved with such victims at all - but all were aware of the need for Victim Support to be so. Most workers said that they received very few domestic violence referrals. Several respondents reported the development of schemes to train volunteers to deal with domestic violence cases. Indeed such training had already been carried out in one of the five force areas. Some respondents felt that it was not appropriate for their Victim Support volunteers to work on such cases until that training had been completed.

Victim Support workers in all five areas described a similar arrangement with the police in that each morning they receive a print-out of the previous day's incidents. Some forces now flag up domestic violence cases and the police seem generally more keen for VS to get involved with domestic violence victims than previously - although in some areas it was thought that the police were still reluctant to pass such cases onto Victim Support.

Most schemes will not contact a victim unless she has given her consent to the police to pass on her details to Victim Support. Victim Support then write to the victim and arrange a meeting - usually on neutral ground (ie not at a police station or the victim's home). One point to note is that most schemes do not allow their volunteers to contact victims of domestic violence if the perpetrator is still at large. This severely restricts the amount of work they can do with domestic violence victims. Several workers felt that they would have to change this policy as referrals increased.

Most respondents felt that Women's Aid were the lead agency for domestic violence and frequently referred victims on to them straight away. Several workers said they thought Women's Aid were better equipped to deal with such cases and Victim Support did not want to be seen to be encroaching on their territory. However, some schemes offered to do home visits for Women's Aid if they were unable to do them.

Views on the police

Overall, Victim Support described an improving police response to domestic violence. However, some thought that the police were not properly trained to deal with domestic violence and that many officers were still unaware of the complexities of domestic violence situations. One respondent thought that, due to the nature of their job, the police became immune to suffering and needed training to understand the suffering of a victim of domestic violence. Another said that standardising practice throughout all forces was the only way in which to ensure a consistent approach to domestic violence incidents.

Contact with DVOs was mixed. Some workers had established a good system whereby the two agencies worked well together and ensured that there was little duplication of effort. Most thought that having a DVO as a contact point within the police was very useful and ensured a better flow of information between the agencies. However, in certain areas there was very little contact between VS and the DVOs and it appeared that no thought had been given to the possibility that there was an overlap in the work they did. In addition, one worker felt that DVOs took on a Victim Support role when dealing with domestic violence cases and that this was inappropriate. This worker also thought that DVOs pushed victims too hard to support a prosecution, instead of offering neutral advice.

Other agencies

As well as interviewing representatives from the core agencies in each area, contact was also made with particular agencies which had developed a role in domestic violence issues in some of the force areas.

Social services refuge liaison officer

Consideration was initially given to interviewing social services representatives in all areas. However, a first meeting with a social services representative showed that social services had little to do with domestic violence cases unless that violence formed part of a general family problem or a child abuse case. However, one area had appointed a refuge liaison officer within their social services community support team, whose job it was to work with refuges and other voluntary agencies to help them improve their services for domestic violence victims.

This liaison officer thought that the police were not sufficiently accountable for their dealings with domestic violence cases and that they continued to apply their discretion in much the same way they did before circular 60/1990 was issued. She was actively involved in training both existing police officers and new recruits about how to deal with domestic violence incidents. She thought that this was beginning to have an effect and that assumptions and stereotypes the police officers held were being effectively challenged.

Women's advice centres

Workers in two advice centres were interviewed. The first was funded by Safer Cities to work as a domestic violence counsellor within a general women's advice centre - offering advice over the phone; running groups for and with domestic violence survivors; and acting as an information resource for women experiencing domestic violence. The other advice centre was run by Women's Aid and offers a crisis intervention facility as well as general advice.

The police had initially contacted the counsellor at the 'general' centre and she now referred women on to the DVOs where appropriate or when requested to do so. While she was very positive about her contact with DVOs she was less so about the general police response. She felt that the police thought that they could not deal with domestic violence effectively and hence would not take cases seriously. She did not feel that the DVOs had impacted on this attitude at all.

The Women's Aid worker said that while the police were now more open and responsive to other agencies asking for help in domestic violence cases, she was less certain that they helped women who did not have the support of these other agencies. In particular, she felt that the police were most reluctant to deal with women who did not conform to a passive victim's role. This worker was also concerned about the inaccuracy of some of the advice police give to victims. She said that the centre had offered to help with training but so far their offer had not been taken up. She also saw a clash of agendas between victims' needs and the police agenda - the victims want protection and the police want prosecutions.

Safer cities

In one area, Safer Cities had identified women's safety as one of their priorities and thus became involved in work on domestic violence. This involvement mainly comprised setting up a support group for workers in the field from various agencies and funding two surveys looking at women's experiences of domestic violence. The coordinator's main criticism of the police was that they went about their work unilaterally and gave the impression that they were the experts and had nothing to learn from other agencies. This was borne out by the fact that they had refused the offer of joint training saying that it was not needed. She made the point, in line with many other respondents, that there was a danger of spending too much time worrying about the role of the police vis-à-vis domestic violence since their role is in most cases very limited.

Solicitors' injunction group

Solicitors in one area have formed a group which has a commitment to dealing with domestic violence victims within 24 hours of them calling, or finding another solicitor to do so if they cannot. The organiser of the group said that the police had come to them for information and advice on the use of injunctions and that she had been involved in training the police about how to use the civil law effectively in domestic violence cases. She felt that it was important to encourage them to appreciate that failure to deploy the criminal law does not amount to failure to deal with that particular case. At present, she feels that the police are very ignorant about injunctions and often think that if an injunction does not carry powers of arrest then there is nothing they can do.

Inter-agency working and inter-agency forums

Most respondents said that the police showed a marked reluctance to be involved in inter-agency working and many felt that they did not have a serious commitment to this kind of work. However, in some areas - particularly those with DVOs - the police were now involved. Indeed, it was sometimes the police who had initiated contact with other agencies.

Much of the inter-agency work was done through various inter-agency groups or forums. Many respondents spoke positively about the role such meetings could take. Bringing the different agencies together was thought to provide a useful forum for information exchange and participants were able to learn more about what other agencies could do and how their roles fitted together. Such meetings were useful in raising awareness about domestic violence and regular meetings helped to keep domestic violence at the top of everyone's agenda. It was thought that inter-agency groups could improve the working relationships between organisations, develop mutual understanding and a common way of dealing with domestic violence. In particular, by developing joint training, a consistent approach to such cases could be developed. By pooling resources, agencies were able to develop initiatives together which they could not do on their own.

On the negative side, respondents criticised inter-agency groups for simply being talking shops and claimed that little of what was said was converted in practice in the agencies represented. Many groups were thought to attend the meetings purely as a public relations exercise and had no intention of changing policy within their own organisations. Some respondents pointed out that as there was very little monitoring, there was no way of knowing whether or not policy was being converted into practice. In addition, the different agendas of each agency can mean developing a common approach is often almost impossible. Finding an agency willing to take the lead in coordinating such a group also seemed to be problematic, as did striking a balance between inviting members who were of enough seniority to have an impact on policy and having people attend who would directly involved in practice.

Some respondents felt that such inter-agency groups had a finite life and if they carried on after, for example, developing a joint policy or training programme, they were in danger of imploding due to internal political wrangling. If they did carry on they were also in danger of preaching to the converted unless they expanded their influence to other groups and other agencies.

DVOs and inter-agency working

Most of the DVOs interviewed for the study had regular contact with other agencies involved with domestic violence. The most frequently contacted were solicitors, housing departments and women's aid/refuges and DVOs were far less reluctant to use women's refuges than their uniformed colleagues. DVOs were rarely in contact with VSS or the probation service. Specialist agencies such as Rape Crisis and counsellors were used less frequently, mainly because fewer victims required their services.

Sixteen of the 24 DVOs were personally involved in an inter-agency group for domestic violence. All of the officers who attended a group found it useful. As one DVO put it:

> yes, very active. All pulling in the same direction. All very interested and genuine. It makes things happen like taking the initiative to work with perpetrators, putting a booklet together, forming the solicitors injunction group.

With one exception those DVOs who did not belong to a group said that they would like to join one:

> *Yes, for feedback from all agencies and to get a better understanding about what they can do and for better liaison.*

The one officer who did not want to belong to a group thought that she could do her job perfectly well without it and said that meeting with other agencies 'hadn't done me any favours'.

Senior police officers and inter-agency working

Fifteen of the 38 senior officers interviewed said that their force was involved in an inter-agency group for domestic violence. Of the remainder, 13 said that they were not and nine did not know[5]. Most of those that were involved in inter-agency working described the main benefits as the sharing of information, knowledge and ideas, and the encouragement of all agencies to pull in the same direction. Others also said that being involved in inter-agency groups had improved the image of the police and encouraged other agencies to use them and to believe that they could and would help. Ten officers voiced some concerns about inter-agency working. These centred around agencies having different agendas and priorities - but most thought that such differences could be dealt with, given time.

Discussion

From the findings reported here, it appears that there is further scope for the development of good relationships between the police and other agencies and in ensuring that other agencies believe the police are dealing with domestic violence incidents properly and effectively. While most respondents accepted that the police had developed good policies on domestic violence, they were less convinced that these had been translated into practice. Relations seemed particularly poor with workers in women's refuges with whom there seemed to be little contact and little mutual understanding.

It was widely thought that DVOs had improved liaison with the police in most areas, and respondents were generally far more satisfied with the response they received from these officers. However, many commented on what little impact the DVOs appeared to have on the general police response.

The CPS appeared to be generally satisfied with both their own response and that of the police to domestic violence cases. However, some said that they could improve their performance by actively supporting victims through the criminal justice process. While insisting that they were prepared to use the full array of charges against defendants in domestic violence cases, most felt that it was better for everyone involved if cases were dealt with in the magistrates' court. By default, this meant they favoured using summary-only offences.

Most respondents saw inter-agency work as having obvious benefits - improving understanding between agencies and developing a more consistent approach for dealing with domestic violence. However, several also felt that inter-agency forums were in danger of becoming simply 'talking shops' and that talk was not translated into practice.

Inter-agency working can improve the response of all agencies in the field of domestic violence, including the police. One of the best ways in which to *actively* cooperate with other agencies appears to be through joint training. This is perhaps the best way to develop a common approach and understanding about domestic violence issues. In addition, inter-agency groups can work well in developing, for example, joint initiatives. Both Nottinghamshire and South Yorkshire police have been particularly active in their inter-agency domestic violence groups and thus have improved relations between the police and other agencies. South Yorkshire have also attempted to reach both practitioners and policy makers through their groups by having individuals forums in each of the force's divisions each of which feeds into a large group for the whole force area.

It is important to bear in mind when developing inter-agency cooperation that very few victims of domestic violence actually go to the police directly (Pahl, 1985) and therefore *all* agencies need to be able to respond as effectively as possible to calls for help. On the other hand, the police offer the only 24 hour emergency service for victims of domestic violence and so by improving their response they may be able to help prevent some of the half a million domestic violence incidents which occur every year in this country[6].

Notes

1. A full report of the findings is contained in Grace, S (1992).
2. The CPS were also asked in more detail about their own practices as these impacted so much on those of the police.
3. At least one representative from each of these agencies was interviewed in each of the five study areas.
4. The infrequent use of Section 23 probably also reflects the very strict conditions which need to be fulfilled before it can be applied.
5. Most of the officers who did not know were shift inspectors and would not therefore have any direct contact with inter-agency work.
6. Estimated by the British Crime Survey, 1992.

References

Dobash, R.E. and Dobash R. (1992) *Women, Violence and Social Change*. London: Routledge.

Hague, G. and Malos, E. (1993) *Domestic Violence: Action for change*. Cheltenham: New Clarion Press.

Home Office circular 60 of 1990 *Domestic Violence*.

Grace, S. (1995) *Policing Domestic Violence in the 1990s*. Home Office Research Study No. 139. London: HMSO.

Mayhew, P.; Aye Maung, N. and Mirrlees-Black, C. (1993) *The 1992 British Crime Survey*. Home Office Research Study No. 132. London: HMSO.

National Inter-Agency Working Party (1992) *Domestic Violence: Report of a national inter-agency working party on domestic violence*. London: Victim Support.

Pahl, J. (1985) *Private Violence and Public Policy*. London: Routledge and Kegan Paul.

15
The probation perspective

A.E.Stelman, B. Johnson, S. Hanley and J. Geraghty

Introduction

In this chapter we attempt to show how the Probation Service
has moved from a position of ignoring the issue of domestic
violence completely to taking a much more active stance towards
working not only with the perpetrators of such violence, but with
victim/survivors and those agencies who work with them as well.
Not only did we spend many years disregarding the widespread
issue of domestic violence as a crime (our justification, in common
with the rest of the criminal justice system, was that there was
no specific offence of domestic violence); we also colluded with
the incidents of domestic violence committed by our clients and
reported to us, by using the rationalisation that we were not
seeing them for that reason and therefore had no business
challenging their attitudes and behaviour towards their partners.
This was the probation equivalent of the 'it's only a domestic'
argument used by other arms of the criminal justice system, and
may well reflect the fact that there are alarmingly few women in
positions of seniority or authority in the criminal justice system
as a whole.

The publication of the Law Commission paper *Domestic
Violence and Occupation of the Family Home* in 1989, followed by
Home Office Circular 60/90 obliged services to recognise that
here was an issue they could no longer disregard. This was
reinforced by the publication of the Victim Support National
Inter-agency Working Party Report and the evidence taken by
the House of Commons Select Committee on Home Affairs. Not
only did that reveal the inadequate responses of Probation

Services in the crime field; worse still, the evidence of many of the Women's Aid organisations pointed up that Probation Services were actually making the problem worse because of their insistence on joint interviewing in cases of separation and divorce where contact or residence arrangements could not be agreed. (This has now been rectified by the National Standard for Family Court Welfare work). All these separate events culminated in the Association of Chief Officers of Probation putting out a position statement about how we should respond to domestic violence in the same year.

Our growing awareness of the issue was helped by the fact that, in many areas of our work, we were having to acknowledge the impact of crime on victims for the first time. In addition we were trying hard to make our involvement in the nebulous concept of crime prevention more hard edged and practical and were beginning to consider how we could offer financial and other resource help to organisations such as Women's Aid.

The national position statement

The basis of the statement is that domestic violence should not be dealt with as a personal pathology, but as an example of the abuse of male power. It follows therefore that training on the politics of gender was viewed as essential and recommended to all services. We know of course that, since that position statement emerged, all work being undertaken by Probation Services and others on the place of women in the criminal justice system has been done against a background of confusion about the impact of the criminal justice system on women offenders.

The statement also recommended that each of the Probation Services in England and Wales should develop a specific policy about domestic violence. At the time of writing about twenty such policies exist.

The position statement also highlights the need to think about employment issues and the likelihood that some women employees will themselves be the victims/survivors of domestic violence. This has implications for work allocation, as well as obliging the organisation to recognise that some of its male employees will also be perpetrators of domestic violence, and that in turn should cause Probation Services to have to consider what measures it would take if such information came to light.

So far we have given an account of how Probation Services

became aware of an issue they had hitherto ignored. What did they actually do about the fact?

Work with perpetrators

Much of the work undertaken with men on the issue of their violence has centred on traditional anger management courses or on voluntary self-help groups, but these approaches have attracted the justifiable criticism that they side-step the basic issue which is an institutionalised and structural belief that men have the right to exert power and control over women. Anger management programmes are predicated on the assumption that people who get angry do so because they have lost control. Domestic violence perpetrators do not lose control. Their behaviour is, in fact a series of methods of gaining control, and is itself very controlled as well as controlling behaviour. Furthermore anger management groups rarely receive the backing of the court by way of a legal requirement to attend.

In the Probation Services which currently run programmes for perpetrators, there is a unanimity of belief that all such programmes should carry a legal requirement. There are two clear reasons for this approach. The first is that clear court sanctions help reassure victim/survivors that the act is being taken seriously and treated as an offence; the second is that we know women endure a very high number of assaults before they finally report to the police. If, as research suggests, those assaults increase in both frequency and degree, then we are talking about a high level of seriousness in terms of offending, repeat victimisation and risk.

The reason for taking such a view is because domestic violence differs from other crime in four major respects.

First, the offence occurs in that most private of institutions, the family home. Secondly, the offender has total or almost total control over the environment in which the offending occurs. This is a factor which makes witness evidence much harder to obtain. Thirdly, and unusually in offending, the victim and perpetrator share the closest possible relationship and often share an enduring mutual responsibility for the upbringing of children. And fourthly, as a consequence of some of the other factors, escape for the victim is difficult or impossible. The unique presence of *all* these factors of course makes domestic violence perfect for formal criminal justice intervention once the necessary work has been done to ensure that women are able to provide evidence in ways that assure their immediate and long-term safety and well-being.

The likelihood of this happening has recently been greatly enhanced by the court of appeal judgement in the case of R v Bird and Holt (October 26 1996). That appeal upheld that when in fear, a defendant should be able to follow the procedure set out in the CPS policy document on domestic violence, and call upon section 23 of the 1988 Criminal Justice Act which permits a decision to be made about evidence being given in written form where fear is an issue for a witness.

So prosecution and additional requirements as part of a probation or combination order is our position, and it is supported by the views of the House of Commons Home Affairs Select Committee where one of the members is reported as saying:

> *What you are saying to the Committee this afternoon confirms all that we have heard so far in this enquiry - that there should be more prosecutions of domestic violence cases...* (para 160).

In working with perpetrators it is essential that the women's perspective is constantly to the fore. Some Probation Services (notably W. Yorkshire) have extended their victim contact scheme to include all offences of domestic violence. We believe that programmes for men should only commence once systems for ensuring that protection for their partners is in place. They also have contact with the domestic violence units in each police division, so that perpetrators' behaviour can be tracked during the currency of the programme itself (thirty weeks), and they can be breached if the police inform the Probation Officers of any incidents to which they have been called. Saying all this however does not necessarily reduce the belief of many refuges that badly needed resources are being put the way of offenders when they need to be used for victim/survivors and their families. In section 4 we outline ways in which Probation Services can offer appropriate support to other agencies and organisations.

The programmes for perpetrators that now operate in many probation services are based largely on the Duluth programmes from Minnesota, distilled by the two Scottish programmes in Edinburgh and Stirling. They are based on a multi-agency approach, utilising the expertise of child centred agencies such as the NSPCC, and Women's Aid. Role play and drama are also used to confront and persuade men to change their behaviour. In a very short time, these programmes have attracted a great deal of positive comment. One example, from Her Majesty's Inspectorate thematic report on probation orders with additional requirements reads as follows:

> *The programme run by x Probation Service was a good example. The offender group was clear, the material and methods very focused and the staff confident about their aims and objectives. This programme, which had rightly gained the respect of sentencers, Probation Officers and offenders, also impressed the Inspectors.* (HMIP, 1995, p60).

The profile of group membership is very diverse. In one of Merseyside's recent groups, Section 39 woundings, rape, and affray were the offences, and two of the offenders (rape and GBH with Intent) were on the programme as part of their prison licence requirement. While physical and/or sexual violence are the offences which bring men onto the programme, their use of all the other forms of abuse such as psychological, economic etc. is alluded to throughout the duration of the programme. A Distance Learning pack on working with domestic violence perpetrators is about to be produced which should be of particular assistance to non specialist practitioners.

Important work is being developed in prisons as well. Leicestershire Probation Service recently ran a group for very violent offenders in HM Prison Gartree, and that needs to be replicated in other places. Probation Service National Standards now require that in all cases in which prisoners are serving 12 months or more for offences of a violent or sexual nature, the Service should seek to trace the victim(s) of those offences for them to be interviewed (if they consent), so that their views can be taken into account in plans for the prisoner's release. Those involved need to be fully aware of the extent to which perpetrators of domestic violence, even when incarcerated, can still seek to use every possible means (including their probation officer) to control the woman or women they have abused.

There are many different groups of stakeholders in the domestic violence programme: victims; offenders; courts; specialist programme providers; referring probation officers; other programme contributors; the Home Office; the community. While each has a different perspective on effectiveness, it is true to suggest that most of the stakeholder groups will be more concerned with outcomes rather than outputs; that is to say, the primary measure of effectiveness is going to be the reduction of re-offending rather than the mere throughput of men on the programme. Measures for offence reduction have to be balanced by qualitative criteria to evaluate effectiveness as well.

Perpetrator programmes must be rigorously evaluated; otherwise the risks to women could well be increased. An in depth research study has been conducted on both the Scottish programmes, and was published recently (Dobash et al, 1996). The research was able to demonstrate programme effectiveness on many different levels. First levels of overt violence were assessed at the time of sentence and then nine months later; secondly other forms of controlling behaviour were reported on; and lastly, the quality of life (using criteria such as fear, self-respect, relaxation etc.) was reported on. The reports came from both perpetrators and victims, and demonstrated that men on the programme performed significantly better on all three dimensions compared with men who had committed similar offences but were sentenced in a variety of different ways, none of which included attendance on the programme.

Because victims \ survivors in domestic violence are so easily identifiable and have such a central part in the process, their views, in terms of impact evaluation are much more relevant than, for example car theft where the offence is largely opportunist and the victim is random not offence specific.

Working with others

The Home Office has done much to encourage and more recently require Probation Services to work in partnership with others, which is particularly relevant in the field of domestic violence, considering out pivotal role with offenders and our involvement with their partners. Our traditional method of doing this has been to try to get other agencies to behave like us. And in respect of the voluntary sector we have a regrettable reputation for colonising agencies and trying to turn them into probation clones.

Perhaps the best example of Probation Services working with others, and in a manner which puts the woman and not the offender at the centre of the picture, is our involvement in domestic violence forums. In the Liverpool forum, the legal subgroup is chaired by a Senior Probation Officer and consists of the police, the CPS, and representatives of local solicitors. The need for a multi-agency approach in a forum is, we think self evident. If we really are serious about the safety of women then we must be prepared to look at offending in its widest dimension and not just focus on the offender.

In the sphere of crime prevention we also have a useful contribution to make. In both Hereford and Worcester and Merseyside the Probation Services have forged partnerships with education departments and helped promote anti-violent relationship programmes in primary and secondary schools. And Merseyside Probation Service's 1A2 programme for perpetrators involves partnership with both Women's Aid and the NSPCC as well as a local drama company.

For many year Probation Services have looked inward and found it hard to link meaningfully with the variety of other organisations and agencies working in the community. Domestic violence has provided an important and timely opportunity to look around and see what others are doing and how we can best contribute. If dealing with domestic violence is central to a community's sense of well-being it is vital that Probation Services focus on how they can contribute. We hope this chapter has outlined some of the ways in which that has been possible and demonstrates the Probation Service's continuing commitment to working with others to combat this long neglected criminal behaviour.

References

Dobash, R., Dobash, R., Cavanagh, K. and Lewis, R. (1996) *A Research Evaluation of Programmes for Violent Men,* Edinburgh: Scottish Office, Central Research Unit

HMIP (1995) *Probation Orders with Additional Requirements.* London: Home Office

Home Office (1990), *Circular 60/90: Domestic Violence.* London: Home Office

House of Commons Home Affairs Committee (1993) *Report of Inquiry into Domestic Violence.* London, Home Office

Law Commission (1992) *Family Law, Domestic Violence and the Occupation of the Family Home.* London: HMSO

National Inter-agency Working Party (1992) *Domestic Violence: Report of a national inter-agency working party on domestic violence.* London: Victim Support.

16
Social service responses to domestic violence: The inter-agency challenge

Audrey Mullender

It is crucial for social services departments (SSDs), and their equivalents in Scotland and Northern Ireland, to engage more fully than has hitherto been the case with the issue of men's abuse of women and its implications for every aspect of assessment, intervention and care. Social services have been slow to recognise the full scope of the changes needed to give women and children the most appropriate forms of help, and they have not been the most active members of inter-agency forums. Nevertheless, it is multi-agency environments which may well provide the spur to action in many areas, allied with pressure from individual staff within social services departments who already understand what is required. This chapter will consider what issues most need to be rethought within social work and what measures can be taken immediately - particularly in the multi-agency contexts of Area Child Protection Committees and inter-agency domestic violence forums - to give women and their children a better chance of living in safety.

Domestic abuse: An unavoidable issue

This country is belatedly facing up to the fact that the abuse of women in intimate relationships is endemic (see, for example, the research by Mooney, 1994). Social workers, like all health and welfare professionals, come into contact with large numbers of women who are experiencing domestic abuse. A half to three quarters of women in refuge samples studied in Britain during the 1980s were found to have sought assistance from the personal social services at some time (Binney *et al.*, 1981, p.19; Pahl, 1985, p.80; Dobash *et al.*, 1985, p.148, Table 10.4) and social workers' reports that at least 1 in 8 of cases involved violence (Leonard and McLeod, 1980, p.44; Borkowski *et al.*, 1983, p.18) were topped by Maynard (1985, p.127) who, as an independent researcher, revealed 1 in 3 of all current case files in a northern town containing 'direct references to domestic violence'. A more recent study, in a multiply deprived London borough, identified woman abuse in 1 in 5 of currently allocated cases (research by Bonnie Miller, cited in London Borough of Hackney, 1994, p.36). Added to this, at least one third of the children on the child protection register there had mothers who were being abused (*ibid.*). Amongst black women, Mama's (1996) research sample of a hundred Asian, African Caribbean and African women in London (who had all experienced housing problems related to domestic violence) included a third overall who had had contact with social services, rising to as many as half the Asian women in the sample.

There is, then, a major challenge to social work to offer an appropriate response to women experiencing abuse, informed by an awareness that particular difficulties are faced by specific groups of women in seeking help. Disabled women, for example, may be trapped at home - where their abuser may also be their carer - without access to information or assistance (London Borough of Hounslow, 1994). Older women may not be taken seriously if they report violence, or may be expected to go on putting up with it because they have done so all their lives, and lesbian women may have particularly strong fears about losing their children because of discriminatory attitudes (Rights of Women Lesbian Custody Group, 1984). Women who have come to this country to marry may be at risk of deportation if they leave the relationship within the first twelve months and can have no recourse to public funds during that time. Training for social workers on violence against women needs to reflect this diversity of situations and needs, as well as the fact that what all women most appreciate from social workers includes practical help - such as direct advice or assistance in getting to a refuge (Binney *et al.*, *op. cit.*, p.20; Pahl, *op. cit.*, p.80; McWilliams and McKiernan, 1993, p.66; Tayside Women and Violence Group, 1994, p.52) and 'knowing the system' well enough to advise on and negotiate with other services if the woman is considering moving on to a new life (Pahl, *loc. cit.*). Women also want the abuse to stop (McGibbon *et al.*, 1989, p.34-5), which may mean helping them to make greater call upon the criminal and civil law to tackle the man's behaviour (albeit in recognition that this may be of limited use until both the law and its implementation are strengthened).

The needs of children living with domestic violence: Messages for Area Child Protection Committees

Often, the first area of work in which social services departments become more aware of domestic violence as an issue, though not necessarily of how to intervene most helpfully, is that of children living in households where men are violent to women. Similarly, one of the inter-agency contexts which is waking up to the issue is that of Area Child Protection Committees which, between them, have a nationwide coverage. This recognition has been slow to come and we are a long way from the child-centred responses to living with violence found in some parts of the USA and Canada - often in multi-agency contexts - such as disclosure work (Children's Subcommittee of the London Coordinating Committee to End Woman Abuse, London, Ontario), therapeutic groups (Mullender, 1994a, 1995), and links with prevention in schools (Mullender, 1994b, though see London Borough of Islington, undated, for an important move in this direction). It has been left to Women's Aid to develop the major national expertise in the UK in work with children who have lived with woman abuse, with the assistance of social services money in some areas (under section 17 of the Children Act 1989) but with more help overall to employ child workers coming from the BBC Children In Need Appeal (letter from Julia Kaufmann to *Community Care*, 11-17 May 1995). Until now there has been a dangerous divide in this country between services for children and services popularly identified as being for women. Yet there are more children than women living in refuges, and Women's Aid has a twenty year history of working with children.

Area Child Protection Committees (ACPCs), in particular - often through a training coordinator with a social services base or background - are beginning to call on Women's Aid for advice and training. Multi-agency events are now the norm. The National Women's Aid Children's Officer had almost daily speaking engagements throughout the Spring of 1997, with a range of academic and professional contributions sharing the platform, and refuge workers, including children's workers, prominent amongst those in attendance alongside every kind of childcare practitioner. Social services department staff and other child protection specialists, including from police and health settings - becoming concerned about the impact of domestic violence on children and the overlap with child abuse - are increasingly able to attend such regional training events.

Often, the most positive approach is to use the occasion to build on work being undertaken by the local ACPC and domestic violence forum, bringing people together to hear about policies being developed and to share their own experiences and expertise. Recent examples include a management-level seminar run by Sheffield ACPC in March 1997, and Birmingham ACPC's well attended training day which has been repeated over several years. Both have made effective use of case study material to encourage professionals to engage with the detail of what needs to change in practice. Major conferences have also been held. One of the largest was organised jointly by Scottish Child and Scottish Women's Aid in the splendid environs of Glasgow City Hall, in June 1995. The pioneers in this field were the Hammersmith and Fulham Domestic Violence Forum and the London Borough of Hackney, both of whom published conference reports (respectively: Holder *et al.*, 1992, and London Borough of Hackney, 1992). These began the flow of UK-produced literature, research and debate which is now actively seeking to meet the needs of children living with domestic violence (see Abrahams, 1994, and particularly Mullender and Morley, 1994).

The impact on children of living with domestic abuse

What is learned at such conferences and from the literature is that considerable emotional disturbance and distress are caused to children by living in environments where their mothers are being abused, but that there is no fixed pattern or syndrome. The NCH Action for Children study (Abrahams, *op. cit.*, pp.34-43) reports effects as diverse as children becoming quiet and clingy, or aggressive and disobedient. Children's responses are affected by factors as divergent as their personalities, their typical reactions to distress, their circumstances and age: for example, pre-school children often demonstrate anxiety in physical ways, such as stomach-aches or headaches, bed-wetting, and sleep disturbance, (Sinclair, 1985, p.88). Indeed, medical services may mistakenly undertake tests to find physical causes for symptoms which are actually the result of living with abuse (Tayside Women and Violence Group, *op. cit.*, p.35) - another reason why agencies need to work hard at learning from one another.

Mothers know that what they suffer personally has an effect on their children; 72 per cent of those interviewed in Evason's research in Northern Ireland (1982) felt there had been an adverse impact. In the NCH Action for Children study (Abrahams, *op. cit.*), eight out of ten women believed their children had become aware of the violence they themselves were experiencing (*op. cit.*, pp.30-32) and 99 per cent knew the children had seen them upset or crying. As many as ten per cent of this sample of women had been sexually abused, and in some cases raped, with children present. It is not the case, therefore, that statutory or voluntary agencies have to discover a 'hidden problem'. What they do need to do is to listen to women and to assist both them and their children to find ways to be safe. Nor do children living with woman abuse fit the currently popular image of 'silent victims'. They use all kinds of coping strategies to try and help their mothers and confront their abusers - from shouting or telephoning for help, to trying to get in the way or force the man to stop. Some social workers may be inclined to interpret this as meaning that the child requires protection through registration or statutory intervention, whereas safety planning with the child and the mother, together with effective action against the man (involving other agencies if appropriate) may be a far more useful course of action to pursue.

Links with child abuse: working with the non-abusing parent

A further reason why inter-agency cooperation in understanding woman abuse is crucial, beyond the impact on children of living with it, is its demonstrated overlap with child abuse; each can be an important indicator for the other - certainly strong enough to point to the need for a fuller social work assessment, and often for safety planning with the parties at risk.

In the recent NCH study (Abrahams, *op. cit.*, pp.30-31), only 44 per cent of mothers said that their partners 'didn't touch the children', that is through deliberate abuse. (See also Bowker *et al.*, 1988 who had even higher figures for overlapping abuse.) Other research (Stark and Flitcraft, 1988; Forman, 1995) has shown that, looked at the other way on, children abused by their fathers also frequently have mothers who have suffered domestic abuse. Yet child protection agencies are not yet making this obvious link or drawing on its corollary: that many more mothers would be able to give their children good care and protection if they themselves were safe. It is a severe indictment of child protection work that abused women in a major American study were, on the contrary, far more likely to have their children removed (Stark and Flitcraft, *op. cit.*, p.106) when the latter were abused than were non-abused women, a clearly punitive response and one which, even in resource, let alone in human terms, does not make sense. These situations of domestic violence are precisely those where there are other options to try which could help a non-abusing parent to parent safely: '[C]ase-workers and clinicians would do well to look toward advocacy and protection of battered mothers as the best available means to prevent current child abuse as well as child abuse in the future' (Stark and Flitcraft, 1985, p.168). This is an important lesson to learn in Britain, where recent research has revealed those child protection cases with the least safety achieved for the child (Department of Health, 1995, p.63, reporting work by Farmer and Owen, 1995) as typically involving violence against the mother. Part of the problem was that the social workers concerned did not know how to tackle the abusive men. Multi-agency forums would seem a good place to begin teasing out how the police and other criminal justice agencies could be brought into the picture so that women and children need not go on living in such extremes of danger.

It is clear from the above that non-abusing abused women are one of our greatest untapped resources for improving what we offer children and, in the present climate, we surely cannot afford to waste such resources. One young mother in a refuge, for example, talked about her abusive partner insisting that their toddler son should remain motionless in his chair whenever he, the man, was around and teasing the child to make him cry. This was not how the woman wanted to care for her son but she had no choice because she was terrified of her abuser. Later, having reached safety in the refuge, she was able to parent to her own standards. The present author saw her little boy running about and playing with other children – a happy child developing normally, simply because his mother has been enabled to care for him.

This does not mean that pressure should be placed on women by social workers to leave, 'for the sake of the children', if this is not what they feel is the best option. It may mean, for example, that the man becomes more unpredictable and dangerous. Women put enormous efforts into shielding and protecting their children, giving them the best care they can manage under the circumstances, and keeping the abuse focused on themselves rather than their children when they can. Domestic violence specialists in local authorities (and, of course, in refuges) often have a more sophisticated understanding of what women are experiencing and how they get themselves and their children through it than do social workers or health visitors. Working together, they may achieve better solutions. One domestic violence coordinator, for example, accompanied a social worker to a case conference which had to decide whether two children's names should stay on the child protection register. The children's developmental milestones and educational achievement were not in question, and their mother was undoubtedly caring, but she continued to suffer severe assaults periodically. Some of the professionals present were arguing for registration to continue. The coordinator helped them to see the woman concerned as a good mother who, under dreadful circumstances, was still managing to provide an acceptable standard of care. She could sense when an attack was coming and get the children out of the way. By thinking things through in more detail, the case conference felt able to take the children off the register and to move into supporting this mother rather than judging her.

There is no research evidence that abused women are more likely to abuse their children and, although conflicts of interest can occur (Debbonaire, 1994), in the majority of cases, working in partnership with mothers is likely to be the best way forward. Furthermore, in cases where women *have* neglected or abused their children, it is always important to consider whether this has been coerced by a male abuser, or otherwise caused by his behaviour. The judgmental accusation against abused women of 'failure to protect' their children, in particular, is not a helpful attribution of blame in situations where it is the abusing man's actions which need to be tackled and where the woman ought to be able to look to the authorities for understanding and support.

When abusive men drag children into the misery, degradation and hurt of domestic violence and abuse, this is their responsibility and not the woman's. It is also the abuser's responsibility when he cuts the woman off from family, community and health and welfare agency supports which could help with child care (London Borough of Hackney, 1994, p.43). It is important in social work and other professional recording of cases that male perpetrators are clearly indicated as such and that there is an end to muddled thinking about 'violent' or 'dangerous families' (Mullender, 1996, Chapter 7). Questions such as 'What is this mother going to do to protect the children from this?' or 'Why doesn't she leave?' are oppressive. More useful questions include: 'What is this man doing to this woman and children?' and 'What are we going to do to confront or control him, while consulting and supporting her?'. Creating the conditions in which non-abusing abused women are empowered to protect themselves and their children (Kelly, 1994) needs to become a major feature of social work intervention and of wider Area Child Protection Committee concerns.

Inter-agency domestic violence forums

In order to improve services, agencies - including social services - need to move forward together, with each developing a clear underpinning policy and a positive programme for change. This is necessary, not least because women often have to approach many different agencies before they receive an appropriate response, and because the most helpful response is multi-faceted. Most of the best practice in social work settings has been developed in a context of inter-agency cooperation. Increasingly, such cooperation is being formalised in inter-agency domestic violence forums, with a wide range of statutory and voluntary agencies in membership.

Where they work well, such forums are an essential way of improving the services abused women receive, by pressing each member agency to be more rigorous in its response to the issue and by coordinating overall responses to women, children and men. At their best, they can identify and tackle the organisational obstacles to confronting male power and empowering women, forge alliances for change, and highlight practice which needs to improve and points at which responses fall down between agencies. For example, social workers cannot effectively help women and children who have nowhere to live and those social workers in Scotland with probation responsibilities who run or refer men to court-mandated programmes rely on the police and Crown Prosecution Service (or equivalent in Scotland) to arrest and prosecute. In other words, a central aim of any forum must be to avoid the situation where, because no one statutory agency has owned the problem, it has been shamefully neglected by all.

From the start, social service and equivalent departments have been invited onto the majority of domestic violence forums but have, not untypically, been slow to recognise why they need to participate so that others have experienced difficulty in getting them effectively on board. Local authorities have often played a less active role through social services than through their women's, or equal opportunities, or community safety units, for example. Housing departments, too, have perhaps been more readily recognised as very centrally involved in domestic abuse issues than have social services. It is extremely rare for SSDs to have played a key initiating role in setting up a forum though, in Leeds, Social Services is one of the originating funders of the Inter-Agency Project.

The increasing specialisation within their own services, and the split between purchasing and providing functions, can tend to mean that social services departments are unsure even who to send when they are invited to join a forum. Some may have begun thinking about its relevance for child protection *or* for community care, so may send a representative of one or other of these spheres, but there is very rarely an across-the-board acknowledgement of its importance. Those local authorities which *have* reached such a recognition and which have produced clear policies and guidelines for social workers on domestic abuse, tend to be amongst those with the most active inter-agency links - for example, Nottinghamshire was early in the field on both counts (with guidelines in 1989 and the conference which spawned its forum in 1990; see Nottinghamshire County Council, 1989 and 1990). And, looked at the other way round, no active inter-agency forum can afford not to involve social services in meetings and in multi-agency training, in view of the scope of its work (Hague *et al.*, 1996, pp.55-56).

Some examples . . .

Leeds

Perhaps the best known and most highly developed multi-agency forum is the Leeds Inter-Agency Forum which manages the Leeds Inter-Agency Project (Women and Violence). Included in well over 100 agencies with which the Project has close links, including several which are women-only and/or black-only projects, are Women's Aid and Sahara, a specialist refuge for black women. Leeds was amongst the first to make advances right across the areas of most concern to social workers, and it has remained a leader in both the clarity of its analysis of the implications of men's abuse for all the public services and its consequent breadth of approach.

In respect of adult services, for example, from the earliest days of the community care reforms, a sub-forum was established on 'Care in the Community: Violence Against Women By Known Men', and the Inter-Agency Project took on the management of a Community Care Partnership Adviser, working specifically with social services and health. Excellent pioneering work was then possible in fostering joint planning by health, social services, housing and the voluntary sector, leading to the inclusion of a specific volume on 'Women Experiencing Violence by Known Men' in the Community Care Plan for the city (Leeds City Council *et al.*, 1992/93 and subsequently). The Project placed confidential counsellors in GP surgeries because many women were seeking treatment or advice from that source, including Asian women who were afraid to go anywhere else for help. It was recognised, too, that a negative impact on women's mental health, as one of the observable results of violence and abuse, can lead to misdiagnosis (Ingram, 1993/94, and see Rosewater, 1988, for research backing for this view), with consequent training needs for approved social workers and other community-based mental health practitioners.

On the child care side, the Inter-Agency Project's Steering Group was one of the first bodies in the UK to emphasise the 'vulnerability of children living in violent homes and the need for coordinated safety strategies with child protection agencies and schools' (Leeds inter-Agency Project, 1993, ch.4, p.1). This approach, in that it emphasises safety planning and not just investigation, remains a model which others could usefully follow. Further positives were the acceptance of responsibility to 'link work to offer support to children, with protection and support for the non-abusing parent', and the recognition that abused women may themselves be survivors of child abuse. The work was strengthened, too, by the involvement throughout of the black women's sub-forum and an emphasis on outreach work to black families.

All relevant organisations were seen, from the start, as having a role to play in 'preventing violence and abuse of women by men known to them' and in 'making women's safety a reality in Leeds'. They have been able to look to the Inter-Agency Project for information, for multi-agency training, and for support with particularly complex cases - all of which are the constant requests of social workers around the country as awareness of men's abuse on women and children continues to rise.

Cleveland

A more recent development, again of keen interest to social workers, is the Cleveland Multi-Agency Domestic Violence Forum. Since 1994, it has employed a Coordinator who is managerially hosted by the Social Services Department (of Cleveland until local government reorganisation, and of Middlesbrough since then), though physically located in an outreach building alongside two voluntary projects. Social services interest in this work has been forthcoming from a senior managerial and elected member level, and has been expressed through active representation on the Forum.

The Coordinator began her task by auditing the existing situation and assessing what needed to change. It was immediately apparent to her that a clear policy was essential, together with guidelines for best practice by staff, and these guidelines were approved in 1995. They are regarded as a crucially important foundation for a complete change of attitude within the delivery of professional services. With the same aim in mind, the Coordinator reached agreement that a member of the training division of the then Cleveland Social Services would be assigned to the Forum. The approach taken was to train this trainer, who would then be able to pass on her learning to at least one immediate colleague and share the task of instituting a thorough-going programme of in-house training. This was backed up by the preparation of an advice pack, along the lines of training and resource materials produced in Hammersmith and Fulham (London Borough of Hammersmith and Fulham, 1991). Input has also been offered, by the Coordinator herself, to local social work qualifying and post-qualifying programmes in higher education settings.

A Children's Sub-Group, linked to a multi-agency task group, began exploring the issue of child protection and domestic violence. One problem of multi-agency relevance recognised by the Coordinator, in the light of a growing (if belated) awareness of the impact of domestic violence on children, was a tendency to place children too readily on the child protection register and a reluctance to remove their names, once on. She identified a need for professionals to become more accustomed to debating the precise implications of domestic abuse for children so that they could judge levels of risk more accurately, and for training on domestic abuse to extend to the highest levels of decision-making.

Overall, as is now beginning to be recognised nationally (Department of Health, *op. cit.*, p.55), there remains a need to make a shift from a predominantly 'section 47' (of the Children Act, 1989) child protection emphasis to a greater balance with 'section 17' family support. The time and effort being swallowed up in child protection work, often of a precautionary nature with little practical outcome for families, should not be outweighing the resources devoted to a broader, preventive approach to recognising children's needs and families' capacities to cope (including those of lone mother families), if they have adequate support. In recognition of this need for a well thought out and consistent approach to the children of abused women (and to the women themselves and their abusers), Cleveland's Area Child Protection Committee established a Domestic Violence Task Group which, in March 1996, launched its practice guidance *Domestic Violence: Whose Problem Is It?* at a well-attended multi-agency event. In this way, it faced the key challenge of rethinking typical responses.

Since the reorganisation of local government, the social services' responsibility in the former Cleveland area has passed to four unitary authorities and this fragmentation has meant that the pace of progress has inevitably slowed, at least for a time. The Forum and the Coordinator now operate across the new authorities, with priorities and levels of commitment and of resourcing inevitably varying between the four. Each has its own district sub-group which may eventually become an autonomous forum. The former Children's Sub-Group of the Forum has not continued in its previous form, but Hartlepool has its own children's sub-group and the Forum as a whole benefits from its work. Perhaps the most positive aspect of the current picture is that the practice guidance launched in 1996 remains in use in three out of the four authorities.

What multi-agency forums can encourage SSDs to achieve

Amongst over 200 inter-agency domestic violence initiatives, the above are necessarily only examples, with some attempt to emphasise social work-related activity and relevance. Whilst no effort to work together for change is likely to be unproblematic (there can be mutual mistrust or self-congratulatory complacence, for example), coordinated inter-agency responses can clearly assist in the establishment of formal policies, in multi-agency training, in fostering best practice, and in improved data collection, collaboration and liaison. All of these are needed in social service settings, as elsewhere.

Those social services departments which have taken the most positive approach have typically started with the introduction of an overall policy statement, or of good practice guidelines, outlining the standard of service which abused women should be able to expect to receive. Social workers in all duty settings, for example, can help those women who may want to leave their partners to access appropriate help from refuge and other temporary accommodation, as well as sources of financial assistance, and sympathetic solicitors, doctors, health visitors, and housing officers. Other important issues highlighted in documents aimed at social work staff include the particular care required with confidentiality (since revealing the woman's whereabouts can be extremely dangerous), as well as the need to support the woman through her approach to other agencies, to keep good records (of potential importance in establishing eligibility for other forms of help), and to undertake safety planning with the woman for herself and her children. Such planning may focus either on reaching safety now, or on being able to do so in any future emergency.

Consistency of help requires raised awareness through training. Inter-agency training can, in addition, help to improve liaison between relevant services. The Leeds Inter Agency Project and the Cleveland Domestic Violence Coordinator are both stressing the need to train the trainers in social services so that there can be a cascade effect of knowledge through the agency. Otherwise, the sheer numbers of staff needing to be aware of the issues is overwhelming. There is no member of a social services' workforce in direct contact with the public who does not need some awareness; domestic violence is not only an issue for duty teams, approved social workers and child care practitioners.

Inter-agency forums therefore probably offer the only possible way of moving forward on the scale required. They also offer the possibility of mounting training events which encompass a more complex and appropriate understanding of women and children's needs and of men's behaviour because they bring together a wide range of experience. Overlapping training needs include: the development of anti-racist services; the use of interpreters; legal, financial and housing rights; and comprehensive assessments of women's needs, including women who are older and/or disabled and/or lesbian.

Agency-wide improvements within social services, and in multi-agency coordination, will only be maximised when there is good quality information as a basis for planning. An enormous amount could be achieved by including domestic abuse as a specific category in referral and assessment forms, and intake or duty records in social services departments; it should also feature in all agency monitoring exercises on the work being undertaken by staff (McGibbon *et al.*, 1989, p.15). None of this is tending to happen currently, with cases being recorded under general headings such as 'family problems' or 'family work'.

One development which can certainly help to keep domestic abuse to the forefront of planning is the establishment of specialist posts. Typically, they concentrate on improving liaison with Women's Aid and other relevant women's groups, including those for black women, as well as working to develop their department's own response. Initiatives around the country have flourished, in particular, where inter-agency work has already been strongly established. The London Borough of Newham, for example, was able to create two social work posts to work half time in Social Services and half time in the voluntary sector - Newham Asian Women's Project and Newham Action Against Domestic Violence - one post designated for an Asian woman and the other for a Caribbean woman. A practice-based role, aimed at supporting and empowering women through direct work with them and their children, combined neatly with an inter-departmental policy development and liaison role. In Bradford, a post of community care officer was introduced, split half time with Keighley Domestic Violence Forum. Its funding base in a health trust was intended to give the post-holder greater freedom to work for change both in social service and in health provision. In Leeds, the Inter Agency Project was an obvious choice to take on the supervision of a post designed to focus on developing training and more effective responses in social services to the issue of men's violence to women.

Liaison within and between the statutory and voluntary sectors is crucial. In inner-city areas, for example, support teams working with women in bed-and-breakfast provision, hostels and homeless families units all need to be brought into the picture. Coordination needs to build on strengths already in place, particularly in women's organisations. Social services departments need to resist the tendency, in forging these links, to act as if they have just invented the issue of domestic abuse and to ensure that they respect external expertise (including in the field of child protection - Singh, 1991, pp.4-5 - where, after all, it was women's groups who were amongst the first to 'hear' and believe survivors' accounts of child sexual abuse), as well as the right of other agencies to arrive at their own policies on confidentiality, appropriate organisational structures, and so on. This remains important, even when social services departments fund posts in refuges and other projects.

Conclusion

Social workers and care managers working with all user groups need a knowledge of domestic abuse and how to respond. This is by no means just a child care matter. Workers may, for example, come across older women who have suffered abuse for years, women with disabilities caused by their abuse or which compound the difficulties of escaping from it, women who have developed mental health problems as a result of abuse, or others who misuse alcohol or other substances to deaden its impact. There is no area of practice where a knowledge of domestic violence is not relevant. Each social services department, as the lead agency for community care, needs to recognise its special responsibility to ensure that women's needs are met in all the above contexts. We can no longer simply say that there is no 'statutory' responsibility for domestic violence; it should form part of comprehensive assessment and intervention in all medical and welfare contexts, so community care planners at authority-wide and individual levels need to know about it. So, also, do those responsible for writing the new children's services plans if they accept the forceful argument that children living with domestic violence are children in need.

There is an urgent need to set appropriate policies and information systems in place in SSDs, so that more effective responses can be established across the board, and to back these with support and training for professional and other staff. A more proactive perspective affords the opportunity to recognise that domestic violence is not a new problem situated in some detached and as yet undiscovered segment of the population. Rather, though it remains true that the full extent of men's abuse of women remains hidden, abused women are already evident in large numbers, scattered across existing caseloads and in the communities of need currently being served. What needs to change is the response they receive.

Increasingly, we can draw on pockets of good practice around the country, developed in a multi-agency context, to demonstrate the way forward. Partnership with other agencies, such as the police, Women's Aid, and housing bodies - including through the burgeoning number of inter-agency forums - is crucial. At the same time, social workers need to work in partnership with women and children as potential survivors of abuse and as the experts on their own lives. Taking a lead in this from women's organisations, being woman-centred as well as child-centred means being non-judgemental of women who are forced to make near impossible choices in life-threatening circumstances. As the statutory sector has traditionally pursued patriarchal agendas, there will always need to be special efforts to keep women's perspectives - and hence women and children's safety - to the fore.

[Editors note: Since this chapter was written the 'Making an Impact' training materials and reader have been produced by the Department of Health (see chapter 4). At the time of publication, good practice with families where there is domestic violence is being mapped by the Joseph Rowntree foundation (by a research team of Audrey Mullender, Marianne Hester, Cathy Humphreys and Gill Hague)]

References

Abrahams, C. (1994) *The Hidden Victims: Children and domestic violence.* London: NCH Action for Children

Binney, V., Harkell, G. and Nixon, J. (1981) *Leaving Violent Men: A study of refuges and housing for abused women.* Leeds: Women's Aid Federation England (Reprinted, Bristol: Women's Aid Federation (England), 1988, with new foreword)

Borkowski, M., Murch, M. and Walker, V. (1983) *Marital Violence: The community response*. London: Tavistock

Bowker, L. H., Arbitell, M. and McFerron, J. R. (1988) 'On the relationship between wife beating and child abuse' in Yllö. K. and Bograd, M. *Feminist Perspectives on Wife Abuse*. Newbury Park, California: Sage

Children's Subcommittee of the London Coordinating Committee to End Woman Abuse, London, Ontario (1994) 'Make a difference: How to respond to child witnesses of woman abuse', in Mullender and Morley, *op. cit.*

Cleveland Area Child Protection Committee (1995) *CACPC Practice Guidance. Domestic Violence: Whose problem is it?* Middlesbrough: CACPC

Debbonaire, T. (1994) 'Work with children in Women's Aid refuges and after', in Mullender and Morley, *op. cit.*

Department of Health (1995) *Child Protection: Messages from research*. London: HMSO

Dobash, R. E., Dobash, R. P., and Cavanagh, K. (1985) 'The contact between battered women and social and medical agencies', in Pahl (1985), *op. cit.*

Evason, E. (1982) *Hidden Violence*. Belfast: Farset Press

Farmer, E. and Owen, M. (1995) *Child Protection Practice: Private risks and public remedies*. London: HMSO

Forman, J. (1995) *Is There a Correlation Between Child Sexual Abuse and Domestic Violence? An exploratory study of the links between child sexual abuse and domestic violence in a sample of intrafamilial child sexual abuse cases*. Lawson's Building, 1700 London Road, Glasgow G32 8XD: Women's Support Project (Reprint of an earlier, undated report)

Hague. G., Malos, E. and Dear, W. (1996) *Multi-Agency Work and Domestic Violence*. Bristol: Policy Press

Holder, R., Kelly, L. and Singh, T. (1992) *Suffering in Silence: Children and young people who witness domestic violence*. London: Hammersmith and Fulham Domestic Violence Forum (Available from Community Safety Unit, Hammersmith Town Hall, King Street, London W6 9JU)

Ingram, R. (1993/94) 'Violence from known men', *OpenMind,* 66, December/January, pp.18-19

Kelly, L. (1994) 'The interconnectedness of domestic violence and child abuse: Challenges for research, policy and practice', in Mullender and Morley, *op. cit.*

Leeds City Council, Leeds Health Authority, Leeds Family Health Services Authority, and Voluntary Action Leeds (1992/93) *Final*

Draft Community Care Plan for Women Subject to Violence by a Known Man, Leeds

Leeds Inter-Agency Project (1993) *Information Pack.* c/o CHEL, 26 Roundhay Road, Leeds LS7 1AB: Leeds Inter-Agency Project

Leonard, P. and McLeod, E. (1980) *Marital Violence: Social Construction and Social Service Response: A pilot study report.* Coventry: Department of Applied Social Studies, University of Warwick

London Borough of Hackney (1993) *The Links between Domestic Violence and Child Abuse: Developing services.* London: London Borough of Hackney

London Borough of Hackney (1994) *Good Practice Guidelines: Responding to domestic violence.* London: London Borough of Hackney, Women's Unit

London Borough of Hammersmith and Fulham (1991) *Challenging Domestic Violence: A training and resource pack for anyone who wants to address domestic violence in their work or community setting.* London: London Borough of Hammersmith and Fulham, Community Safety Unit

London Borough of Hounslow (1994) *Domestic Violence - Help, Advice and Information for Disabled Women.* London: London Borough of Hounslow

London Borough of Islington (undated) *STOP - Striving to Prevent Domestic Violence: An activity pack for working with children and young people.* London: London Borough of Islington, Women's Equality Unit

Mama, A. (1996) *The Hidden Struggle: Statutory and voluntary Sector responses to violence against black women in the home.* (2nd Ed.) London: Whiting and Birch

Maynard, M. (1985) 'The response of social workers to domestic violence' in Pahl (1985), *op. cit.*

McGibbon, A., Cooper, L. and Kelly, L. (1989) *'What Support?' Hammersmith and Fulham Council Community Police Committee Domestic Violence Project. An exploratory study of Council policy and practice, and local support services in the area of domestic violence within Hammersmith and Fulham. Final report.* London: Child Abuse Studies Unit, Polytechnic of North London

McWilliams, M. and McKiernan, J. (1993) *Bringing It Out In the Open: Domestic violence in Northern Ireland.* Belfast: HMSO

Mooney, J. (1994) *The Hidden Figure: Domestic Violence in north London.* London: London Borough of Islington, Police and Crime Prevention Unit

Mullender, A. (1994a) 'Groups for child witnesses of woman abuse' in

Mullender and Morley, *op. cit.*

Mullender, A. (1994b) 'School-based work: education for prevention' in Mullender and Morley, *op. cit.*

Mullender, A. (1995) 'Groups for children who have lived with domestic violence: learning from North America', *Groupwork*, 8(1), pp.79-98.

Mullender, A. (1996) *Rethinking Domestic Violence: The social work and probation response.* London: Routledge

Mullender, A. and Morley, R. (eds.) (1994) *Children Living with Domestic Violence: Putting men's abuse of women on the child care agenda.* London: Whiting and Birch

Nottinghamshire County Council (1989) *Domestic Violence - Guide to Practice: Practice guidelines to assist staff dealing with situations involving domestic violence.* West Bridgford, Nottingham: Nottinghamshire County Council

Nottinghamshire County Council (1990) *Domestic Violence Conference Report.* West Bridgford, Nottingham: Nottinghamshire County Council

Pahl, J. (ed.) (1985) *Private Violence and Public Policy: The needs of battered women and the response of the public services.* London: Routledge and Kegan Paul

Rights of Women Lesbian Custody Group (1984) *Lesbian Mothers on Trial: A report on lesbian mothers and child custody.* London: Rights of Women

Rosewater, L. B. (1988) 'Battered or schizophrenic? Psychological tests can't tell' in Yllö, K. and Bograd, M., *Feminist Perspectives on Wife Abuse.* Newbury Park, California: Sage

Sinclair, D. (1985) *Understanding Wife Assault: A training manual for counsellors and advocates.* Toronto, Ontario (from Ontario Government Bookstore, Publications Services Section, 880 Bay Street, Toronto, Ontario M7A 1N8)

Singh, T. (1991) 'Working Together Under the Children Act': WAFE Submission to the Department of Health, Bristol: Women's Aid Federation (England)

Stark, E. and Flitcraft, A. (1985) 'Woman-battering, child abuse and social heredity: What is the relationship?' in Johnson, N. (ed) *Marital Violence.* London: Routledge and Kegan Paul

Stark, E. and Flitcraft, A. (1988) 'Women and children at risk: A feminist perspective on child abuse' *International Journal of Health Services*, 18(1), 97-118

Tayside Women and Violence Group (1994) *Hit or Miss: An exploratory study of the provision for women subjected to domestic violence in Tayside Region.* Dundee: Tayside Regional Council, Equal Opportunities Unit

17
Inter-agency work with children and young people

Davina James-Hanman

In the development of inter-agency working on domestic violence, it is rare that either work with children and young people or the provision of services for them have been in the forefront. Work has tended instead to focus on services used by women; improving the police response, providing training for local authority staff, producing information and so on. This work is clearly necessary but it has meant that not only have the effects of domestic violence on children and young people traditionally taken second place but also that work on domestic violence generally has focused on improving services to women who have already experienced domestic violence rather than on preventative work. The lack of education initiatives aimed specifically at children and young people becomes even more marked when Britain's experience is compared with other countries such as Australia, Canada, New Zealand and several states in the USA. In these areas, much more extensive work has taken place not only to explicitly support children and young people who are experiencing or witnessing domestic violence but also to educate children and young people generally about the issue.

This is not to say that the issue has been ignored altogether in this country. Women's Aid, more than any other single agency has developed work in this area over the past decade but even here, it has historically taken second place to services to women. This has been less because of the importance placed by Women's Aid on the issue and more because funding for employing Children's Development Workers has been so poor. For example, in London, the main funder of refuges is the

London Borough Grants Committee who only fund refuge workers and do not fund staff to work with children. Hence most London refuges must raise funds each year for the salaries of any Children's Workers despite the fact that children represent two-thirds of refuge residents. The annual BBC Children in Need appeal gives more money to support children's work in refuges than every Social Services department in the country added together. This chronic underfunding means that Children's Development Workers are rarely in a position to undertake extensive educational work externally to the refuge although there are several outstanding examples of support work which has been developed internally in refuges and in rare instances, with external bodies.

Just as refuge workers working with women have become involved in lobbying, publicising and training on domestic violence in other agencies which are commonly used by their residents, Children's Development Workers in refuges have begun doing the same with agencies with whom the children and young people in the refuge have contact. Thus, Children's Development Workers have been liaising with and giving talks in schools, running workshops and lobbying Education Departments and Youth Services to put the issue of domestic violence and children on their agenda. However, this inter-agency work has tended to exist outside of any formal structures which may exist to coordinate a multi-agency approach to domestic violence. Education departments are rarely represented on inter-agency fora unless a specific initiative is being undertaken.

Nevertheless, as a consequence of the efforts of Women's Aid, along with other initiatives such as several research projects concerning domestic violence and children being published within a relatively short period of time, there has been an explosion of interest in the effects of domestic violence on children and young people over the past few years.

This has led to some inter-agency domestic violence fora turning their attention to educational projects aimed at children and young people as part of their work. One of the first to do this was Hammersmith and Fulham's Domestic Violence Forum who, in 1992, hosted a conference called 'Suffering in Silence?'. The conference, which later produced a report of the same name, focused specifically on the impact of domestic violence on children.

Other fora around the country have followed suit and have

also begun inter-agency work on education including Charnwood, Cleveland, initially Edinburgh and now the Central Regional Council, Fife, Hackney, Islington, Keighley, Leeds, Rugby, and Wolverhampton as well as others.

What sort of projects have there been?

Below is a selected sample of some of the inter-agency projects which have been developed around the country:

Charnwood Domestic Violence Panel
In this area, the work was initiated by a local secondary school who liaised with the local Domestic Violence Forum. Pupils from all years participated in learning about domestic violence and whole school assemblies were held.

Cleveland Domestic Violence Forum
In Cleveland, the Domestic Violence Forum formed a children's sub-group which ran support groups for children directly affected by domestic violence. Out of this work came a need to do more general educational work and a pack for training teachers was developed.

Welsh Women's Aid
XYZero, an inter-agency project initiated by Welsh Women's Aid and Save The Children, was established to produce an educational pack for young people in the age range of 11 - 14. To begin this process, extensive consultation took place involving childcare workers, social workers, refuge workers and other organisations working to produce educational packs. In addition, survivors of domestic violence were also consulted as were young people within the target age range. The project was established for three years.

Edinburgh
Edinburgh District Council Women's Unit was the first council to try to research children and young people's knowledge of and attitudes towards the issue of domestic violence. They targeted adolescents in their survey and their published summary of the results, reproduced below, makes for sobering reading:

- Knowledge of adolescents about domestic violence is poor.

Guessing responses and error rates are high.

- Boys of all ages are more accepting of violence towards women than are girls.
- The presence of a rationalisation ending to domestic violence scenarios (i.e. where an 'excuse' is offered) affects the rating of them so as to make the violence more acceptable. Such 'rationalisations (e.g. 'she made me do it') are typically made by male abusers.
- *Only a minimal exposure to information about domestic violence is required* (my emphasis) to influence attitudes in the direction of decreasing its acceptability.
- Violence directed towards non-marital partners is rated as less acceptable than the same action directed towards wives.
- Both girls and boys report that they are very likely to use physical violence in their own personal relationships in the future.
- A large majority of students report personal experience of the use of physical force in family relationships and friendships.
- As students get older, there is an increase in the use of physical force by parents and guardians against girls and a decrease in its use against boys. The highest level of the use of physical force by parents and guardians is against year 1 boys and year 5 girls.

These results make it clear as to why educational work on domestic violence is so important not only in terms of providing support to children for whom domestic violence is part of their lives, but also to educate children who currently have no or incorrect information and knowledge about the issue.

Fife Zero Tolerance Campaign

The Zero Tolerance campaign, itself an inter-agency initiative, worked in conjunction with Fife Education Services to develop a comprehensive youth strategy which involved a range of work including:

- production of a young persons information and support pack
- a peer education theatre project
- an Elastica concert
- an arts project produced by child and adolescent sexual abuse survivors

- workshops with children and young people
- cascade training for part-time youth workers
- an extremely successful youth conference

Different styles

The nature of inter-agency educational initiatives in this country have varied enormously in both their scope and impact. The following factors have been the major variables which are explained in more detail below:

- the location of the individual or organisation who initiated the process;
- the scale of the work envisaged or accomplished;
- the degree to which the work was located within a formal educational framework;
- whether the work was carried out by a specific, and often external, group or whether the initiative aimed to equip teachers and / or youth workers to do the work themselves;
- whether the aim was to educate children and young people or to offer support to those children and young people experiencing or witnessing domestic violence;
- whether the work directly or indirectly addressed the issue of domestic violence.

Who started it?

The location of the initiating individual or organisation appears to be a crucial element in both shaping the framework of the work and in impacting on likely success. For example, in some areas the initiative began from the local authority, sometimes within the Education Department itself and sometimes from other departments, most likely, Women's Equality Units or Women's Officers within Equal Opportunities Units. In other areas the initiative has come from individual schools or from inter-agency projects with paid staff and in still others, the initiative has come from the local Women's Aid group.

The position both of the individual within their own organisation and the position of their organisation within the local area impacted on how successful subsequent work was. In some areas contact between Women's Aid workers and local teachers was very successful in 'by-passing' the bureaucracy and getting something done. In other areas (e.g. Charnwood), the school invited in other agencies which was much less problematic than the situation in those areas where a local domestic violence forum was trying to get into schools. In the case of the latter, success was highly dependent on the willingness of local head teachers, governing bodies and the education department to embark upon this work.

How big was it?

In some areas, the project was carefully planned and had pre-determined limits so that it became difficult to respond to unforeseen needs. For example, in one area, the project had not considered supporting children who became distressed as a consequence of domestic violence being discussed in their school or youth club. When it became clear that support services were needed, all available resources for the project had been allocated and the project was thus unable to respond to this newly identified need. In other areas, a single school or youth club initiated the process and as such the project never grew beyond the confines of that particular school.

In most cases, however, the projects evolved into new areas of work as it became obvious that the current limits would not be sufficient to achieve the initial objectives. In such projects, there was more flexibility, particularly within resource terms, to respond to new data as it was gathered and as the projects progressed, more and more agencies were drawn into the process.

How formal was the work?

It appears that work falls primarily within two major areas; either work began in a policy context and developed into direct work with children and young people or initiatives began with direct educational work and in a few instances, later became formalised at a policy level.

In terms of embedding the work into the educational system in such a way that the initiatives were maintained, it would seem from experience to date that beginning the work at a policy level is more successful. However, it must be remembered that this is only one definition of what constitutes success and there are other criteria which should be considered before assuming that policy work is the only way to begin. For example, it is also true that beginning at this point means that the implementation process takes far longer and that there may be considerably more resistance with which to cope than if the initiative began from a practitioner level. Indeed, any fora considering embarking upon education work, will need to discuss at length what 'success means and how it can be evaluated.

Who did the work?

In some areas, it was an external group which put together a 'package' to take into schools and youth clubs. All that was required from the Educational Department or individual schools was permission and the allocation of time. In other areas, materials have been developed for teachers and youth workers themselves to use. Both approaches have advantages and drawbacks. External groups going into schools and youth clubs have the advantage of lessening the work required by teachers or youth workers. It is also easier to retain control over the content of what is taught and in most cases they have the advantage of being interesting and new to the children and young people.

The second approach which requires teachers and youth workers to educate themselves about the issues and monitoring the style or content of the programme is much more problematic. However, professionals have the advantage of, in most cases, having an on-going relationship with the children and young people which makes for higher levels of trust and also means that work can continue over a period of time rather than in a short burst which may not be sufficient for the attitudinal changes we are seeking.

Support or educate?

In one inter-agency forum with a paid coordinator, (Keighley) the work began with the aim of educating children and young people but soon expanded into providing direct support to young people so that they had somewhere to go with their feelings that the work evoked. The Keighley Domestic Violence Forum thus provided support and training to local youth counselling projects so that they could take up the role of supporting individual young people. This lasted throughout the life of the project.

The project quickly found itself overwhelmed with requests for information and invitations to speak as their work was something of a rarity and they found themselves performing a balancing act to ensure that their primary aim of producing a resource led by young people was achieved.

Nevertheless, the project did become involved in policy development and actively contributed to policy initiatives being undertaken by the local authority. The project was extremely successful in achieving its primary aims and objectives in youth work, but had much less success, with one notable exception, within the schools system. The project lasted three years and towards the end, schools were finally beginning to respond. This serves to highlight the length of time that needs to be allocated to building up good relationships with agencies (in this instance, schools) who have not to date played a full role in inter-agency responses to domestic violence.

In another area (Wolverhampton), the initiative to work with children and young people arose from the collaborative efforts of the local domestic violence forum, a theatre company and a 'Workers-in-training' scheme. Here too, the aim was to raise awareness and educate children and young people about domestic violence. Although at its end, the project identified that support services were clearly needed, this was not an objective of the project and indeed was not addressed as part of it. Surprisingly, therefore, the project had much greater success with schools (who were their primary target) than the previous project mentioned although it is likely that this can be attributed to other factors, in particular, the use of a theatre group to introduce the topic of domestic violence to children and young people rather than relying on teachers to take the initiative.

Yet a third approach was taken in another project (Cleveland) where the work began as a way of providing support to children and young people who were experiencing or witnessing domestic violence. The project has now moved on to developing an educational resource for teachers and youth workers to raise the issue of domestic violence with children and young people who had had no personal experience of it.

Direct or oblique approach?

In one area, all of the educational work with children and young people was conducted without any direct reference to domestic violence. Instead, children and young people were taught skills on assertiveness and conflict resolution. As a consequence, children and young people were not exposed to information about domestic violence or the gender dynamics involved in this issue. This clearly brings us back to the debate about how success is defined.

Although this oblique approach was not the aim of another project which ran support groups for children personally affected by domestic violence, the workers soon discovered that the children were sometimes reluctant to directly discuss their experiences. As part of the philosophy of the project involved allowing the children and young people to direct the agenda, the workers soon stopped trying to encourage children to talk openly and directly about their experiences and approached it indirectly via related issues.

In yet another project, the initiating agency was put under considerable pressure to avoid including 'too much domestic violence' in the educational pack! Regular alternative suggestions of developing a pack on bullying or racism were made and dismissive comments were made about exercises which dealt directly with domestic violence. Nevertheless, the initiating agency resisted this pressure and materials dealing directly with the issue were eventually produced.

Summary

The issues discussed above are the major differences between the projects although there are undoubtedly many more. As so many of these projects are relatively new or even in some cases, not yet fully completed, it is not yet possible to state with any certainty which structure or approach is more likely to be successful and indeed, what constitutes success is still not commonly agreed. A starting point, however, is to look at the responses to the projects and how the positives can be accentuated and potential problems minimised.

Responses to the projects

Achievements

In all areas where work with children and young people has been undertaken, valuable lessons have been learned even if the original purpose behind doing such work was not achieved.

In some areas, all original aims and objectives were achieved although the work may have thrown up additional work which was unidentified at the project start.

Resistance

Almost every project consulted for the writing of this chapter spoke at length about the resistance and backlash they had encountered when trying to introduce work on domestic violence to children and young people. This was particularly true within the formal educational system (e.g. schools) and to a much lesser extent in youth clubs.

Resistance took many forms; a selected sample illustrates the problems and issues raised:

- in one area teachers wanted to consult with abusers about the content of lessons to ensure the materials was 'unbiased!;
- admission to schools was refused in another area on the grounds that domestic violence was an inappropriate topic for children and young people;
- permission was refused to place domestic violence within a context of other power and control issues such as racism or in particular, homophobia;
- differing demands and perspectives from funders, the wider inter-agency forum and local communities affected the initiative to such an extent that work was delayed or even lost completely;
- a belief that the scarcity of support systems available to children and young people who were experiencing or witnessing domestic violence meant that the issue should not be raised at all;
- refusal to allow the issue of domestic violence to be 'named', which led to classes or workshops on bullying or conflict resolution skills without making explicit the links with domestic violence. This makes it clear why training and awareness raising is needed for teachers and youth workers.

The Islington experience

In Islington, the Inter-agency Domestic Violence Working Party set as an objective to produce an educational pack for teachers and youth workers to use to raise the issue of domestic violence with children. A small sub-group was established which included coopting several new members who were not otherwise involved in the Domestic Violence Working Party. Following extensive discussions, a proposed outline was drafted which aimed to fulfil the following criteria:

- it would contain sufficient information for teachers and youth workers to use it even though they may have little previous knowledge of domestic violence;
- exercises would be included that could be used with relatively

little or no preparation to encourage people to use the pack
- the pack would discuss and give guidance to teachers and youth workers on some of the difficulties they may encounter when raising the issue of domestic violence.
- the pack would aim to include exercises that could be used outside of an already over-burdened PHSE curriculum.

The supporting information and guidance was drawn up but the development of curriculum materials proved more difficult. A review of existing materials revealed that for children aged under 16 there was almost nothing available which directly addressed domestic violence. The main exception to this were materials aimed specifically at children and young people who had witnessed / experienced domestic violence and was therefore aimed at dealing with their feelings rather than educating them about the topic.

To develop curriculum materials, a study day was organised of 12 women who had experience either in curriculum development *or* of working with children who had experienced / witnessed domestic violence. Participants spent the day working together to brainstorm ideas for potential exercises.

The result evolved into the S.T.O.P. (Striving *TO Prevent*) Domestic Violence pack which was widely consulted and piloted in several schools and youth clubs before a final version was published. The pack was than introduced to educators within the Borough via an INSET training programme and development work took place with Education Welfare Officers and Social Services staff to ensure that support systems were in place before teachers and youth workers began using the pack with children and young people.

The pack has since been purchased by several other local authorities some of which have simply reproduced the contents and some of which have used it as a basis on which to further develop the ideas (e.g. Hackney - now known as the 'Respect Pack).

Conclusions

Although so far limited, there are some important conclusions that we can draw from the experiences of various inter-agency education initiatives to date.

- The two issues of educating children and young people about domestic violence and providing support services for those children to whom it is occurring, cannot be separated.
- Building up relationships with schools is very important if they are to be fully involved.
- Employing people to go into schools and youth clubs to at least begin the initiative seems to be helpful in getting any project off the ground.
- Teachers and youth workers are as subject to the myths and stereotypes around the issue of domestic violence as the rest of the population. Thus, training for teachers to increase their awareness and understanding before they teach children and young people about the subject is essential.
- Education of children and young people will not, on its own, lead to an effective prevention strategy. Educational initiatives must occur at the same time as the rest of society is being educated if it is to have any impact. In addition, children and young people should not be left feeling that they are the only generation which needs to change.
- A careful balance needs to be found between empowering children and young people to feel that they can be part of the solution in preventing domestic violence and being unrealistic or undermining of the personal experiences of children and young people living in violent homes of being disempowered either by the failure of their own efforts to stop the violence or the failure of agencies to which they or their mothers may have turned to for help.

[Editor's note: Since this chapter was written, several more education packs have been produced. The Islington S.T.O.P. Domestic Violence Pack continues to be widely used.]

Appendix 1

The Education Reform Act states that the schools curricula should:

- Promote the spiritual, moral, cultural, mental and physical development of pupils at the school and of society;
- Prepare such pupils for the opportunities, responsibilities and experiences of adult life.

It also notes:

> The 'topic of domestic violence is also a fruitful area of study within the National Curriculum and one that involves studying a range of issues relevant to many traditional school subjects as below.

The cross curricular theme - 'Citizenship' includes the following suggestions for study:

> Learning about duties, responsibilities and rights is central to this component. Rights include civil, political, social and human rights and how these may be violated by various forms of injustice, inequality and discrimination, including sexism and racism.

It goes on to say:

> Pupils' experience and appreciation of family life is varied. This component encourages pupils to understand the nature of family life in all its forms and to distinguish myths and stereotypes from reality. It helps them to examine their current roles, to anticipate future roles as partners and parents and to become more effective in their relationships'.

The activities may also be used to develop core skills such as:

- problem solving
- decision making
- communication
- personal and social skills
- language
- life skills

Specific issues that could form the basis of study might include:

'sources of information and organisations to contact'.
'challenges facing family units, e.g. separation, divorce, domestic problems......'
'the basic principles of the legal system'
'how civil and criminal law differ'
'how criminal and civil courts work'
'how legal advice may be obtained, including legal aid'
'legal responsibilities, rights'
'Police, public and the law'
'How public services people need are provided in different ways e.g. private, voluntary, public etc.'.

All of these areas can be explored in a 'project' based approach to the issue of domestic violence. In addition domestic violence as a topic can be studied in English, Drama, Social Studies, History, Art, Law, Politics, Sociology and General Studies.

The Department of Employment states in its document *United Nations Fourth World Conference on Women-Beijing 1995, Report of the United Kingdom of Great Britain and Northern Ireland*:

Schools may address issues of relevance to tackling domestic violence through the National Curriculum, their programme of sex education and in the wider curriculum through their programmes of personal, social and health education.

While it may seem appropriate to address the issue of domestic violence in the upper age range of secondary education, in fact the power relationships between the sexes (and in other relationships) are often topics explored in personal and social education in the first/second and third years of secondary schools. Violence and conflict, bullying and conflict resolution are frequently explored in junior schools and domestic violence as an issue could be raised within this context. Above all the impact of domestic violence will be significant and dramatic, no matter what the age of the child.

Appendix 2

One of the outcomes of the Fife Zero Tolerance Youth Conference was the creation of a young peoples' Charter which is reproduced below.

We are young people in Fife who have been brought together by the Zero Tolerance campaign to explore some of the issues around domestic violence, child sexual abuse and rape and sexual assault. This is our Charter towards creating a world where the abuse of women and children doesn't happen anymore.

Young people should have education from an early age to help understand what abuse is, why abuse happens and how to get help. We believe that all young people need to know that bullying, hurting and frightening other people to get your own way is never OK. We believe that adults should not be allowed to treat children and young people in this way.

Young people and children should have the same rights to respect and equality as anyone else. Adults need to accept this.

We believe that adults need to find ways to help young people which respects their privacy and their fears. All adults who work with children and young people need to learn about the feelings and difficulties of young people who experience abuse by listening to young people themselves.

Young people and children should have a right to protection from abuse and help and support to recover from abuse. It should be respected that young people can make decisions that affect their lives. Young people who experience abuse need support services that do not make them stand out as 'victims'.

These services for young people and children should be easy to get without having to have lots of adults make decisions about them. Services which help should be available in all communities. We believe that the best people to help young people come to terms with the effects of abuse in their lives are often other young people who have experience and an understanding of their own.

We expect that mothers who face abuse should have access to support, refuge and safe housing so that they can protect themselves and their children.

Young people and children themselves should have the right to safe housing and refuge.

Children and young people should have a right to expect justice from the criminal justice system and abusers should be sent a strong message that domestic violence, child sexual abuse and rape and sexual assault are not acceptable in our world.

We believe that adults, especially those who run services for children and young people should listen to us.

Our voices are the voices of the future.

Collected references

Aboriginal Affairs Department (1995). *Royal Commission into Aboriginal Deaths in Custody*. Perth: Government of Western Australia

Abrahams, C. (1994) *The Hidden Victims: Children and domestic violence*. London: NCH Action for Children

ABS (1996). W*omen's Safety Australia*. Canberra: Australian Bureau of Statistics, Office of the Status of Women, Department of Prime Minister and Cabinet

Arblaster, L., Conway, J., Foreman, A. and Hawtin, M. (1996) *Asking the Impossible? Inter-agency working to address the housing, health and social care needs of people in ordinary housing*. Bristol: The Policy Press

Argyle, M. (1969) *Social Interaction*, London: Tavistock Publications

Arden, A. and Hunter, C. (1997) *Homelessness and Allocation*. London: Legal Action Group

Astor, H. (1991). *Mediation and Violence against Women*. Canberra: National Committee on Violence Against Women, Office of the Status of Women, Department of the Prime Minister and Cabinet

Atkinson, J. (1996). *A Pebble in the Pond and a Hole in the Blanket. Moving On: Traditional wisdom in contemporary practice*. Brisbane: unpublished

Attorney General's Department. (1996). *Family Law Reform Act 1995: Overview*. Canberra: Family and Administrative Law Branch, Commonwealth Attorney-General's Department

Ball, M. (1990) *Children's Workers in Women's Aid Refuges: A report on the experience of nine refuges in England*. London: National Council for Voluntary Childcare Organisations

Ball, M., (1992) *An Evaluation of the National Children's Worker Post and a Report on Children's Work in Seven Refuges Funded by the BBC Children In Need Trust*. Bristol: Bristol: Women's Aid Federation of England/Children In Need (unpublished)

Ball, M. (1994) *Funding Refuge Services*. Bristol: Women's Aid Federation of England.

Ball, M. (1995) *Domestic Violence and Social Care: A report on two*

conferences held by the Social Services Inspectorate.
London: Department of Health Social Services Inspectorate

Barron, J. (1990) *Not Worth the Paper? The effectiveness of legal protection for women and children experiencing domestic violence.*
Bristol: Women's Aid Federation of England

Barron, J. Harwin, N. and Singh, T. (1992) *Written Evidence to the House of Commons Home Affairs Committee Inquiry into Domestic Violence.* Bristol: Bristol: Women's Aid Federation of England

Bindle, J., Cook, K. and Kelly, L. (1995) 'Trials and tribulations: Justice for women, a feminist campaign for the 1990s', in Griffin, G. (ed) *Feminist Activism in the 1990.* London: Taylor and Francis

Binney, V., Harkell, G. and Nixon, J. (1981) *Leaving Violent Men: A study of refuges and housing for abused women.* Leeds: Women's Aid Federation of England [Reprinted, 1988, with new foreword. Bristol: Women's Aid Federation of England]

Blazejowska, L. (1994). *Court Support Schemes: Improving women's access to the legal system. Challenging the legal system's response to domestic violence.* Brisbane

Bolger, A. (1991). *Aboriginal Women and Violence.* Darwin: Australian National University North Australia Research Unit

Borkowski, M., Murch, M., and Walker, V. (1983) *Marital Violence: The community response.* London: Tavistock

Bourlet, A. (1990) *Police Intervention in Marital Violence.* Milton Keynes: Open University Press

Bowker, L. H., Arbitell, M. and McFerron, J. R. (1988) 'On the relationship between wife beating and child abuse' in Yllö. K. and Bograd, M., *Feminist Perspectives on Wife Abuse.* Newbury Park, California: Sage

Bradburn, H. (1994) *Home Truths: Access to local authority and housing association tenancies. Responses to the consultation paper.* London: Shelter

Bridge Child Care Consultancy Service (1991) *Sukina: An evaluation of the circumstances leading to her death.* London: Bridge Child Care Consultancy Service

Broadhurst, R. G., A. M. Ferrante, et al. (1992). *Crime and Justice Statistics for Western Australia: 1992.* Perth: Crime Research Centre, University of Western Australia

Bull, J. (1993), *Housing Consequences of Relationship Breakdown.* London: HMSO

Cain, M. & Smart, C. (1989). Series Editor's Preface in Smart, C. and Sevenhuijsen, S. (eds.). *Child Custody and the Politics of Gender.* New York: Routledge

Campbell, B. (1988) *Unofficial Secrets.* London: Virago

Campbell, B. (1995) 'A question of priorities', *Community Care*, 24-30 August, pp18-19

Charles, N. (1993), T*he Housing Needs of Women and Children Escaping Domestic Violence.* Cardiff: Tai Cymru (Housing for Wales)

Chief Justice's Taskforce (1994). *Report on Gender Bias and the Law.* The Hon Mr. Justice D.K. Malcolm AC: Chief Justice of Western Australia

Children's Subcommittee of the London Coordinating Committee to End Woman Abuse, London, Ontario (1994) 'Make a difference: How to respond to child witnesses of woman abuse', in Mullender, A. and Morley, R. (eds.) *Children Living With Domestic Violence: Putting men's abuse of women on the child care agenda.* London: Whiting and Birch

Christian, C. (1981) *Policing by Coercion.* London: GLC

Clark, A. (1993) *Homeless Children and their Access to Schooling: A Bristol case study.* Bristol: SPACE Trust

Cleveland Area Child Protection Committee (1995) *CACPC Practice Guidance. Domestic Violence: Whose problem is it?* Middlesbrough: CACPC

Crawford, A. (1994) 'The partnership approach to community crime prevention: Corporatism at the local level', *Social and Legal Studies,* 3

Debbonaire, T. (1994) 'Work with children in Women's Aid refuges and after', in Mullender, A. and Morley, R. (eds.) *Children Living With Domestic Violence: Putting men's abuse of women on the child care agenda.* London: Whiting and Birch

Department of Health (1995) *Child Protection: Messages from research.* London: HMSO

Department of Health (1997) *Local Authority Circular: Family Law Act 1996, Part IV Family Homes and Domestic Violence.* London: Department of Health

Department of the Environment (1993) *Report and Recommendations of the Working Party on Relationship Breakdown.* London: HMSO

Department of the Environment (1994) *Access to Local Authority and Housing Association Tenancies.* (Consultation Paper) London: HMSO

Dixon, M. (1976). The *Real Matilda.* Melbourne: Penguin Books

Dobash, R.E. and Dobash, R.P. (1980), *Violence against Wives.* London: Open Books

Dobash, R.E. and Dobash, R.P. (1992) *Women, Violence and Social Change.* London: Routledge

Dobash, R.E., Dobash, R.P. and Cavanagh, K. (1985) 'The contact between battered women and social and medical agencies', in Pahl, J. (ed.) (1985) *Private Violence and Public Policy: The needs of battered women and the response of the public services.* London: Routledge and Kegan Paul

Dobash, R.E., Dobash, R.P., Cavanagh, K. and Lewis, R. (1996) *A Research Evaluation of Programmes for Violent Men,* Edinburgh: Scottish Office, Central Research Unit

DOE 0919 (1996) *Housing England and Wales: The Homelessness (Suitability of Accommodation) Order 1996.* London: HMSO

DOE 1086 (1997) *Housing, England and Wales: The Allocation of Housing (Reasonable and Additional Preference) Regulations.* London: HMSO

Domestic Violence Task Force (1986). *Break the Silence.* Perth: Women's Interests Division, Department of the Premier and Cabinet, WA

Dominy, N. and Radford, L. (1996) *Domestic Violence in Surrey: Developing an effective inter-agency response.* Kingston: Surrey County Council and Roehampton Institute

Downes, R. *Unravelling Criminal Justice.* London: Macmillan

Dublin Women's Aid (1995) Discussion Document on an Inter-Agency Approach to Domestic Violence. Unpublished

Dunhill, C (1989) *The Boys In Blue: Women's challenge to the police.* London: Virago

Easteal, P. (1990). *Doctors and Spouse Assault Victims: Prevention or perpetuation of the cycle of violence.* Canberra: Criminology Research Council, Australian Institute of Criminology

Easteal, P. (1992). *Rape. Violence prevention today.* Canberra: D. Chappell/Australian Institute of Criminology

Easteal, P. (1993). *Killing the Beloved: Homicide between adult sexual intimates.* Canberra: Australian Institute of Criminology

Easteal, P. (1994a). 'Homicide between adult sexual intimates in Australia: Implications for prevention', *Studies on Crime and Crime Prevention: Annual Review* 3

Easteal, P. (1994b). 'Violence against women in the home: How far have we come? How far to go?', *Family Matters,* 37, pp86-93

Edleson, J.L. & Syers, M. (1991) 'The effects of group treatment for men who batter: An 18-month Follow-Up Study', *Research in Social Work Practice,* 1, pp227-243

Edwards, S. (1989) *Policing Domestic Violence.* London: Sage

Egger, S. and J. Stubbs (1993). *Effectiveness of Protection Orders in Australian Jurisdictions,* Canberra: National Committee on Violence Against Women

Evans, A. (1991) *Alternatives to Bed and Breakfast, Temporary*

Housing Solutions for Homeless People. London: National Housing and Town Planning Council

Evans, A. and Duncan, S (1988) *Responding to Homelessness: Local Authority Policy and Practice*. London: HMSO

Evans, R. (1992). 'A gun in the oven: Masculism and gendered violence'.in K. Saunders and R. Evans (eds) *Gender Relations in Australia: Domination and negotiation*. Sydney: Harcourt Brace

Evason, E. (1982) *Hidden Violence*. Belfast: Farset Press

Family and Domestic Violence Task Force (1995). *It's Not Just a Domestic: An action plan on family and domestic violence*. Perth: Western Australian Government

Family Law Act 1996. London: HMSO

Farmer, E. and Owen, M. (1995) *Child Protection Practice: Private Risks and Public Remedies - Decision making, intervention and outcome in child protection work*. London: HMSO

Ferrante, A., F. Morgan, et al. (1995). *Measuring the Extent of Domestic Violence*. Melbourne: Federation Press

Forman, J. (1995) *Is There a Correlation Between Child Sexual Abuse and Domestic Violence? An exploratory study of the links between child sexual abuse and domestic violence in a sample of intrafamilial child sexual abuse cases*. Lawson's Building, 1700 London Road, Glasgow G32 8XD: Women's Support Project (Reprint of an earlier, undated report)

Gardiner, J. (1996). *From Private to Public: Creating a coordinated approach to preventing wife abuse: The Armadale Domestic Violence Intervention Project*. Perth: Criminology Research Council, Australian Institute of Criminology

Gilroy, R. and Woods, R. (1994) *Housing Women*. London: Routledge

Gordon, P, (1987) 'Community Policing: Towards a Police State', in Scraton, P. (ed) *Law, Order and the Authoritarian State*. Buckingham: Open University Press

Grace, S. (1995) *Policing Domestic Violence in the 1990s*. Home Office Research Study No. 139. London: HMSO

Greve, J. (1991) *Homelessness in Britain*. York: Joseph Rowntree Foundation

Greve, J. and Currie, E. (1990) *Homeless in Britain*, Housing Research Findings, No. 10, February. York: Joseph Rowntree Foundation

Hague, G. (1997) 'Smoke-screen or leap forward', *Critical Social Policy*, 17(4)

Hague, G., Kelly, L., Malos, E and Mullender, A. (1996) *Children, Domestic Violence and Refuges: A study of needs and responses*. Bristol: Bristol: Women's Aid Federation of England

Hague, G. and Malos, E, (1993), *Domestic Violence; Action for change*.

Cheltenham: New Clarion Press

Hague, G. and Malos, E. (1994) 'Domestic violence, social policy and housing', *Critical Social Policy*, 42

Hague, G. and Malos, E. (1996) *Tackling Domestic Violence: A guide to developing multi-agency initiatives.* Bristol: The Policy Press

Hague, G. and Malos, E. (1997) 'The police: Inter-agency initiatives as a response to domestic violence', *Police Journal*, LXX, 1

Hague, G. and Malos, E, (1998a) *Domestic Violence; Action for change.* (2nd Ed) Cheltenham: New Clarion Press

Hague, G. and Malos, E. (1998b) 'Inter-agency approaches to domestic violence and social services', *British Journal of Social Work*, 28, pp369-386

Hague, G., Malos, E. and Dear, W. (1995), *Against Domestic Violence: Inter-agency initiatives,.* Working Paper 127. Bristol: SAUS, University of Bristol

Hague, G., Malos, E. and Dear, W. (1996) *Multi-Agency Work and Domestic Violence: A national study of inter-agency initiatives.* Bristol: Policy Press

Hague, G. and Wilson, C. (1996) *The Silenced Pain: Domestic violence 1945 - 1970.* Bristol: The Policy Press

Hanmer, J. and Saunders, S. (1984) *Well Founded Fear: a community study of violence to women.* London: Hutchinson

Harwin, N. (1998) *Families without Fear: Womens Aid agenda for action on domestic violence.* Bristol: Bristol: Women's Aid Federation of England

Harwin, N. and Barron, J. (forthcoming) 'Domestic violence and social policy: perspectives from Women's Aid' in Itzin, C. and Hanmer, J. (eds) *Home Truths.* London: Routledge

Hester, M. and Radford, L. (1996) *Domestic Violence and Child Contact Arrangements in England and Denmark.* Bristol: Policy Press

Hester, M., Harwin, N. and Pearson, C. (1998) *Making an Impact.* London: Department of Health/Barnados

Higgins, G. (1994) 'Childrens Accounts' in Mullender, A. and Morley, R. (eds.) *Children Living With Domestic Violence: Putting men's abuse of women on the child care agenda.* London: Whiting and Birch

HMIP (1995) *Probation Orders with Additional Requirements.* London: Home Office

Holder, R. (1996) 'Creating Unholy Alliances: Policy developments on domestic violence in the UK' in *Making a Difference: Proceedings of a national conference,* Perth, Australia

Holder, R., Kelly, L. and Singh, T. (1992) *Suffering in Silence? Children and young people who witness domestic violence*. London: Hammersmith and Fulham Domestic Violence Forum (Available from Community Safety Unit, Hammersmith Town Hall, King Street, London W6 9JU)

Home Office (1986) *Circular 69/86: Violence against Women*. London: Home Office

Home Office (1990), *Circular 60/90: Domestic Violence*. London: Home Office

Home Office (1994a) *Consultation Document on Inter-agency Responses to Domestic Violence*. London: Home Office,

Home Office (1994b) *Criminal Statistics: England and Wales 1993*. London: HMSO

Home Office (1995) *Inter Agency Circular: Inter-agency Co-ordination to Tackle Domestic Violence*. London: Home Office and Welsh Office

Homer, M.., Leonard, L., and Taylor, P. (1984) *Public Violence, Private Shame*. Bristol: Women's Aid Federation (England)

Hopkins, A. and H. McGregor (1991). W*orking for Change: The movement against domestic violence*. North Sydney: Allen & Unwin

House of Commons Home Affairs Committee (1993) *Report of Inquiry into Domestic Violence*. Vols. I and II. London, Home Office

Housing Act 1996. HMSO: London

Ingram, R. (1993/94) 'Violence from known men', *OpenMind*, 66, pp.18-19

Jaffe, P., Wolfe, D.A. and Wilson, S.K. (1991) *Children of Battered Women*. California: Sage

Jones, T., Newburn, T. and Smith, D.J. (1994) 'New policing responses to crime against women and children' in *Democracy and Policing*. London: Policy Studies Institute

Kelly, L (1994a) *Abuse of Women & Children: a feminist response,* London: University of North London.

Kelly, L. (1994b) 'The interconnectedness of domestic violence and child abuse: Challenges for research, policy and practice' in Mullender,A. and Morley, R. (eds.) *Children Living With Domestic Violence: Putting men's abuse of women on the child care agenda*. London: Whiting and Birch

Kelly, L. (1996) 'When does the speaking profit us? Reflections on the challenges of developing feminist perspectives on abuse and violence by women' in Hester, M., Kelly, L. and Radford, J. (eds) *Women, Violence and Male Power*. Buckingham: Open University Press

Law Commission (1992) *Family Law, Domestic Violence and the Occupation of the Family Home*. London: HMSO

Leeds City Council, Leeds Health Authority, Leeds Family Health
Services Authority, and Voluntary Action Leeds (1992/93) *Final
Draft Community Care Plan for Women Subject to Violence by a
Known Man*. Leeds
Leeds Inter-Agency Project (Women & Violence) (1991) *Violence
Against Women by Known Men Multi-Agency Training Pack*. Leeds:
LIAP
Leeds Inter-Agency Project (Women & Violence) (1992), *Information
Pack*. Leeds: LIAP
Leeds Inter-Agency Project (1993) *Information Pack*. c/o CHEL, 26
Roundhay Road, Leeds LS7 1AB: Leeds Inter-Agency Project
Leonard, P. and McLeod, E. (1980) *Marital Violence: Social
Construction and Social Service Response: A Pilot Study Report*.
Coventry: Department of Applied Social Studies, University of
Warwick
Liddle, M. & L Gelsthorpe, L. (1994) *Inter-agency Crime Prevention:
Organising local delivery,* Crime Prevention Unit (No.52), *Crime
Prevention & Inter-agency Cooperation* (CPU No 53), and *Inter-
agency Crime Prevention: further issues* (CPU supplement to Nos
52 & 53). London: Home Office
Lloyd, C. (1994) *The Welfare Net*. Oxford: Oxford Brookes University
Logan, F. (1986) *Homelessness and Relationship Breakdown: How the
law and housing policy affects women*. London: One Parent Families
London Borough of Hackney (1992) *The Links Between Domestic
Violence and Child Abuse: Developing services*. London: London
Borough of Hackney
London Borough of Hackney (1994) *Good Practice Guidelines:
Responding to domestic violence*. London: London Borough of
Hackney, Women's Unit
London Borough of Hammersmith & Fulham (1990) *Policing Domestic
Violence in Hammersmith & Fulham*. London: London Borough of
Hammersmith & Fulham
London Borough of Hammersmith and Fulham (1991) *Challenging
Domestic Violence: A Training and Resource Pack for Anyone Who
Wants to Address Domestic Violence in Their Work or Community
Setting*. London: London Borough of Hammersmith and Fulham,
Community Safety Unit
London Borough of Hounslow (1994) *Domestic Violence - Help, Advice
and Information for Disabled Women*. London: London Borough of
Hounslow
London Borough of Islington (undated) *STOP - Striving to Prevent
Domestic Violence: An Activity Pack for Working with Children and
Young People*. London: London Borough of Islington, Women's

Equality Unit

London Co-ordinating Committee to End Woman Abuse (1992) *An Integrated Community Response to Prevent Violence against Women in Intimate Relationships*. London (Ontario): LCCEWA

Lusgarten, L. (1986) *The Governance of Police*. London: Sweet & Maxwell

Malos, E. (1993) *'You've got No Life' : Homelessness and the use of bed and breakfast hotels*. Bristol: University of Bristol, School of Applied Social Studies

Malos, E. and Hague, G. (1993) *Domestic Violence and Housing*. Bristol: Women's Aid Federation (England) and University of Bristol, School of Applied Social Studies

Mama, A. (1996) *The Hidden Struggle: Statutory and voluntary responses to violence against black women in the home*. (2nd Ed) London: Whiting and Birch

Mayhew, P.; Aye Maung, N. and Mirrlees-Black, C. (1993) *The 1992 British Crime Survey*. Home Office Research Study No. 132. London: HMSO

Maynard, M. (1985) 'The response of social workers to domestic violence' in Pahl, J. (ed) *Private Violence and Public Policy*. London: Routledge and Kegan Paul

McFerren, L. (1990). 'Interpretation of a frontline state. Australian women's refuges and the state', in Watson, S. *Playing the State: Australian feminist interventions*. Sydney: Allen and Unwin

McGibbon, A., Cooper, L. and Kelly, L. (1989) *'What Support?' Hammersmith and Fulham Council Community Police Committee Domestic Violence Project. An exploratory study of Council policy and practice, and local support services in the area of domestic violence within Hammersmith and Fulham. Final report*. London: Child Abuse Studies Unit, Polytechnic of North London

McMahon, M. & Pence, E. (1995). 'Doing more harm than good?' in Peled, E., Jaffe, P. G. and Edleson, J.L. (eds.). *Ending the Cycle of Violence*. Thousand Oaks, CA: Sage Publications

McWilliams, M. and McKiernan, J. (1993) *Bringing It Out In the Open: Domestic violence in Northern Ireland*. Belfast: HMSO

Mooney, J. (1994) *The Hidden Figure: Domestic violence in north London*. London: Islington Police and Crime Prevention Unit

Morley, R and Mullender, A. (1994) *Preventing Domestic Violence to Women*. Police Research Group, Crime Prevention Unit Series, Paper 48. London: Home Office Police Department

Morley, R. (1993) 'Recent responses to "domestic violence" against women: A feminist critique', in Page, R. and Baldock, J. (eds) *Social Policy Review 5*. Nottingham: Social Policy Association

Moylan, H. J. M., Minister for the Status of Women (1997). *National Directions: How to move our decisions forward*. WESNET National Conference, University of NSW, Randwick

Muir, J. and Ross, M. (1993) *Housing The Poorer Sex*. London: London Housing Unit

Mullender, A. (1994a) 'Groups for child witnesses of woman abuse', in Mullender, A. and Morley, R. (eds) *Children Living with Domestic Violence: Putting men's abuse of women on the child care agenda*. London: Whiting and Birch

Mullender, A. (1994b) 'School-based work: education for prevention', in Mullender, A. and Morley, R. (eds) *Children Living with Domestic Violence: Putting men's abuse of women on the child care agenda*. London: Whiting and Birch

Mullender, A. (1995) 'Groups for children who have lived with domestic violence: learning from North America', *Groupwork*, 8(1), pp.79-98

Mullender, A. (1996) *Rethinking Domestic Violence: The Social Work and Probation Response*. London: Routledge

Mullender, A. and Morley, R. (eds.) (1994) *Children Living with Domestic Violence: Putting men's abuse of women on the child care agenda*. London: Whiting and Birch

National Clearinghouse for the Defense of Battered Women (1995) *Statistics Packet* (3rd Ed) Philadelphia: National Clearinghouse for the Defense of Battered Women

National Inter-Agency Working Party (1992) *Domestic Violence*. London: Victim Support

NCH Action for Children (1994) *The Hidden Victims: Children and domestic violence*. London: NCH Action for Children (*see also:* Abrahams, C., 1994)

NCVAW (1992). *National Strategy on Violence Against Women*. Canberra: National Committee on Violence against Women, Office of the Status of Women, Department of the Prime Minister and Cabinet

NCVAW (1993). *Training in the Area of Violence against Women: incorporating National Training Guidelines; Training of key occupational groups; and train the trainer programs*. Canberra: National Committee on Violence against Women, Office of the Status of Women, Department of the Prime Minister and Cabinet

Nicholls, R. (1993). *Address to Domestic Violence Action Groups of Western Australia*. Annual General Meeting of Domestic Violence Action Groups of Western Australia, Inc., Perth, Western Australia

Norwich Consultants on Sexual Violence (1988) 'Claiming Our Status as Experts: Community Organising' *Feminist Review*, 28, 144-149

Nottinghamshire County Council (1989) *Domestic Violence - Guide to*

Practice: Practice guidelines to assist staff dealing with situations involving domestic violence. West Bridgford, Nottingham: Nottinghamshire County Council

Nottinghamshire County Council (1990) *Domestic Violence Conference Report.* West Bridgford, Nottingham: Nottinghamshire County Council

O'Hara, M. (1994) 'Child deaths in contexts of domestic violence: Implications for professional practice', in Mullender, A. and Morley, R. (eds) *Children Living with Domestic Violence: Putting men's abuse of women on the child care agenda.* London: Whiting and Birch

Office of Population Census and Statistics (1997) *Social Trends*, 27. London, HMSO

Office of the Status of Women (1995). *Community Attitudes to Violence against Women: Detailed report.* Canberra: Department of the Prime Minister and Cabinet

Office of the Status of Women (1997). *Partnerships Against Domestic Violence.* Canberra: Department of Prime Minister and Cabinet

Pahl, J. (ed.) (1985) *Private Violence and Public Policy: The needs of battered women and the response of the public services.* London: Routledge and Kegan Paul

Parliamentary Select Committee on Violence in Marriage (1975) *Report from the Select Committee on Violence in Marriage, Together with the Proceedings of the Committee,* Vols.1-2. London: HMSO.

Pascall, G. and Morley, R. (1996) 'Women and Homelessness, 1: Proposals from the Department of the Environment: Lone mothers', *Journal of Social Welfare and Family Law*, 18(2)

Pascall, G. and Morley, R. (1996) 'Women and Homelessness, 2: Proposals from the Department of Environment: 'Domestic violence', *Journal of Social Welfare and Family Law*, 18 (3)

Pearson, G., Blagg, H., Smith, D., Sampson, A. and Stubbs, P. (1988) 'Crime, locality and the multi-agency approach', *British Journal of Criminology,* 28(4)

Pence, E. & Paymar, M. (1993). *Education Groups for Men Who Batter: The Duluth Model.* New York: Springer

Pence, E. (1985). *The Justice System's Response to Domestic Assault Cases: A Guide for policy development.* Minneapolis: Minnesota Program Development

Pizzey, E. (1974) *Scream Quietly or the Neighbours Will Hear.* Harmondsworth: Penguin

Pollock, S. & Sutton, J. (1985). 'Father's rights, women's losses', *Women's Studies International Forum,* 8, 593-599

Queensland Domestic Violence Task Force (1988). *Beyond These*

Walls. Queensland Department of Family Services and Welfare Housing

Ralph, A. (1992). *The Effectiveness of Restraining Orders for Protecting Women from Violence*. Perth: Western Australian Office of the Family

Rights of Women Lesbian Custody Group (1984) *Lesbian Mothers on Trial: A report on lesbian mothers and child custody*. London: Rights of Women

Robertson, N. and R. Busch (1993). *Two Year Review*. Hamilton , NZ: Hamilton Abuse Intervention Pilot Project

Rose, H. (1985) 'Women's refuges: Creating new forms of welfare?', in Ungerson, C. (ed) *Women and Social Policy*. London: Macmillan

Rosenau, P. (1992) Post-*Modernism and the Social Sciences: Insights, inroads and intrusions*. Princeton NJ: Princeton University Press

Rosewater, L. B. (1988) 'Battered or schizophrenic? Psychological tests can't tell' in Yllö, K. and Bograd, M., *Feminist Perspectives on Wife Abuse*. Newbury Park, California: Sage

Ross, M. (1990) *A Summary of Research into Women and Homelessness*. London: London Housing Unit

Russell, D. (1982) *Rape in Marriage*. New York: Collier

SAAP (1997). *Case Management with Children in SAAP Services: A family oriented approach*. Canberra: Supported Accommodation Assistance Program, Commonwealth Department of Health and Family Services

Sampson, A. et al (1988) 'Crime, localities and the multi-agency approach', *British Journal of Criminology*, 28(4), pp.478-493

Sampson, A., Smith, D., Pearson, G., Blagg, H and Stubbs, P. (1991) 'Gender issues in inter-agency relations: Police, probation and social services', in Abbott, P. and Wallace, C. (eds) *Gender, Power and Sexuality*. London: Macmillan

Saunders, A., Keep, G. and Debbonaire, T. (1995), *It Hurts Me Too: Children's experiences of domestic violence and refuge life*. Bristol: Bristol: Women's Aid Federation of England/ChildLine/NISW

Saunders, D. G. (1992). 'Women Battering', in Ammerman, R.T. and Hersen, M. (eds.) *Assessment of Family Violence: A clinical and legal sourcebook*. New York: Wiley

Scarman, L.G. (1986) *The Brixton Disorders, 10-12 April 1981: Report of an enquiry by Lord Scarman*. (cmnd 8422). London: HMSO

Scottish Women's Aid (1995) *Children, Equality and Respect: Children and young people's experience of domestic violence*. Edinburgh: SWA

Scraton, P. (ed) *Law, Order and the Authoritarian State*. Buckingham: Open University Press

Seddon, N. (1992) *Domestic Violence in Australia: the legal response*.

Sydney: The Federation Press

Sexty, C. (1990) *Women Losing Out: Access to housing in Britain today*. London, Shelter

Sherman, L. W. (1992). *Policing Domestic Violence: Experiments and dilemmas*. New York: Free Press

Sinclair, D. (1985) *Understanding Wife Assault: A training manual for counsellors and advocates*. Toronto, Ontario (from Ontario Government Bookstore, Publications Services Section, 880 Bay Street, Toronto, Ontario M7A 1N8)

Singh, T. (1991) *'Working Together Under the Children Act': WAFE submission to the Department of Health*. Bristol: Women's Aid Federation (England)

Sivanandan, A. (1985) 'Racial awareness training and the degradation of black struggle', *Race and Class,*, 26(4)

Smith, L. (1989) *Domestic Violence: An overview of the literature*. Home Office Research Studies 107. London: HMSO

Smith, R., Gaster, L., Harrison, L., Martin, L., Means, R. and Thistlewaite, P. (1993) *Working Together for Better Community Care*. Bristol: SAUS Publications

Southall Black Sisters (1989) 'Two struggles: Challenging male violence and the police' in Dunhill, C. (ed) *The Boys in Blue: Women's challenge to the police*. London: Virago

Stanko, E. (1995) 'Desperately seeking safety: Problematising policing and protection'. Paper delivered at the British Criminology Conference, Loughborough

Stark, E. and Flitcraft, A. (1985) 'Woman-battering, child abuse and social heredity: what is the relationship?', in Johnson, N. (ed) *Marital Violence*. London: Routledge and Kegan Paul

Stark, E. and Flitcraft, A. (1988) 'Women and children at risk: A feminist perspective on child abuse', *International Journal of Health Services*, 18(1), pp97-118

Statistics Canada (1993). *The Violence Against Women Survey*. Ottawa: Statistics Canada

Straus, M. and Gelles, R. (1988) *Intimate Violence: The causes and consequences of abuse in the American family*. New York: Simon & Schuster

Straus, M. and R. Gelles, Eds. (1990). *Physical violence in American families: Risk factors and adaptations to violence in 8,145 families*. New Brunswick, NJ: Transaction Publishers

Summers, A. (1994). 'Feminism on two continents: The women's movements in Australia and the United States', in Grieve, N. and Burns, A. *Australian Women: Contemporary femininst thought*. . Melbourne: Oxford University Press

Taylor, G. (1993). 'Child custody and access', *Vis-à-Vis: National Newsletter on Family Violence,* 10(3) Canadian Council on Social Development

Taylor, M. (1994) *Housing and Domestic Violence in Scotland.* Scotland: Scottish Women's Aid

Tayside Women and Violence Group (1994) *Hit or Miss: An exploratory study of the provision for women subjected to domestic violence in Tayside Region.* Dundee: Tayside Regional Council, Equal Opportunities Unit

Thomas, A. and Niner, P. (1989) *Living in Temporary Accommodation: A survey of homeless people.* London: HMSO

UN Department of Information (1993) *Convention on the Elimination of Discrimination Against Women: Directive on Violence Against Women.* New York: United Nations

UN Department of Information (1995) *The Beijing Declaration and The Platform for Action.* New York: United Nations

Ungerson, C. (ed) (1985) *Women and Social Policy.* London: Macmillan

UNICEF (1997) *The Progress of Nations.* London: UNICEF

V-Net (1995). *Stopping Men's Violence in the Family: A manual for running men's groups.* Melbourne: Victorian Network for the Prevention of Male Family Violence

Victim Support (1992) *Domestic Violence: Report of a national inter-agency working party on domestic violence.* London: Victim Support

Watson, S. (1984) 'Definitions of homelessness: A feminist perspective', *Critical Social Policy,* 11

Watson, S. and Austerbury, H. (1983a) *Women and Housing Research: Future directions for the next decade.* London: SSRC

Watson, S. and Austerberry, H. (1983b) *Women on the Margins: A study of single women's housing problems.* London: The City University

Watson, S. and Austerberry, H. (1986) *Housing and Homelessness: A feminist perspective.* London: RKP

Wearing, R. (1992). 'Family violence: has anything changed in 4 years?' *The National Centre for Socio Legal Studies:* 4-5

Wearing, R. (1992). *Monitoring the impact of the Crimes (Family Violence) Act 1987.* Melbourne: La Trobe University

Welsh Women's Aid (1989) *Report of the International Women's Aid Conference.* Cardiff: Welsh Women's Aid

West Yorkshire Police (1993) *Domestic Violence Survey.* Leeds: West Yorkshire Police

Wetheritt, M. (1987) 'Community policing now' in Wilmott, P. (ed) *Policing and the Community.* London: Policy Studies Institute

Wilmott, P. (ed) (1987) *Policing and the Community.* London: Policy

Studies Institute

Women and Children in Refuges (1988) *You Can't Beat a Woman.* Bristol: Women's Aid Federation of England

Women's Aid Federation of England (1996) *Report from Annual Survey of Refuges and Helpline Services* (unpublished)

Women's Aid Federation of England (1997) *Annual Report.* Bristol: Bristol: Women's Aid Federation of England

Women's Education Project (1989) *Breaking Through: Women surviving male violence.* Bristol: Women's Aid Federation of England

Women's National Commission and Equal Opportunities Commission (1996) *National Agenda for Action.* London: Department of Employment

Women's Research Centre (Vancouver), (1988) *In Women's Interest: Feminist activism and institutional change.* Vancouver: WRC

The Women's Unit (1999) *Living Without Fear. An integrated approach to tackling violence against women.* London: Cabinet Office.

Index